Special Needs and Early Years

Education at SAGE

SAGE is a leading international publisher of journals, books, and electronic media for academic, educational, and professional markets.

Our education publishing includes:

- accessible and comprehensive texts for aspiring education professionals and practitioners looking to further their careers through continuing professional development

- inspirational advice and guidance for the classroom

- authoritative state of the art reference from the leading authors in the field

Find out more at: **www.sagepub.co.uk/education**

Special Needs and Early Years

A Practitioner's Guide

Third Edition

Kate Wall

Los Angeles | London | New Delhi
Singapore | Washington DC

Third edition published 2011

Second edition published 2006
Reprinted 2007

First edition published 2003
Reprinted 2004

SAGE Publications Ltd
1 Oliver's Yard
55 City Road
London EC1Y 1SP

SAGE Publications Inc.
2455 Teller Road
Thousand Oaks, California 91320

SAGE Publications India Pvt Ltd
B 1/I 1 Mohan Cooperative Industrial Area
Mathura Road
New Delhi 110 044

SAGE Publications Asia-Pacific Pte Ltd
3 Church Street
#10-04 Samsung Hub
Singapore 049483

Library of Congress Control Number: 2010928639

British Library Cataloguing in Publication data

A catalogue record for this book is available from the
British Library

ISBN 978-1-84920-132-2
ISBN 978-1-84920-133-9 (pbk)

Typeset by Dorwyn, Wells, Somerset
Printed and bound by CPI Group (UK) Ltd, Croydon, CR0 4YY
Printed on paper from sustainable resources

Contents

Foreword

Let us hope that as the new Coalition Government is led by two fathers of young children – and both the Prime Minister and Deputy Prime Minister appear to be highly involved parents compared with many politicians of years ago – the increased interest in ensuring every child matters is maintained, despite the severe economic climate we are experiencing and which may persist for some time.

Kate Wall details for us once again in this gem of a book, the need for a period of calm. A time of consolidation, with developments in training for Early Childhood Education and Care (ECEC) professionals to ensure we move, as a society, to the kind of inclusion which would mean young children would no longer be deemed to have 'special needs'. Inclusion would be taken for granted, a matter of course. As Kate says, good inclusive practice is 'just good practice'.

When those of us on the team drafted the research review for *Birth to Three Matters* (David, Goouch, Powell and Abbott, 2003), what surprised us was, firstly, the simplicity of the conclusions we could draw and secondly that two of our three main conclusions – that all young children need loving, sensitive key persons around them and that they need to be respected as people – remained intact in the published report. Our fear that these conclusions would be altered or cut was based on the fact that no government can ensure these. They are the responsibility of the whole society and especially of those who work with families, particularly vulnerable or isolated families. At that time we were very fortunate to have Kate read, comment on and add influential suggestions to our synthesis of analysis of some 500-plus publications. I believe that Kate's work is founded on those same messages.

Both the previous editions of Kate's book have been greeted enthusiastically by practitioners and received glowing reviews by many colleagues. Kate's ability to blend theory, research evidence, policy and a wealth of practical knowledge helps ECEC professionals to work meaningfully with all the children and families with whom they become involved. Once again, in updating the book, Kate keeps us abreast of developments in all those aspects of this important field.

This third edition of Kate's book moves us on yet again and will, no doubt, benefit many children because it will provoke new insights in practitioners, students, researchers and policy makers. It will be a book colleagues read and enjoy but also return to, as they constantly review their work in order to ensure inclusive practice. However, I guess Kate is really hoping that a fourth edition will be unnecessary – because maybe after all her efforts we will have become able to value and build on every child's individual talents, sharing the joy of their achievements with parents and other family members.

Tricia David
Emeritus Professor of Education,
Canterbury Christ Church University, and
(2003–2009) Emeritus Professor of
Early Childhood Education, University of Sheffield
July 2010

Reference

David, T., Goouch, K., Powell, S. and Abbott, A. (2003) *Birth to Three Matters: A Review of the Literature*. Research Report 444. London: DES.

Acknowledgements

My thanks go to all those who have supported me in my writing endeavours, specifically Pia Parry and all my colleagues at the University of Chichester who have been very aware of the difficulties and time pressures placed on me over recent months. I must also thank Jude Bowen at Sage, and her team, for their hard work and support throughout the writing process. My greatest thanks are to Michael, Sam and Tracy for their unfailing belief in me, and this time I need to give huge thanks to Sam in particular who has painstakingly read, re-read and tracked changes along with me – she has also tried to teach me about apostrophes but has failed along with everyone else – sorry, Sam!

As always, this book is dedicated to my mum.

About the Author

Kate is a Principal Lecturer at the University of Chichester and Programme Leader for the BA (Hons) Early Childhood Studies with Practitioner Options Degree. She is a member of the Advisory Board for NASEN, the Members Forum for NCB and regularly speaks at conferences across the UK and abroad. Kate is also an external examiner and regularly engages as an external expert in validation events and periodic reviews at other HE institutions. Kate spent over 20 years as an early years teacher, beginning as a reception class teacher then progressing through a range of interesting and challenging posts before moving into the field of special education supporting children aged 2–8 years with special needs and disabilities and their families. Her last role before moving into HE was leading practice in an early years special unit. Since entering HE, Kate has also actively worked as an author, publishing many articles and several books related to special needs and working practice. Her interest in children with autism stems from her own working experiences which challenged yet rewarded her greatly. Kate is passionate about effective integrated working, the early years workforce and improving provision for young children with special needs, but also for their families who, she feels, are often overlooked. She is always ready to challenge policy and to suggest possible ways forward for the benefit of children and families.

Glossary of Acronyms

ACE   Advisory Centre for Education
ADHD   Attention deficit hyperactivity disorder
AHDC   Aiming High for Disabled Children
AIT   Auditory Integration Training
ASD   Autistic spectrum disorder
CAF   Common Assessment Framework
CLIC   Cancer and Leukaemia in Children
CSIE   Centre for Studies on Inclusive Education
CWDC   Children's Workforce Development Council
DCSF   Department for Children, Schools and Families
DfEE   Department for Education and Employment
DfES   Department for Education and Skills
DoH   Department of Health
DRC   Disability Rights Commission
ECM   Every Child Matters
EEC   Early Excellence Centres
ELG   Early Learning Goals
EP   Educational psychologist
ES   Early Support
ESN   Educationally subnormal
EYAT   Early Years Advisory Teacher
EYDCP   Early Years Development and Childcare Partnership
EYFS   Early Years Foundation Stage
EYP   Early Years Professional
EYPS   Early Years Professional Status
EYQISP Early Years Quality Improvement and Support Programme
GP   General Practitioner

HEI	Higher Education Institution
HV	Health Visitor
IBP	Individual Behaviour Plan
IDP	Inclusion Development Programme
IEP	Individual Education Plan
IPSEA	Independent Panel for Special Education Advice
IQ	Intelligence quotient
IT	Information technology
LA	Local authority
LEA	Local education authority
LSA	Learning support assistant
MLD	Moderate learning difficulties
NAS	National Autistic Society
NASEN	National Association of Special Educational Needs
NEET	Not in education, employment or training
NNEB	Nursery nurse
NSF	National Service Framework
NVQ	National Vocational Qualification
OECD	Organisation for Economic Co-operation and Development
OFSTED	Office for Standards in Education
OT	Occupational therapist
PBCL	Pre-school Behaviour Checklist
PECS	Picture Exchange Communication System
PLA	Pre-School Learning Alliance
PPS	Parent Partnership Scheme
PSED	Personal, social and emotional development
RBA	Removing Barriers to Achievement
SEAL	Social and emotional aspects of learning
SEN	Special educational needs
SENCO	Special educational needs coordinator
SENDA	Special Educational Needs and Disability Discrimination Act
SENDIST	Special Educational Needs and Disability Tribunal
SLCN	Speech, language and communication needs
SLD	Severe learning difficulties
SLT	Speech and language therapist

SMART	Specific, measurable, achievable, relevant and time bound
SN	Special needs
SPELL	Structure; Positive approaches and expectations; Empathy; Low arousal environments; and Links with parents
SSD	Severely subnormal difficulties
SSD	Social services department
TAC	Team around the Child
TDA	Training and Development Agency for Schools
TEACCH	Treatment and Education of Autistic and Related Communication Handicapped Children
TfC	Together for Children
TfDC	Together for Disabled Children

Definitions

The following terminology is used throughout this book:

Early years/young children are those aged 0–8 years, but this book will focus predominantly on the under 5s or pre-school children as there is a plethora of information available on children of statutory school age.

Early years provider/provision/setting refers to any practitioner or establishment providing opportunities and/or support to 0–5-year-old children. This will include pre-school groups, nurseries, nursery classes, childminders, daycare, special needs units/classes/schools, early excellence centres, Children's Centres, wrap-around care, Sure Start centres and educare groups.

Parents refers to any person, parent or otherwise, assuming 'parental responsibility' for the child.

Professionals/practitioners refers to any person working with children in any setting, whether or not they hold professional qualifications.

Special educational needs (SEN) are any difficulties experienced by a child requiring additional or different educational provision to be made. *Special needs* (SN) are those difficulties experienced by a child that do not necessarily result in a special educational need.

Special needs, additional needs or individual needs?

I would suggest that all children, like all adults, have individual needs that will change in type, severity or nature during different phases of their lives. It should be our aim, therefore, as early years practitioners to enable all children to achieve their optimum potential whether they are identified as having 'special needs', 'special educational needs', or not. However, in the current early years arena, despite discussions around 'additional needs' and 'individualised' or 'personalised learning', policy still uses the term 'special educational needs' (e.g. Code of Practice, DfES, 2001c) so for this reason the term 'special educational needs' will be used throughout this book.

1

Legislation and policy

Introduction

The term 'special needs' is frequently used in a generic manner and has become indicative of a separate and discrete area of education and wider society, yet we are currently experiencing increasing societal changes that promote inclusion in all aspects of our lives. It could be suggested that all people have needs and that these needs will vary as their lives develop and change, some having severely traumatising effects demanding very specific short- and/or long-term support, but at other times causing less impact. At times we all require very specific, individual support but this does not necessarily imply that we are different, or have special needs, more that we are human. We should therefore strive to provide effectively for the individual needs of *all* children at *all* times, enabling each child to achieve his/her full potential. Provision should ensure that each child is offered a range of appropriate, challenging experiences to support development at his/her own pace and thus ensure success. High-quality early years provision would

1

then respond to the needs of all children, whether or not any of the children have identified special needs.

Development of nursery provision in the UK

Within the UK, there is a well-documented diverse range of early years provision that has undergone periods of growth and expansion, mostly on a needs-led basis (for example, Abbott and Langston, 2005; Baldock et al., 2005; Maynard and Thomas, 2009). Here, key developments will be briefly explored.

The late 1800s to the early 1900s

At the beginning of the twentieth century, there was no statutory preschool provision in the UK, although in Europe the importance and value of preschool provision had been identified and early years settings were encouraged. As far back as 1869, the French government supported the development of crèches and continued to support further expansion and development. Van der Eyken commented:

> What we see throughout the nineteenth century in Europe therefore, is a ferment of ideas, of quick development and of official recognition for the world of the young child, and by 1908 it was possible to say that half the children between two and five in Belgium, a quarter of those in France and between 2 and 10 per cent in Germany were regularly attending institutions of some kind. (Van der Eyken, 1967: 60)

In the UK at this time, there was no such perceived need for early years provision. Few women worked, with most remaining at home to fulfil their duties as wives and mothers. However, some 3- and 4-year-old children were placed in elementary classes alongside their older peers, remaining seated for the majority of the school day and following inappropriate curricula set for older children. Learning, sometimes in classes of 60 children, was by rote and severe punishments were administered for misdemeanours. In 1908, the Education Act gave local education authorities (LEAs) the power to offer free nursery education in nursery classes housed within elementary schools. However, without legislation to enforce such provision, this did not secure nursery education for all 3- to 5-year-olds, simply those living near to schools which offered the service. Subsequent governments have followed a similar pattern, although currently we are seeing support for free nursery places for all young children whose parents desire it.

Some early pioneers

Throughout history, despite the lack of government support, early years pioneers have recognised, very clearly, the value of early years education. There was an increasing need to provide for the growing population of children requiring daycare, owing to a continuing increase of the female workforce, but also for children with special needs. These special needs could be the effects of poverty and war, major factors of the time, resulting in 'over-crowding, malnutrition, poor hygiene, disease and the ravages of poverty' (Van der Eyken, 1967: 65).

Robert Owen (1771–1858) was one of the earliest and most influential early years pioneers. A cotton-mill manager in New Lanark, Scotland, Owen reduced the working hours of young children in his mill and set up a school for the children of mill workers. Owen, according to David (1990: 18), 'believed that environmental factors, particularly during the earliest years of life, shaped the future citizen, and what he worked for was the education of an engaged future citizenry, not a subjugated and underachieving one'. Although we may question Owen's motives, his school encouraged children to explore play activities within a philosophy similar to Froebel, a German educator who was responsible for opening Germany's first kindergarten in the mid-1800s. He acknowledged the importance of play for young children and advocated kindergartens that encouraged exploratory play using appropriate resources to stimulate and extend children's knowledge. This philosophy still exists today but is, in the eyes of some, compromised by the introduction of the Early Years Foundation Stage, which they view as too formal and structured for 3- and 4-year-old children in the UK. In 1906, sisters Rachel and Margaret McMillan were instrumental in the introduction of the school meals system and in 1913 opened their first nursery school in Deptford with its own outdoor play space, which prospered rapidly. Owing to the poor general state of the nation's children at the time, the McMillan sisters were providing for many children with special needs and at the same time campaigned for nursery education for all, as Bradburn summarised:

> She (Margaret) realized that poverty, ignorance and disease were not only harming an adult population but mortgaging the growth of the next generation also. She yearned to change the system which created the conditions she abhorred. At the same time she realized that sick children could not wait for political reform. She fought to cure the dirt and disease that she saw everyday in the mothers and children around her, and kept up the fight for political reform as well. (Bradburn, 1976: 45–6)

The McMillan sisters continued throughout their lives to work for a nationwide nursery education system for all children.

Maria Montessori, founder of the Montessori Education system, first published her work 'the Montessori Method' in 1912, based on observations of her own young children and placing the child at the heart of the learning process. Within a Montessori classroom, the adult is a guide to the child, supporting the child's exploration and discovery but not intervening or imposing. A range of Montessori materials (didactic teaching materials) enable the child to explore, develop skills and self-check. These central materials are part of a broader range of stimulating experiences offered to the child. Beaver et al. (2000) summarise the method:

> The child is at the centre of the Montessori method. She (Montessori) believed that children learn best through their own spontaneous activity and that they have a natural inquisitiveness and eagerness to learn. The role of the adult is to provide a planned environment that will allow the child the opportunity to develop skills and concepts. (Beaver et al., 2000: 81)

The early to mid-1900s

In 1907, and again in 1916, a case for separate and discrete early years provision was raised, as was the suggestion that children should not be compelled to commence formal education at the age of 5, but without positive results. It was, however, the beginning of an understanding that a different form of education was required for our youngest children.

In 1918, the Maternal and Child Welfare Act separated daycare and education, placing responsibility for daycare provision within the remit of the Department of Health (DoH), with education remaining under the Board of Education. At the same time, the 1918 Education Act gave local authorities the power to support nursery education for children aged 2 to 5 years, specifically to promote healthy physical and mental development.

By the late 1920s, the UK government appeared to view nursery education from a more positive perspective with an education enquiry committee report in 1929 recognising the different needs of under 5s and identifying a need for separate nursery education.

Grace Owen (1928: 15), the honorary secretary to the Nursery Schools Association, concluded at the time that: 'It cannot be long before nursery schools for children between two and five years of age are the accepted instrument for securing adequate nurture for very young children'. This is an ideal yet to be achieved in the twenty-first century.

Until the start of the Second World War, there was little change in the range of provision available. Benefits to children, short and long term, were still not well researched and children's developmental needs and the importance of appropriate early years provision not recognised by all. Robson (1989: 4) highlighted: 'The developmental needs of the child seemed secondary to political, economic and social factors and the pamphlet (Nursery Schools and Nursery Classes 1936) described the under-fives "problem" as being due to modern housing conditions, the growth of traffic and all kinds of pressing social, industrial and financial considerations'.

In 1943, the Board of Education White Paper again highlighted a need for nursery provision, concluding that nursery schools were needed nationwide to offer appropriate educational experiences to the very young. The 1944 Education Act that followed continued to support the notion of nursery education, but sadly the country then experienced economic difficulties and the expansion of nursery provision was severely compromised.

During the Second World War, the government supported pre-school provision by way of grants, predominantly to release women to war-related workplaces as the majority of the male workforce was fighting for their country. In addition, the women needed to supplement the poor wages sent home by their husbands. Once the grants were removed after the war, many of the nurseries closed, thus returning the nation to a diversity of pre-school provision and most parents to a lack of useful provision, dependent on where they lived and their financial status.

The 1950s to 1970s

After the end of the Second World War, growth in pre-school provision continued in an ad hoc manner but availability varied geographically. Throughout the 1950s and 1960s, when the population was fast overtaking available housing, the sheer lack of available space for housing development resulted in the building of many high-rise flats. This produced additional concerns for young children and families as the basic design of such accommodation limited socialisation for adults and children alike and left many families isolated from friends, family and their local community. Over the years, many of these tower blocks became run-down and high-rise estates were often known (and in some cases still are known) for their problems of vandalism, crime, drug and alcohol abuse, anti-social behaviour and social deprivation. At a time when nursery provision was still not available to all, the quality of opportunities and experiences offered to these children could be described as minimal and lacking challenge.

The Plowden Report (CACE, 1967) highlighted the value of early years provision that led to some expansion of nursery provision, but these developments were predominantly in inner-city areas deemed to have exceptional needs (educational priority areas). Additional expansion at this time came mainly from the private sector and voluntary agencies, with an increase in campaigning for more provision for the under-5s.

The playgroup movement

Throughout the 1960s, the playgroup movement expanded nationally, responding directly to local need and the lack of state provision. Van der Eyken concluded:

> The efforts of these groups have done a great deal to stimulate concern about the under-fives. No one, however, would suggest that these self-help solutions are in any way an alternative to the provision of proper facilities and trained supervision for young children. They have arisen out of a growing recognition by parents of the needs of their children. At considerable personal sacrifice these parents are doing what they can to fill a void that they recognise exists. Inevitably their efforts can only alleviate the need. To satisfy that need is the responsibility of society as a whole. (Van der Eyken, 1967: 83)

Often being held, and still being held, in church halls or community centres, playgroups were predominantly run by mothers who maintained a rota to attend and supervise 3- to 4-year-olds at play, charging a nominal fee to cover expenses. Few of these mothers had formal training, qualifications or experience of such work. Since the first playgroups were introduced, the Pre-School Play-groups Association (now the Pre-School Learning Alliance – PLA) has been instrumental in providing guidance, training and support to all playgroups as well as continuously campaigning for the early years.

The 1970s to 1990s

In 1972, the Conservative government boldly pledged to provide free nursery education for every 3- and 4-year-old within ten years, another government commitment to early years education that was to remain unfulfilled. By the mid-1980s, little progress had been made, as highlighted within the Policy Analysis Unit report which concluded that:

In Britain there is hardly any provision at all for two year olds and part-time care only for 20 per cent of three year olds. Low priority has been given by successive Governments to child-care for under-fives, and there is no longer any statutory responsibility on local authorities to provide facilities for pre-school children, except those 'at risk'. (Policy Analysis Unit, 1986: 2)

The Children Act (1989) brought together preceding public and private law relating to children and identified a core value of the welfare of the child being 'paramount'. The Act also reinforced the importance of the family and of those who have 'parental responsibility' for children, trying to redress the balance between 'the needs and rights of children and the responsibilities and rights of parents' (Beaver et al., 2000: 196).

The Children Act defined 'children in need' and made clear how local authorities should provide for them, enabling children to remain at home with their families whenever appropriate. In addition, regulations were set for daycare providers covering such issues as space available, staffing ratios and qualifications of staff, all of which were monitored via the annual inspection process.

The terminology within the Children Act (children in need) should not be confused with educational terminology (special needs or educational needs).

1990–1997

From this point in time, there was little change in early years provision offered to 3- to 4-year-old children until 1996 when the Conservative government passed The Nursery Education and Grant Maintained Schools Act (1996) which formalised the Nursery Voucher Scheme and offered parents of children in their pre-school year vouchers to exchange for sessions with local providers.

Instead of the anticipated expansion of available provision offering greater choice to parents, many playgroups were forced to close. The incentive of monetary gain encouraged schools to open empty classrooms as nursery classes and some parents, perhaps misguidedly, perceived pre-school provision in schools as more 'educational' and thus 'better than' playgroups. Some schools added to parents' dilemmas by guaranteeing reception class places to nursery class attendees only. Playgroups were also subject to inspection by the social services department (SSD), whereas nursery classes on school premises were not.

For voluntary sector providers, registering with the scheme meant increased income, without which they were no longer financially viable, but also brought about the introduction of Office for Standards in Education (OFSTED) inspections demanding changes in methods of assessment, monitoring, recording and policy production. Groups registered on the scheme were expected to follow the Desirable Learning Outcomes (SCAA, 1996), outlining six areas of learning to be addressed with the children.

At this changeable time, training for playgroups and other voluntary providers was instigated around the country, as was support for groups to cope with the extra administrative tasks. As from 2000, Desirable Learning Outcomes were replaced by *Early Learning Goals* (QCA, 1999) as part of the Foundation Stage of Learning designed to prepare children from the age of 3 years until the end of the reception year in primary school for the National Curriculum following school entry.

1997–2010

In 1997, a new Labour government, with their commitment to progression in the early years, was elected. At this point, initial guidance emerged regarding the evolution of Early Years Development and Childcare Partnerships (EYDCPs) and a requirement for authorities to produce Early Years Development and Childcare Plans, from April 1998. Also in 1998, the government issued its National Childcare Strategy and at the time it was considered 'more ambitious in scope than anything produced by the previous government' (Baldock et al., 2005: 22), which identified the five key areas of focus within the strategy:

- tackling child poverty in the UK
- supporting increased partnerships in the early years
- encouraging further expansion and innovative practice
- breaking down the division between 'care' and 'education' and placing responsibility within the Department for Education and Employment (DfEE)
- improvements in the regulation of provision nationwide.

This National Childcare Strategy was seen as a positive step towards improved services for all young children and their families, and in 1999 the Working Tax Credit was introduced to encourage parents to return to work if they wished to, although parents faced a small mountain in trying to complete the forms and gain access to the money. Sure Start was a key element of the revised programme of change which offered interagency provision in areas designated as socially deprived: 'The development of Children's Centres is based on establishing holistic services for children under five, aiming to provide ... integrated service provision to better meet the needs of all children and families and to provide early assessment and intervention for children with additional needs' (Baldock et al., 2009: 43). Parents were involved from the start in the planning and implementation of the local community setting to ensure the needs of the community were heard, respected and included. Following the initial establishment of Sure Start pilot settings, the government has continued to roll out the programme nationwide over subsequent years. Integrated settings, with interagency philosophies, became a further area for government expansion with the intention of providing interagency and integrated settings in every community in England. This was combined with the establishment of the National Professional Qualification in Integrated Centre Leadership, to ensure effective leadership of such centres.

Following the re-election of the Labour government in 2001, the speed of change in early years, which some felt had already been considerable, seemed to take on renewed vigour. Building on their previous term's raft of changes, the commitment to continue with their policies was clear.

The Education Act 2002 implemented the recommendations from the White Paper, 'Schools: Achieving Success'. This act 'is a substantial and important piece of legislation intended to raise standards, promote innovation in schools and reform education law' (DfES, 2003b). Relating to early years, the key areas of change lay in:

- the introduction of the Foundation Stage profile to replace baseline assessment
- the role of the LEA in childcare and early education
- changes to the inspection process for childminders, daycare and nursery education
- renewed focus in promoting and safeguarding the welfare of children.

While emphasis had been placed on pre-school children (generally aged 3–5 years) up until this point, the government's next major initiative was the *Birth to Three Matters* framework (DfES/Sure Start Unit, 2002), offering structure to working with the very youngest children for the first time.

Practitioners viewing the child holistically was fundamental to this framework, within which four aspects of early childhood were identified: a strong child, a skilful communicator, a competent learner and a healthy child. The framework further divides the child developmentally, with each section of activities being age appropriate:

1   Heads up, lookers and communicators (0–8 months).

2   Sitters, standers and explorers (8–18 months).

3   Movers, shakers and players (18–24 months).

4   Walkers, talkers and pretenders (24–36 months).

In 2003, the Children's *National Service Framework* (NSF) evolved – 'a 10-year programme intended to stimulate long-term and sustained improvement in children's health … the NSF aims to ensure fair, high quality and integrated health and social care from pregnancy right through to adulthood' (DoH, 2009a). Offering a set of standards to be achieved, standard 8 refers specifically to disabled children and children with complex needs, so is particularly relevant to this text.

Arguably the most significant document to reach our desks has been *Every Child Matters* (ECM) (DfES, 2003a). Reviewing the situation and research at that time, the government revealed the following facts relating to young children (DfES, 2003a):

• There had been a fall in the number of children living in relative low income (from 34 per cent in 1996/97 to 28 per cent in 2002/03).

• This has been matched by a fall in the number of children living in absolute poverty (from 34 per cent in 1996/97 to 17 per cent in 2002/03).

• Three million of the 12 million children in this country have experienced the separation of their parents.

• As of January 2004, 1.4 million (17 per cent) of school children had special educational needs (SEN), of whom almost 250,000 (3 per cent) have a statement.

• There are at least 500,000 disabled children in England.

• As of 31 March 2004, there were 61,000 looked after children in England.

• As of 31 March 2004, there were 26,300 children on Child Protection Registers.

Such findings encouraged the government to maintain their drive to improve outcomes for all children, and in 2004 a barrage of supplementary guidance documents emerged outlining the changes planned for the future of all children and young people in an attempt to improve their outcomes through the ECM framework (see the timeline at the end of the chapter).

The ECM framework set out the national agenda for change from central government through local authorities to practitioners and parents, with the NSF being integral to all developments. Following ECM's considerable consultation process, the Children Bill was 'the first step in a long-term programme of change, creating the legislative spine for developing more effective and accessible services focused around the needs of children, young people and their families' (DfES, 2004a: s. 2.2). The central aims were to:

- establish the five outcomes across the full range of services for all children – to be healthy, stay safe, enjoy and achieve, make a positive contribution and achieve economic well-being

- appoint a Children's Commissioner for England to lead on and monitor developments

- ensure that at local level partnerships between all relevant parties exist to inform planning and provision

- ensure the safety of all children at all times

- establish Children's Trusts which will 'secure integrated commissioning leading to more integrated service delivery and better outcomes for children, young people and their families' (DfES, 2004a: s. 2.20). EYDCPs are likely to be incorporated within the new Children's Trusts

- establish a Director of Children's Services in each authority, 'to ensure clear accountability across the children's services functions of the local authority' (DfES, 2004a: s. 2.28).

The ECM framework supports the view that while many children are successful and achieve their potential, there are many who do not, so at a more local level the overarching aims are to be addressed through supporting families, giving children a positive start in life, early intervention and effective provision, integrated inspections, combined with reforms of the children's workforce to ensure higher-qualified staff who are able to provide effectively for all children. The ECM framework of change is further supported by the Children Act (DfES, 2004b) which legislated for some of the key changes, such as

Directors of Children's Services, improved interagency working systems and practices, integrated inspections and the Children's Commissioner. The Act also reviewed child protection procedures and identified strategies to reduce the number of children 'slipping through the net'. Another indication of the government's commitment to change in early years came in the form of *Choice for Parents, the Best Start for Children: A Ten Year Strategy for Childcare* (HM Treasury, 2004). In recognition of the growing wealth of research highlighting the vital importance of the earliest years in a child's life, the strategy addresses family issues surrounding work and family life.

The *Children's Workforce Strategy* (DfES, 2005a) emerged from the ECM framework and builds on the ten-year strategy claiming that: 'Success depends in a large part on the capacity and quality of those people who plan, manage and deliver services at the front line. We need a skilled and more stable workforce in sufficient numbers, led and deployed around the needs of children and young people' (DfES, 2005a: 3). This ambitious and long-awaited reform was to address issues such as qualifications, pay and conditions, retention and recruitment, and strong leadership. The reform documentation was followed by the *Common Core of Skills and Knowledge for the Children's Workforce* documentation (DfES, 2005b) which set out the levels of required knowledge in each of six key areas:

• effective communication and engagement

• child and young person development

• safeguarding and promoting the welfare of the child

• supporting transitions

• multi-agency working

• sharing information. (DfES, 2005b: 4)

In 2006, we saw the Childcare Act emerge which formalises:

the important strategic role local authorities play through a set of new duties. These duties will require authorities to improve the five Every Child Matters (ECM) outcomes for all pre-school children and reduce inequalities in these outcomes; secure sufficient childcare for working parents; and provide better parental information services. (Sure Start, 2008)

The Children's Plan was launched in 2007 (DCSF, 2007a), again building on ECM, and aiming to:

strengthen support for all families during the formative early years of their children's lives, take the next steps in achieving world class schools and an excellent education for every child, involve parents fully in their children's learning, help to make sure that young people have interesting and exciting things to do outside of school, and provide more places for children to play safely. (DCSF, 2007a cited in Wall, 2010: 20)

Next was the *Early Years Foundation Stage* (EYFS) (DCSF, 2008d) which brought guidance for the education and care of all children aged 0–5 years. This combined the earlier *Birth to Three Matters, Curriculum Guidance for the Foundation Stage* and the *National Standards for Under 8s Daycare and Childminding* and again incorporated the principles of ECM offering a smooth transition for provision covering the under-5s. However, with it arrived its critics stating that prescriptive planning for the very youngest children could lead to misinterpretation of the guidance and thus less appropriate provision for our children. The EYFS was a central focus within both the *Choice for Parents, the Best Start for Children: A Ten Year Strategy for Childcare* (HM Treasury, 2004) and *Childcare Act 2006* (Sure Start, 2008). So we saw a continuation of rapid and considerable change to our early years planning and provision. The five ECM outcomes were to be met through:

- setting the standards for the learning, development and care of children

- ensuring equality of opportunity and anti-discriminatory practice

- creating the framework for partnerships with parents and other professionals

- improving quality and consistency across the sector

- laying secure foundations for the future of the children.
  (Adapted from DfES, 2007: 7)

Throughout all these changes and developments, the profile of parents has been consistently raised, culminating in *Every Parent Matters* (DCSF, 2007b) outlining how crucial the parenting role is and how we need to identify gaps in our current supporting systems and ways forward, to ensure all parents are valued, have access to the services they need and are involved in decision-making processes.

During this period of time, the government was also developing the children's workforce strategy and the Children's Workforce Development Council (CWDC) was established. In 2008, the government launched its targets for the workforce in the *2020 Children and Young People's Workforce Strategy* (DCSF, 2008a) focusing on: '… ensuring that people in the workforce have the skills and knowledge they need to support children who are particularly vulnerable, including those who are looked after, are disabled or have mental health needs' (DCSF, 2008a: 7).

In the same year, the guidance to support the Childcare Act of 2006 was published: *Raising Standards – Improving Outcomes* (DCSF, 2008b) demanding that all Local Authorities (LAs) work to: 'improve the five Every Child Matters outcomes of all young children (aged 0–5) in their area and reduce inequalities between them, through integrated early childhood services' (DCSF, 2008b: 3). Following on from the *Raising Standards – Improving Outcomes* strategy of 2008, the government produced the *Early Years Quality Improvement Support Programme (EYQISP)* (DCSF, 2008c) which offers guidance to LA early years officers and leaders of settings with a set of 'tools' to enhance existing quality assurance mechanisms they may have in place. Five principles underpin the guidance:

- Strengthening leadership for learning
- Developing practitioner learning
- Facilitating partnerships for learning and development
- Supporting progress, learning and development
- Securing high quality environments for learning and development.
  (DCSF, 2008c: 6–7)

As part of the ongoing commitment to improved partnerships with parents, provision for children and interagency working, the government updated the EYFS in 2008 in light of feedback received from 'local authorities, schools and early years providers' (DCSF, 2008d).

Early in 2009 saw a health focus emerge with the arrival of *Healthy Lives, Brighter Futures: The Strategy for Children and Young People's Health* (DCSF, 2009a), established to improve the health of our youngest children, leading to healthier lifestyles as adults. We also saw the *Next Steps for Learning and Childcare* (DCSF, 2009b) which updated the ten-year childcare strategy and called for improved support for families, increased access to early learning opportunities, improved quality of all provision, increased information for all parents and more financial support for those families in greatest need.

Shortly after, schools became the focus of government attention, culminating in the publication *Your Child, Your Schools, Our Future: Building a 21st Century Schools System* (DCSF, 2009c). The vision is one of a system that:

provides a great start in life for every child in every school. A system that responds to the global economy, a changing society, rapid technological innovation and a changing planet. A system in which every child can enjoy growing up, and which develops the potential and talents of every child and young person and gives them the broad skills they need for the future. And a system which breaks down the link between deprivation, disadvantage, disability and low educational achievement and so impacts upon intergenerational poverty.

Also in 2009, the government developed and piloted ContactPoint (DCSF, 2009d) as an outcome of Lord Laming's report on child protection issues following the tragic death of baby Peter. ContactPoint is a new online directory which: 'provides a quick way for authorised practitioners in different services to find out who else is working with the same child or young person. This will make it easier for them to work as a team and deliver faster, more coordinated support' (DCSF, 2009d). Also stemming from Lord Laming's report came a review of the work of health visitors, aiming to highlight their changing role and suggest ways forwards to address the needs of all young families and their children across the country more effectively. *Getting it Right for Children and Families* (DoH, 2009b) outlines changes needed at national and local levels to ensure improved services to support the healthy development and care of every child. Working in the same area, the government's guidance on Information Sharing also stemmed from the Laming report and strives to set the way for improved services so no child can 'slip through the net'. The guidance (DCSF, 2009e), for practitioners and managers working in all agencies, advises on when information should be shared, plus the mechanisms to do this effectively: 'To support early intervention and preventative safeguarding or child protection situations' (DCSF, 2009e).

The range of early years settings

As can be deduced from the preceding section, the range of early years settings has grown considerably and continues to grow. While under the umbrella of making more choice available for parents, the considerable array could present as a confusing range which will still not ensure equality of access for all parents and their children as all communities are unlikely to be able to offer the 'full range' of services.

Historically, providers could be divided into three broad categories and have been well documented (for example, Maynard and Thomas, 2004; Pugh, 2001). The range of provision now includes schools, day nurseries, childminders, nannies, preschool groups, nursery classes, Children's Centres, extended provision, Sure Start centres and many more.

Now, in the twenty-first century, many of our Sure Start settings have been developed into Children's Centres. When this is combined with the increase in schools offering breakfast clubs and after-school clubs, we can see the beginnings of more flexibility for families, which many would view as positive. However, there are some issues:

- If you live in a rural location without transport, how accessible will your nearest integrated setting be in reality?

- How can we ensure parents have sufficient information to make informed decisions and choices when the rate of change is so rapid and the range of settings is considerable?

In conclusion, early years provision has developed according to need and at varying rates, owing to a lack of consistent government funding. The current range of provision is only now becoming more unified following very recent legislation, guidance and increased funding.

The historical development of special needs provision and legislation in the UK

An exploration of the development of special needs provision will highlight key chronological events, indicating a progression from eighteenth-century perspectives to the present day, however it is not possible to explore all legislation and policy within this chapter so readers are referred to the timeline at the end of this chapter for further information.

During the eighteenth century, the first public schools for the deaf and the blind were opened, followed in the early nineteenth century by the development of asylums for 'idiots'. Throughout this historical period, children with special educational needs were, for the most part, unacceptable to society. For religious, societal and/or cultural reasons, parents often experienced great shame and tremendous guilt, and in some cases either abandoned their children or kept them hidden from society.

Armstrong (2007) summarises the position for young children with disabilities in the early 1800s:

> many disabled children from poorer families were sent to workhouses, reformatory or industrial schools where they received basic education and training. There were also the lunatic asylums where children and adults diagnosed as insane or 'mentally defective' were placed, and where they sometimes received

education and training, but the residential special schools, which were located in asylums controlled by doctors, psychiatrists and philanthropists, were detached from the education sector and the influence of educationists. (2007: 554)

In 1870, *Forster's Education Act* provided education for all children – a significant move forwards. In the 1890s, LEAs were required to make special provision for all blind and deaf children, and were given the option to provide for 'mentally defective' children. School meals and medical inspections were introduced under the 1909 Education Act in an attempt to alleviate future problems with the nation's health.

Throughout the 1920s and 1930s, Freud's work became established, offering explanations for adult behaviours and feelings, and linking them back to early childhood experiences. This highlighted implications for the importance of those early experiences. At this time, the first child guidance clinic was founded to respond to the prevalent problems of poverty and lack of work, and their impact on the young children of the time.

The Education Act 1944 instigated the appointment of a Minister for Education and the formation of the Ministry of Education, and stated that LEAs 'should have regard to the need for securing that provision is made for pupils who suffer from any disability of mind or body by providing special educational treatment' (Ministry of Education, 1944: 5). The Handicapped Pupils and School Health Regulations of 1945 identified 11 categories of disability: blind, partially blind, deaf, partially deaf, delicate, diabetic, educationally subnormal, epileptic, maladjusted, physically handicapped and with speech defects. At this stage, medical practitioners undertook diagnoses and children were placed in the most appropriate facilities, resulting in many children being sent away from their homes to boarding schools. Within the 1950s, many parents rebelled against this 'medical model' of diagnosis as their children, often very vulnerable, were transported considerable distances from their families and local communities resulting in the children becoming even more vulnerable.

The 1970 Education (Handicapped Children) Act (DES, 1970) placed the responsibility of special needs provision within the remit of LEAs and, as a result, special schools were established.

Perhaps one of the earliest references specifically regarding special needs within the early years was the Court Report of 1976 which highlighted the need for focus on the screening of health and development in the early years to identify difficulties within a developmental framework.

In 1978, the *Warnock Report* (DES, 1978) was published, having examined in great detail the provision available at the time for all 'handicapped children and young people'. This report, innovative at the time, was to inform subsequent legislation and significantly change the face of special needs provision. One of the key issues raised was that all children have the right to an education and, as society was now more accepting of 'difference', that for children experiencing difficulties we should be committed to 'educating them, as a matter of right and to developing their full potential' (1978: 1.11). The fact that this basic principle needed stating reflects somewhat negatively on the education system and societal perspectives prior to 1978. The report continued to suggest a continuum of special needs as opposed to children fitting into one or more categories. The report clarified that children can experience short- and/or longer-term needs, and that provision must be flexible to accommodate change.

Within the report were clear recommendations for LEAs (not health authorities) to assume responsibility for assessing and identifying young children with possible special needs. Furthermore, methods of assessment were detailed to move forwards from the sole use of intelligence quotient (IQ) tests. The report made clear that a variety of methods should be employed to ensure the most effective provision according to need and that within child factors should be considered in conjunction with additional possible causal factors, including those within the school/setting.

Parental partnerships were seen as crucial for effective provision if all children with special needs were to achieve their full potential. The child should be assessed as an individual with a differentiated curriculum reflecting this, if appropriate.

The ensuing Education Act 1981 echoed the key principles of the Warnock Report and placed special educational needs provision firmly on the legislative agenda. Key points included:

- LEAs were given the responsibility of identification and assessment of special educational needs.
- Multidisciplinary assessments could lead to a formal assessment of special educational needs, culminating in a statement of special educational needs, which would be reviewed annually.

- A focus should be placed on individual needs rather than on categories of need.

- Provision for children with special educational needs to become the responsibility of the LEA.

- All categories of handicap were removed.

- Effective parental partnerships should be established.

- Integration should occur wherever practicable.

In addition, definitions of special educational needs were consolidated (DES, 1981, s. 1.1):

> Children have a learning difficulty if:
>
> They have significantly greater difficulty in learning than the majority of children of their age, or
>
> They have a disability which prevents or hinders them from making use of the educational facilities generally provided in schools, for children of their age. It continued, that a child has a learning difficulty if he/she:
>
> Has a learning disability which requires educational provision that is additional to, or otherwise different from, the educational provision made generally available within the school, or: If he/she has a physical disability.

The Children Act (1989) consolidated previous public and private laws regarding the welfare of children. Additional definitions and revised terminology were clarified:

> A child shall be taken as 'in need' if:
>
> He is unlikely to achieve or maintain, or to have the opportunity of achieving or maintaining, a reasonable standard of health or development without the provision for him by services by a local authority under this Part; His health or development is likely to be significantly impaired, or further impaired, without the provision for him of such services;
>
> Or,
>
> He is disabled. (DoH, 1991: s. 2.3)

The Children Act also clearly identified a need for effective multidisciplinary working systems, as summarised by Anderson-Ford (1994: 20): 'The Children Act, like the 1981 Act, clearly defines the need for communication between teachers, the school health service and social services departments (SSDs) as well as between the LEA and SSDs at a senior management level'.

The Education Reform Act 1988 (DfEE, 1988) introduced the National Curriculum, outlining core and foundation subjects, with flexibility for modification to accommodate the learning needs of children with special educational needs. A key focus of the Act was to ensure that all children had equal access to a broad and balanced curriculum.

The Disability Discrimination Act, in 1995, demanded that all schools should have admission statements for children with special educational needs, but specifically for those with physical disabilities. Schools needed to ensure that all pupils had equal access to facilities, resources and curriculum, and that an anti-discriminatory philosophy existed. One may have argued, however, that the limitations, general conditions and planning of some school and pre-school buildings rendered this Act difficult to adhere to, despite the best of intentions of staff and governors alike.

Part three of the 1993 Education Act (DfEE, 1993) addressed problems and issues that had arisen since the implementation of the 1981 Act. Major reviews of the 1981 Act highlighted key areas for change, as outlined by Lindsay (1997: 20): 'The Act was inconsistent, inefficient and clearly did not meet the objective of ensuring each child with SEN received a quality assessment, and provision to meet the needs identified'. In summary, the 1993 Education Act revised the 1981 Act and introduced the following changes:

• School SEN policies must reflect the new approach.

• Greater responsibility should be given to parents within positive, effective working partnerships.

• An independent tribunal system should be established.

The *Code of Practice* (DfEE, 1994) guidance document (as opposed to legislative) was introduced in 1994, detailing the responsibilities previously laid down within the 1993 Act. It offered LEAs and practitioners very clear and specific guidelines on all aspects of special educational needs provision, including identification, assessment, a five-staged approach to assessment and statementing, reviews and the new role of the Special Educational Needs Coordinator (SENCO).

One of the key issues for all early years practitioners was that provision for children below the age of five years was included within section 5 of the Code of Practice, giving support to the philosophy of early identification and intervention within a multidisciplinary framework.

At that particular time, with playgroups dominating pre-school provision, these requirements were considerable as, although very skilled and knowledgeable adults staffed such groups, they often lacked formal qualifications and, more specifically, special needs training. Training programmes were introduced nationwide, mainly through either LEAs or the Pre-School Playgroup Association, to ensure that all children's needs could be addressed.

The newly created role of SENCO (DfEE, 1994: para. 2.14) brought with it considerable requirements and responsibilities, as summarised by Smith (1996: 9):

- taking responsibility for the day-to-day operation of the school's SEN policy
- liaising with and advising fellow teachers
- coordinating provision for pupils with SEN
- maintaining the school's SEN register and overseeing the records of all pupils with SEN
- liaising with parents
- contributing to staff in-service training
- liaising with external agencies.

In reality, many SENCOs were already full-time practitioners and these responsibilities were therefore additional, although in some instances new appointments were created. However, pre-school providers also had to maintain a SENCO and, with many playgroup employees remaining in post for relatively short terms, this created ongoing difficulties for many groups.

The five stages of assessment from identification through to formal statements detailed within the Code applied to children from birth, although the Code did not expect special educational needs to arise during the first two years of a child's life, unless the child had a specific condition from birth and/or major health and development difficulties.

The Code outlined the requirements for effective planning of provision for individual children on the special needs register (Individual Education Plans – IEPs), which could include such information as a summary of the difficulties, steps taken to accommodate those needs, details of parental views, resources (materials and human) required, detailed targets for future working, and information on assessments, monitoring and reviewing the provision.

2000 onwards

The Special Educational Needs and Disability Act 2001 incorporated further changes for education and as a result the Special Educational Needs Code of Practice 2001 was published, followed by the Disability Discrimination Code of Practice.

The Special Educational Needs Code of Practice (DfES, 2001c) included a section on identification, assessment and provision of special educational needs in early education settings. The five-staged approach from the 1994 Code was now replaced by a 'graduated response' incorporating Early Years Action and Early Years Action Plus:

> Once practitioners have identified that a child has special educational needs, the setting should intervene through *Early Years Action*. If the intervention does not enable the child to make satisfactory progress the SENCO may need to seek advice and support from external agencies. These forms of intervention are referred to (below) as *Early Years Action Plus*. (DfES, 2001c: s. 4.11)

The new Code of Practice (DfES, 2001c) identified key changes from the original Code of Practice (DfEE, 1994) as:

- a stronger right for children with SEN to be educated at a mainstream school

- new duties on LEAs to arrange for parents of children with SEN to be provided with services offering advice and information and a means of resolving disputes

- a new duty on schools and relevant nursery education providers to tell parents when special educational provision is being provided for their child

- a new right for schools and relevant nursery education providers to request a statutory assessment of a child. (DfES, 2001c: iv)

Another area emphasised within the new Code of Practice was the value of and need for effective multidisciplinary working systems, providing for the needs of children within a 'seamless' service that addressed the needs of children as well as their parents. However, practitioners and organisations such as NASEN have identified possible shortcomings within the guidance, including the lack of provision for non-teaching time for SENCOs to allow for planning, preparation and record-keeping (although the guidance suggests that this should be reviewed within settings), plus the recurring issue of training and funding. Considerable importance is placed on parental partnerships and multidisciplinary working, but these place additional demands on SENCOs' time to create, monitor, review and maintain systems and processes. It could be that without the alloca-tion of specified time to undertake such activities the outcomes may be limited, although working practices inform us that many SENCOs achieve this despite the time implications. This will be further explored in Chapter 7.

The other half of the SENDA 2001 related to disability discrimination and it was at this stage that early years providers became responsible for meeting the set requirements. The guidance (CDC, Sure Start and NCB, 2003: 2) comprised two key duties:

- not to treat a child less 'favourably' for any reason related to their disability

- to make 'reasonable adjustments' for disabled children, such as arranging staff training to ensure a child with a particular condi-tion can be provided for appropriately following entry to the setting.

The Audit Commission published their review of SEN provision in 2002 entitled *Special Educational Needs: A Mainstream Issue* which explored the progress of authorities and settings in managing and providing quality services for children with SEN and concluded that: 'Whether and how children's needs are identified appears to be influ-enced by a range of factors, including their gender, ethnicity and family circumstances, where they live and which school they attend ... Some continue to face considerable barriers to learning' (Audit Commission, 2002: 51). The report made ten recommendations for improvement.

Together from the Start: Practical Guidance for Professionals Working with Disabled Children (Birth to 2) and their Families was published by the DfES and DoH in 2002 and explored the delivery of services for the very youngest children with disabilities. While the common themes appeared – early identification and provision, partnerships with parents and interagency working – it also highlighted the need for strategic direction for this particular age group. Noticeably, three key barriers to existing provision were highlighted: a lack of sensitivity at the time of diagnosis, inconsistent patterns of provision and the lack of coordination between multiple service providers which it addressed in more detail (DfES and DoH, 2002: 3). Within an inclusive climate, the guidance suggests that as most birth-to-two-year-olds will spend most of their time within the family home, priority must be given to authorities ensuring effective and respon-sive intervention within an effective partnership system with parents and other agencies.

The same year saw the publication of *Supporting Families Who Have Children with Special Needs and Disabilities* (Sure Start, 2002) which used the Together from the Start definition of special needs (Sure Start, 2002: 5):

A child under four years of age has a disability or special needs if she or he:

- is experiencing significant developmental delays, in one or more of the areas of cognitive development, physical development, communication development, social or emotional development and adaptive development; or

- has a condition which has a high probability of resulting in developmental delay.

The purpose of the guidance was to ensure 'access to a good quality service from Sure Start programmes; ensure issues of access and quality; help develop awareness of the needs of families and how to respond appropriately; build on and share knowledge and information about special needs services' (2002: 3). The document continued to outline procedures and effective provision, taking into account interagency working, parent partnerships, early assessment and intervention. The need to respect and value contributions of parents, other professionals and the whole community emerge as ongoing themes.

Sure Start then issued their guidance entitled: *Area Special Educational Needs Coordinators (SENCOs) – Supporting Early Identification and Intervention for Children with Special Educational Needs* (Sure Start, 2003). This guidance 'sets out the envisaged role and practices of Area SEN-COs as they empower all those working with children in the early years to create inclusive and effective early learning environments' (2003: 2). Aiming at a target of one Area SENCO to every 20 non-maintained early years settings by 2004 (2003: 2), the guidance continued to identify the roles he/she will adopt and what knowledge and skills are necessary to undertake the job. Interestingly, the original intention of ensuring Area SENCOs were qualified teachers was later removed from the draft document and senior managers had the right to set their own qualifying criteria.

The Early Support Pilot Programme, which adopted the main principles from Together from the Start, was piloted in 2003 and offered guidance for all professionals, across agencies, working with young children with disabilities. Focusing on early identification and appropriate intervention, Early Support has now become the government's mechanism for improving interagency working and streamlining systems in support of all families with a child or children with a disability. The government states the programme will 'make a real difference to the lives of disabled children and their families' (DCSF, 2004).

The National Service Framework (2003) referred to earlier, contained 11 standards to be met, with standard 8 specifically relating to children with disabilities and/or complex health needs. This standard states that: 'Children and young people who are disabled or who have complex health needs receive coordinated, high quality child and family centred services which are based on assessed needs, which promote social inclusion and, where possible, which enable them and their families to live ordinary lives' (DoH, 2004). The standard then identifies key themes to support the standard:

- services which promote social inclusion
- access to hospital and primary health care services
- early identification
- early intervention and support
- palliative care
- safeguarding young children
- multi-agency transition planning. (DoH, 2004)

Also in 2004, *Removing Barriers to Achievement: The Government's Strategy for SEN* (RBA) was published (DfES, 2004c). Dovetailing with the government's array of early years and children's strategies at that time, but most specifically the ECM, the RBA strategy outlined the government's vision for continued improvements in SEN provision. Chapters focused on early identification, removing barriers to learning, raising expectations and achievements, delivering improved partnerships and interagency working. The strategy 'sets out the Government's vision for giving children with special educational needs and disabilities the opportunity to succeed. Building on the proposals for the reform of children's services in Every Child Matters, it sets out a new agenda for improvement and action at national and local level' (DfES, 2004c). We also saw the establishment of a team of *National SEN Advisers* in 2004 to work with local authorities in an advisory capacity.

It should be noted that many of the changes in early years already discussed in this chapter also make reference to special needs provision. For example, the National Service Framework, Every Child Matters and the Code of Practice all share common aims of improving early identification and intervention, family support, inclusive services, working with parents, skilled early years workforce and interagency working. Early in 2005, the government produced their report, entitled *Improving the Life Chances of Disabled People*, with the ambitious aim that: 'By 2025, disabled people in Britain should have full opportunities and choices to improve their quality of life and will be respected and included as equal members of society' (Cabinet Office, 2005). Of the four key areas identified, one relates specifically to families with young children with disabilities, ensuring that provision is tailor-made to respond to individual child and family needs and that parents should have access to their own individualised budgets, offering them greater choice and control over their provision. This links directly to the government's Direct Payments Scheme (DoH, 2004) which offers parents of disabled children (aged 0–17 years) the option of receiving direct payments from the government to arrange their own package of services to respond to their child's needs. Currently, social services and/or LEAs provide funding and set up and pay for the services offered.

Baroness Warnock, the original leader of the Warnock committee in the 1970s, also contributed to the inclusion debate in 2005 by producing a leaflet suggesting a U-turn in her original views from the 1970s. She concluded that: 'pressure to include pupils with problems in mainstream schools causes "confusion of which children are the casualties"' (Behaviour4Learning, 2005). Special schools, she claims, still have a place, as inappropriate placement in mainstream school does not guarantee successful inclusion. She continues to suggest that it would be more financially viable to retain some special schools as opposed to closing them all and attempting to replicate their provision in every mainstream school. Attracting much media attention at the time, her views received considerable criticism. The Independent Panel for Special Educational Advice (IPSEA) suggested that: 'Mary Warnock's 2005 attack on statements needs to be commented on because she is accorded the status of special educational needs guru by politicians and the media, and this risks her recent contribution to the debate being accorded a significance which it does not merit' (2005: 9).

The Disability Rights Commission published the *Special Schools Debate* in July 2005 (DRC, 2005) which examined 'educational opportunities for disabled children'. Highlighting that significant improvements had been made, the report concluded that children with disabilities 'continue to experience inequality in the education system' (DRC, 2005). Schools are seen as critical to future progress in three specific areas:

- providing children and young people with the opportunity for self-development, reaching their individual potential and successful transition to independent adult life and becoming contributory citizens

- transmitting society's values to children and young people

- offering a place and a reason for interaction between different children and communities. (DRC, 2005)

The report supports the government's progress and recommendations in documentation such as RBA and clearly defines a need for society, government and practitioners to end discussion relating to where children should be educated (special or mainstream) and begin developing our thinking and practices to support an education system 'which fosters and promotes disabled people's belonging and inclusion' (DRC, 2005).

This report was closely followed in October 2005 by an *Inquiry into Special Education Needs* by IPSEA. While summarising the current situation relating to SEN assessment and provision, the report highlighted some areas for improvement, such as improved DfES responses to complaints about LEAs, possible changes to the SENDIST service and an improved role for government itself in leading future changes.

The Disability Discrimination Act of 2005 (DCSF, 2007c) updated previous versions and laid down the requirements for all public bodies to:

- eliminate discrimination

- eliminate harassment based on disability

- promote equality of opportunity between disabled people and other people

- promote positive attitudes towards disabled people

- encourage participation by disabled people in public life

- take steps to take account of disabled people's disabilities even where that involves treating disabled people more favourably than other people. (DCSF, 2007c)

The Act makes clear that all schools must now create, monitor and review their work to ensure they meet their Disability Equality Duty and a wealth of useful guidance is available, with one area focusing on the early years (DCSF, 2009f).

In 2007, we saw the emergence of *Aiming High for Disabled Children: Better Support for Families* (AHDC) (HM Treasury, 2007), highlighting the government's commitment to improving services for young children with disabilities and their families. Having acknowledged that:

> disabled children are less likely to achieve their full potential without appropriate and improved support systems the government invested £340 million to ensure progress in the following areas:
> * increased access to services
> * more responsive support, and
> * higher quality support for all children. (adapted from Wall, 2010: 21)

In the same year, the *Inclusion Development Programme* (IDP) was published, building on the Removing Barriers to Achievement strategy of 2004 and incorporating Early Support approaches. The IDP (DCSF, 2007d) aims to improve provision (and therefore outcomes) for all children with special needs and disabilities and is funded over a four-year period (until 2011), with each academic year taking a different focus – for example, in 2009/10 the focus is on autistic spectrum disorders, and in 2010/11 it will focus on behavioural, emotional and social needs. Through offering support and professional development materials to practitioners, it is hoped that the workforce will become more highly trained to accommodate the needs of all children in an inclusive manner. There is also specific guidance for the early years phase (DCSF, 2008e) which practitioners could find particularly useful. However, the materials are online and while a practitioner can enrol and gain a certificate if they successfully complete the modules, we need to ask how many practitioners have the time to access these crucial materials.

In 2008, John Bercow reviewed provision for children with speech, language and communication needs (*The Bercow Report*, DCSF, 2008f), identifying that improvements were needed in the following areas:

* understanding the importance of the need to communicate

* improved early identification and intervention

* services to respond to the needs of the family

* joint working between agencies, and

* improved equity of access to appropriate support. (adapted from Wall, 2010: 22)

Forty recommendations were made in the report and the follow-up action plan, *Better Communication* (DCSF, 2008g), clearly outlines the means by which these will be met.

2008 also saw the publication of the *Quality Standards for SEN and Outreach Services* (DCSF, 2008h), which although not mandatory, offer guidance on how to:

- illustrate good practice in the provision of SEN support and outreach services

- help guide the development of local provision and support

- assist local authorities in determining appropriate resources and arrangements, and

- assist in the monitoring and evaluation process. (DCSF, 2008h: 2)

Following on from the AHDC in 2007, the government published *Aiming High for Disabled Children: Best Practice to Common Practice* (DCSF, 2009g) which highlighted the progress to date in each of the identified areas from the original document and the next stages of work to take place. By using case studies, it is hoped that the examples of excellent practice will encourage further developments nationwide to improve provision and access to provision for all young children with disabilities and their families.

The Lamb Inquiry was requested by the government to explore parental satisfaction in SEN provision. Sir Brian Lamb's report (DCSF, 2009h) highlighted numerous areas where parents felt less than satisfied with their experiences of the SEN system, stating that:

> The failure to comply with statutory obligations speaks of an underlying culture where parents and carers of children with SEN can too readily be seen as the problems and as a result parents lose confidence in schools and professionals. As the system stands it often creates 'warrior parents' at odds with the school and feeling they have to fight for what should be their children's by right; conflict in place of trust. It does not and should not have to be like this. (DCSF, 2009h: 2)

The 11 recommendations will require considerable change from all those involved in SEN provision but hopefully should lead to significant improvements in years to come, if successfully implemented.

The CWDC has also produced updated guidance for all practitioners on the use of the Common Assessment Framework (CAF) with a specific focus on early identification, assessment and intervention (CWDC, 2009a). This non-statutory guidance covers all aspects of the CAF and its uses to ensure proactive and interagency provision is in place to avoid any more children 'slipping through the net' of provision. Reflecting the key principle that early identification and intervention make a difference, the guidance builds on all other policy initiatives stemming from ECM.

Within this chapter, I have only touched the surface of the documentation that has emerged and for this reason a supplementary timeline is offered at the end of this chapter with further legislation, guidance and policy documents included. An online search would direct the reader to each document.

When considering the expanse of documentation published since 2001, the reader can begin to understand how and where many of these initiatives begin to dovetail and build on the anticipated success of each other. Through a comprehensive review and a clear vision, the government is hoping to enable greater choice and flexibility for families and their children as well as ensuring high-quality and effective provision for all children, within frameworks specifically designed to address the needs of each child, at each stage of their formative years. At all times, the safety and protection of children is seen as of paramount importance. However, while this array of change may appear to be highly desirable and of great value to all, there are many criticisms that could be raised, such as how are early years practitioners expected to find time to access, read and assimilate the complex information contained within the vast array of publications? How will the changes be implemented at local level and will there be equity nationwide regarding funding? Time will tell, but I am sure that, despite the innovations that have emerged, each with commendable justification, problems and difficulties are also likely to emerge.

Summary

Early years provision has changed considerably over the past century to offer a diverse range of opportunities to young children and their families, and all registered early years providers must now have due regard to the Special Educational Needs and Disability Act 2001 (DfES, 2001b), hopefully ensuring appropriate special educational provision for all children within an interagency framework. However, issues such as funding, training, resources and accommodation can impact on the levels of provision available and the range offered in different areas of the country and in different settings, so we are still a long way from a system that offers equity to all children at all times. Huge strides have been made, but further progress is still needed to ensure optimum achievement for all very young children.

Special educational needs provision, both generally and in the early years, has received more national attention over the past 20 years than ever before and, while we can acknowledge that the central aim is to strive continuously to improve systems and provision, the current situation (and relevant legislation and guidance) is not necessarily the answer to ensure equal and appropriate provision for all. As Farrell concludes, we are currently in a situation balancing both positive and negative aspects:

> On the positive side parents now have a much louder voice, there are more mechanisms to support them and they have far greater rights of appeal ...
>
> Perhaps more important are the continued problems associated with the bureaucratic and cumbersome statutory assessment procedures which, despite the proposed changes in the new Draft Code, still seem to be a millstone round the necks of all those involved in striving to provide the best quality education to pupils with SEN and their families. (Farrell, 2001: 8)

While we are definitely moving in the right direction, we still have a *long* road ahead.

The reader is recommended to access directly documents referred to in this chapter for more detailed information, as only the briefest of overviews has been possible.

Points for reflection

- Assess the training needs of all practitioners in your setting with regard to special educational needs.
- Identify any training needs and how to address them.
- Ensure your setting meets all current government requirements.

Suggested further reading

Farrell, M. (2004) *Special Educational Needs: A Resource for Practitioners.* London: Paul Chapman Publishing.

Hayward, A. (2006) *Making Inclusion Happen.* London: Sage.

Maynard, T. and Thomas, N. (eds) (2009) *An Introduction to Early Childhood Studies*, 2nd edn. London: Sage.

Wolfendale, S. (2006) *Meeting Special Needs in the Early Years: Directions in Policy and Practice.* London: David Fulton.

TIMELINE OF KEY LEGISLATION, REPORTS AND GUIDANCE SINCE 2000

For further information, internet searches should take you directly to the documents

Date	Author	Title
2001	DfES	SEN Code of Practice
2001	DfES	Inclusive Schooling: Children with SEN
2002	DfES	Education Act
2002	Sure Start	Supporting Families who have Children with Special Needs and Disabilities
2002	LGA	Serving Children Well: A New Vision for Children's Services
2002	DfES	Birth to Three Matters
2002	DfES and DoH	Together from the Start: Practical Guidance for Professionals Working with Disabled Children and their Families
2003	DfES	Report of the Special Schools Working Group
2003	Sure Start	Area SENCOs: Supporting Early Identification and Intervention for Children with Special Educational Needs
2003	Audit Commission	Special Educational Needs: A Mainstream Issue
2003	DoH	National Service Framework
2003	DoH	Assessing Children's Needs and Circumstances: The Impact of the Assessment Framework
2003	DfES	Every Child Matters (ECM)
2004	DfES	ECM: Change for Children
2004	DfES	ECM: Change for Children in Schools
2004	DfES	ECM: Change for Children in Social Care
2004	DfES	ECM: Change for Children in Health Services
2004	DfES	ECM: Working with Voluntary and Community Organisations to Deliver Change for Children and Young People
2004	DfES	ECM: Next Steps
2004	DfES	Children Act
2004	DCFS, DoH & Sure Start	Early Support Programme
2004	DfES and DoH	Disabled Children and Young People and those with Complex Health Needs
2004	HM Treasury	Choice for Parents, the Best Start for Children: A Ten-year Strategy for Childcare
2004	OFSTED	Special Educational Needs and Disability: Towards Inclusive Schools
2004	DfES	Management of SEN Expenditure
2004	National Strategies	Learning and Teaching for Children with SEN in the Primary Years
2004	DfES	Removing Barriers to Achievement – The Government's Strategy for SEN
2004	DfES	Introduction of SEN Expert Advisers
2005	DfES	The distribution of resources to support inclusion
2005	Prime Minister's Strategy Unit	Improving the Life Chances of Disabled People
2005	DRC	Special Schools Debate
2005	DCSF	Higher Standards: Better Schools for All, More Choice for Parents
2005	House of Commons Education & Skills Committee	Special Educational Needs: Third Report of Session 2005–06
2005	OFSTED	Removing Barriers: A Can-Do Attitude
2005	DCSF	Disability Discrimination Act
2005	DCSF	Disability Equality Duty guidance
2005	DfES	Common Core of Skills and Knowledge for the Children's Workforce
2006	DCSF	Children's Workforce Strategy
2006	DfES	Children Act
2006	CWDC	The Lead Professional: Manager's Guide
2006	DCSF	The Rose Review
2007	DfES	Early Years Foundation Stage
2007	DfES	Every Parent Matters
2007	DCSF	Inclusion Development Programme
2007	DCSF	Children's Plan
2007	HM Treasury/DfES	Aiming High for Disabled Children: Better Support for Families
2007	DCFS, DoH & Sure Start	Best Practice in Key Working: What do Research and Policy Have to Say?
2007	DCFS, DoH & Sure Start	Team Around the Child

2007	DCFS, DoH & Sure Start	Information Sharing, the Common Assessment Framework and Early Support
2007	DCFS, DoH & Sure Start	Working with Parents in Partnership
2007	DCFS, DoH & Sure Start	Improving Access and Inclusion in Early Years Services
2007	DCFS, DoH & Sure Start	Family Structures
2008	DCSF	The Education (Special Educational Needs Coordinators) (England) Regulations 2008
2008	DCSF	Bercow Review
2008	APPGA	Half-way There Report
2008	DCSF	2020 Children and Young People's Workforce Strategy
2008	DCSF	21st Century Schools: A World Class Education for Every Child
2008	DCSF	Better Communication: An Action Plan to Improve Services for Children and Young People with Speech, Language and Communication Needs
2008	DCSF	Quality Standards for SEN Support and Outreach Services
2008	DCSF	The Education of Children and Young People with Behavioural, Emotional and Social Difficulties (BESD) – revised guidance
2008	DCSF	Early Years Foundation Stage Profile Handbook
2008	DCSF	SEN – A Guide for Parents and Carers
2008	National Strategies	Attainment and progress for pupils with SEN/LDD
2008	DCSF	Every Child a Talker
2008	DCSF	Raising Standards, Improving Outcomes
2008	DCSF and Cabinet Office	Families in Britain: an evidence paper
2008	DCSF	What is a Children's Trust?
2008	DCSF	The Impact of Parental Involvement on Children's Education
2008	DCSF and National Strategies	Social and Emotional Aspects of Development: Guidance for Practitioners Working in the Early Years Foundation Stage
2008	CDC	Inclusion Policy
2008	DCSF and National Strategies	Early Years Quality Improvement Support Programme (EYQISP)
2008	DCSF and National Strategies	Inclusion Development Programme – Supporting Children with Speech, Language and Communication Needs: Guidance for Practitioners in the Early Years Foundation Stage
2009	DCSF	Healthy Lives, Brighter Futures: The Strategy for Children and Young People's Health.
2009	HM Government	Next Steps for Early Learning and Childcare
2009	DCSF	Aiming High for Disabled Children: Best Practice to Common Practice
2009	DCSF	Progression Guidance 2009–10
2009	QCA	Planning, Teaching and Assessing the Curriculum for Pupils with Learning Difficulties: General Guidance
2009	DCSF	Introduction of Contact Point
2009	EDCM	Disabled Children and Health
2009	DCSF	Lamb Inquiry
2009	DCSF	The Education (Special Educational Needs Coordinators) (England) (Amendment) Regulations 2009
2009	House of Commons	National Curriculum Fourth Report of Session 2008–09: Volume 1
2009	House of Commons	SEN and Disability Bill (2nd reading)
2009	United Nations	Rights of Persons with Disabilities
2009	QCA	Planning, Teaching and Assessing the Curriculum for Pupils with Learning Difficulties
2009	DoH	Getting it Right for Children and Families: Maximising the Contribution of the Health Visiting Team
2009	DfES	Safeguarding Disabled Children
2009	CWDC	The Common Assessment Framework for Children and Young People: Early Identification, Assessment of Needs and Intervention: A Guide for Practitioners
2009	DCSF	Your Child, Your Schools, Our Future: Building a 21st Century Schools System
2009	DCSF	Progress Matters: Reviewing and Enhancing Young Children's Development
2009	DCSF/HMO	Information Sharing: Guidance for Practitioners and Managers
2009	DCSF	The Cambridge Primary Review
No date	NASEN	Policy on Partnership with Parents and Carers
No date	NASEN	Policy document on Inclusion
No date	NASEN	Policy on Assessment
No date	NASEN	Policy on Partnership Working
No date	NASEN	Policy on the Inclusive Curriculum

2

Families of children with special needs

Chapter objectives

To develop awareness of:
- the impact of a child with special needs on family members
- parental views on the support and provision they and their child receive
- key issues for practitioners
- pointers for effective practice.

Introduction

Having a baby or a young child with special needs can be traumatic in many ways such as:

- working through feelings of grief and loss

- being confronted with a diverse range of 'expert' professionals, each having their own perspective on your child

- having feelings of lost control over decision making

- experiencing confusion within an unfamiliar and complex system.

Different family members are likely to deal with these issues in their own way and their own time, so it is important that early years practitioners understand and respect each and every individual involved. If we support the needs of each family member then, indirectly, we also support the child. Effective parental partnerships and interagency working will support this process but it is imperative that we do not make assumptions about parents' needs and views. We should listen to, and attempt to understand and respect, their perspectives and feelings.

Children and their families

Today's family is often far from the stereotypical image of two parents with two children. In the mid-twentieth century, there were fewer broken marriages and more extended family members who usually lived nearby and supported their families, particularly the young and elderly.

In my early childhood perhaps I was fortunate to live with both parents, behind the family shop. Both parents were, for the most part, on hand at all times, but when they were ill or away from the house, my grandmother, who lived locally, was available to help out. Similarly, when I had my own children, my mother was able to support me when I returned to full-time work, so neither my own children nor myself required daycare provision. In contrast, my own daughters, who do not live nearby and who have a mother who is still working full time, will need early childhood services for their children. So it can be seen that family life has changed considerably.

Besides these fundamental changes, the structure of families has also changed dramatically and we should reflect briefly on the range of family structures that currently exist and in which the children we work with are growing up. Barnes (1995) suggests five key family structures: conjugal nuclear; non-conjugal nuclear; lone parent; reconstituted or 'blended'; and extended. Today, however, we also need to consider gay/lesbian parents, adoptive families, foster families and care homes.

Therefore, if family structures vary considerably and, if we accept that family members have significant influence upon the children growing up, we must understand family issues that are raised through having a child with special needs as there are important considerations for early years practitioners.

How does a family impact on a child?

What is a family? Barnes suggests:

> 'Those who have loved us' may be parents, siblings, grandparents, other relatives, teachers or peers. Although other groups and social factors affect socialisation, the family is typically seen as the most influential agency in the

socialisation of the child. It is the context within which the most direct and intimate relationships are forged. Our concept of family is greatly influenced by our personal experiences and our culture. (Barnes, 1995: 84)

While accepting this perspective, society should also acknowledge that, sadly, not all children are loved in this way. However, if, as Barnes suggests, 'family' comprises those people who love us and each member is a great influence on our development, then we need to begin to explore all those individuals and groups that impact on the lives of children which will extend far beyond the primary notion of the immediate family. Bronfenbrenner's ecology of human development (1979) extended beyond the immediate family to national and societal levels through four distinct levels:

1   Microsystem – comprising all family members, the home environment and early years providers, all of whom spend considerable amounts of time with the child. Thus, each of their behaviours informs the child's development.

2   Mesosytem – extending beyond the home and provider, where links and interaction develop between them.

3   Exosystem – including the social networks of the family, the local neighbourhood and the employment of family members, each of which can directly or indirectly affect the child.

4   Macrosystem – relevant national policies, education and welfare systems, economic systems and cultural systems.

While we may initially consider that only the immediate family affects the child, it is clear to see that, directly or indirectly, there are many influences on a child's life on which we should reflect.

Goldenberg and Goldenberg (1985: 136) highlight key family features: 'Families are systems influenced by many factors: the ethnic and cultural backgrounds; the stage of the family life cycle; environmental events; external factors; individual relationships and the personal and collective experiences of family members'. Therefore, when considering a child's development, we should consider all positive and negative influencing factors, including the family. The changing faces of any one family must also be considered, as the family itself is an evolving entity that will change, develop and grow through interaction with significant others and wider society. In current times, we need to consider issues such as unemployment, health and housing.

Government initiatives for family support – Sure Start

The government Sure Start initiative has been an investment in young families specifically aimed at alleviating deprivation. Millions of pounds have been spent on developing Sure Start programmes across the country in an attempt to 'deliver the best start in life for every child by bringing together early education, health and family support' (DCSF, 2009i). The key philosophy is one of empowerment. Through giving initial direction and professional support, staff work to enable families to develop their own support and provision. The government summarises its intentions:

> Sure Start Children's Centres are building on existing successful initiatives like Sure Start programmes, neighbourhood nurseries and early excellence centres, and bringing high quality integrated early years services to the heart of communities. By 2010, there will be 2500 children's centres, so that every family has easy access to high-quality integrated services in their community and the benefits of Sure Start can be felt nationwide. (DCSF, 2009i)

Reflecting on the whole child

If we are to consider the individual, and sometimes special needs of each of the children with whom we work, we should understand their differing backgrounds and the resulting effects in order to assess the 'whole child' in a holistic manner. In some instances, specific familial issues may compound a child's difficulties and be beyond our control, yet if we are aware of and acknowledge these difficulties we can still support the child effectively.

Children with special needs and their families

Perspectives of families of children with special needs

While the preceding discussion of the family equates to all families, those bringing up children with special needs undergo a range of experiences that can have additional positive and/or negative effects on individuals. Parents of children with special needs may have different perspectives on development, learning, opportunities and the future for their children, themselves and their family as a whole. Russell suggests that:

> Socially they are identified as different from the main population of parents, through the identification of their child's disability, and are therefore perceived to require help to fulfil their role as a parent. Emotionally many will need support to adjust to their new-found situation and the continued care of their child. Intellectually they need to learn and understand a new body of knowledge relating to their child's diagnosis and the systems designed to support them. (2003: 144)

Research is readily accessible to identify and support individual family needs (Carpenter, 2005; Flewitt and Nind, 2007; O'Connor et al., 2005; Rogers, 2007; Swick and Hooks, 2005; Whitaker, 2007), identifying a need for professionals to acknowledge and understand the perspective of each family member. Carpenter (2000b: 49) concluded that: 'Where professionals can enable support for the whole family, including siblings, then parents are more likely to acquire better adjustment. Often the child with disabilities is the focus for the professionals involved but this may only be one of the family's concerns'.

It has become increasingly clear over the past few years that families of children with special needs require very specific support to avoid the SEN system placing yet more obstacles in their path. Together from the Start identifies that:

> There are many common issues for parents of disabled children, but no two families are the same or have identical needs. Families can be diverse in terms of their experience, resources and expectations as well as their cultural, religious and linguistic influences. (DfES/DoH, 2003: 9)

Further, Carpenter (with Egerton, 2007) reminds us that when a child with a disability is born it is the birth of a child that should be celebrated, and that the parents will love their child no less because of their disability and will strive for their child to grow into a happy adulthood, that is, they are simply parents. They are, however, parents that are about to face a different journey through life than they had previously expected and are likely to have one or two battles along that journey. Carpenter suggests that:

> The reality for the family of a child with special educational needs is that they face recurrent and unpredictable challenges. Not only do they require appropriate Early Intervention, but they require access to ongoing support at points when they need to push the button. The families of children with special educational needs do not seek sympathy, do not want to be patronized. They do want to be valued and treated as equals. They are not interested in being converted to particular educational ideologies or medical or therapeutic doctrines. They desire recognition of the individuality of their child and the uniqueness of their family. (Carpenter, 2007: 19)

So it becomes clear that we have a responsibility to address the needs of the whole family as well as individual family members, as this in turn will support our direct work with the child. Lee (2005: 65) suggests that: 'Parents of young children with special needs often tread a path that is steep, rocky and fraught with pitfalls', a sentiment we should remember.

Within our thinking about parents of children with special needs, we perhaps need to focus more on the role of fathers as they can often be overlooked. When we, as early years practitioners refer to 'parents', I would suggest we predominantly mean 'mothers', as they are the parents we most often deal with, but the impact of fathers on their children is now well documented, as illustrated by Towers (2009) who informs us that:

> there is a growing body of research that has looked at the influences of fathers generally on their child's development (Fatherhood Institute, 2008). A systematic review of studies (Pleck and Masciadrelli, 2004, cited in Fatherhood Insistute, 2008) found that 'positive' father involvement was associated with a range of desirable outcomes for children and young people. (2009: 10)

We also need to reflect on cultural issues here as within some cultures great shame is associated with having a child with a disability and often the mother (and/or father) can be blamed by the extended family. This can extend to the point where the family 'hides' the child from the extended family and sometimes the wider community, but hopefully attitudes are changing for the better.

The father's perspective

Current national processes and systems for the identification, assessment and intervention of special needs occur most frequently during the working day, immediately prohibiting attendance and participation for many working fathers. Their understanding of discussions is therefore often second-hand and may lack clarity and/or depth. As one of the main carers for children, and therefore a key influence, it is imperative that fathers are fully included in all decision-making and information-giving meetings. Carpenter (2000a: 137) concluded that: 'They (fathers) need to be offered increased access to information and support, to be provided with opportunities to network with other fathers and to have their need for information and support within the family addressed. In order to achieve these aims, greater training and awareness among professionals is necessary'.

While we may not be able to accommodate paternal involvement at all meetings and discussions, or to change paternal working conditions, we should at least address the issues by ensuring that local systems are in place to inform and support fathers more adequately.

A recent report by Towers, for the Fatherhood Institute (2009), highlights specifically the importance of supporting fathers of children with disabilities, stating that:

> It (the report) provides statistical data that validates the previous findings that fathers play a key role and that their needs should be considered and responded

to. The report also develops the discussion about these fathers as carers. They show how valuable a resource their care is for their partners and children, that many want to provide more of it, and that this would be enormously beneficial. They identify the barriers these fathers face in fulfilling their aspirations and describe policy and practice changes that are needed if their contribution in terms of providing both 'cash and care' to their families are to be optimized. (2009: 2)

The report suggests four key recommendations around the involvement and inclusion of fathers in discussions and decision making; improvements in access to information and services for fathers; steps to ensure the health and well-being of fathers; and improved family support through including fathers to ensure the health of the family as a unit.

The professional perspective

Mallett (1997) highlighted that as professionals we enter a chosen career and those who work with children with special needs often progress to this work after an initial period of working within mainstream settings. We therefore choose to work with children and families experiencing difficulties and many are paid an arguably respectable salary. Ongoing training and support are available and, theoretically, we can leave work behind at the end of the day (although in reality few achieve this).

Parents, on the other hand, may have had little or no advance warning of having to bring up a child with special needs and, in many cases, were expecting a healthy child for whom they had plans and aspirations. Suddenly, their dreams and expectations are changed and they are faced with a barrage of professionals, confusing systems, some lack of control of events, possible rejection by their friends, community and family, and a possible overwhelming feeling of failure and disappointment.

The way parents are supported is crucial to their future, their child's future and the future of other family members and will require considerable sensitivity on behalf of the professionals diagnosing the difficulty and those supporting the family. The Early Support materials (DCSF, 2009j) state that:

It is not easy for parents to hear that all is not well with their child and it's not easy to be the person telling them. Where a concern or condition is detected at or very soon after birth, there are obvious and particular sensitivities.

Professionals should also reflect on the findings of the Lamb Inquiry

(DCSF, 2009h: 2), requested by the government to explore parental and professional views on current SEN systems and to suggest how 'parental confidence' in these systems could be improved. Making 51 recommendations, the Inquiry found that while some children had made good progress and their parents felt well supported, others felt that their lives had been full of constant battles with the system to secure the necessary support for their child(ren). Overall Lamb concluded that:

> I am not recommending anything that is not being done by the best teachers, schools and local authorities across the country already. I argue that it is not the current framework that is at fault but rather the failure to comply with both the spirit and the letter of the framework. (DCSF, 2009k: 6)

Key areas highlighted were:

- The crucial importance of early identification.
- The culture of low expectations for children with SEN must change.
- Improved expertise needed among teachers.
- Parents' voices and children's voices must be heard.
- SEN systems must work from the child's individual needs and circumstances.
- SEN systems must be more accountable.

Parental acceptance of special needs at or soon after birth

Children experiencing complex disabilities are often diagnosed at or soon after birth, as are children with specific conditions such as Down's syndrome. Sometimes parents may have known during the pre-natal period, but to many the news will be totally unexpected and will arrive at a time when they are already experiencing tremendous emotional turmoil.

During the first days and weeks following childbirth, parents experience major adjustments to a totally new way of life. There is extreme joy and celebration of the event plus excitement and anticipation for the future, but this sometimes conflicts with the overburdening sense of responsibility for this brand new, totally dependent life. When one parent is feeling that the responsibility is overwhelming, hopefully their partner will be able to support them, and vice versa. Extended family and friends will be visiting, so time for the new family can often be interrupted and compromised by well-meaning visitors. So what happens when this turbulent period is interrupted by the news that the much loved, newborn child has special needs? Dale (1996: 49) suggests: 'Parents rarely expect their child's disabling condition or life-threatening illness. The confirmation or diagnosis, whether at birth or later, often creates an immense crisis of changes, expectations and hopes, and parents may experience intense reactions during the early days'.

The impact of the initial diagnosis

Undoubtedly, parents need to know if their child is experiencing difficulties and to be informed as soon as practically possible by a professional who is aware of the implications of the specific difficulties and able to respond to any questions or issues raised, but at this emotional time the sensitive handling of this initial discussion will be crucial. Coming to terms with an early diagnosis can be made easier or more difficult by professionals and there are many reports highlighting parents' negative experiences, resulting in increased difficulties over and above the natural turbulence of emotions at the time. Birrell offers such a report, highlighting one family's passage from delivering an apparently healthy little girl to discovering she has considerable difficulties:

> Then he (the paediatrician) requested that we got Iona dressed before telling us, in a gentle voice: 'I am afraid it appears that Iona is profoundly brain-damaged.' They (the words) seemed to reek of despair, of hopelessness, of her condition being incurable, her life unbearably bleak. Our hopes for her, and for us, seemed to plunge further into the abyss with each echo. (Birrell, 1995: 1)

Such examples only begin to give professionals an inkling of the feelings parents experience. Unless we have actually been through a similar experience, and naturally there are practitioners who have, we cannot fully appreciate the implications and effects on each and every member of the family. Carpenter (2000a: 135) suggests that too often at this very difficult time: 'The professional approaches were insensitive and ill-timed as they did nothing to enhance their quality of life or parenting confidence'.

The Sure Start guidance, *Supporting Families Who Have Children with Special Needs and Disabilities*, offers advice and guidance on this difficult period for parents, as well as generally, highlighting that:

> How a parent is told of their child's special needs or disability can significantly affect their subsequent view of support services and have a positive or negative influence on their willingness to use them. News of a disability will come as a

shock to many parents, but it is possible to lessen the potential impact of this event by giving information in a way that shows respect for the parents and their child. (Sure Start, 2002: 14)

What we must remember is that we need to consider the impact of the diagnosis on the parent and give them time to assimilate this information before embarking on a discussion of what happens next and/or in the future – sensitivity is again the key. Carpenter summarises this point succinctly:

At the point of diagnosis of a child's disability, a parent's question is hardly likely to be about the local early childhood intervention services. These families are frightened, disturbed, upset, grieving and constantly vulnerable. The role of the professionals involved with them is to catch them when they fall, listen to their sorrow, dry their tears of pain and anguish, and, when the time is right, plan the pathway forward. (2007: 136)

Including the father

In this difficult period, professionals often spend most time with the mother who is seen as the primary carer. Fathers can too easily be overlooked as they are expected 'to be the strong one'. Herbert and Carpenter's study of seven fathers highlighted this 'marginalisation' of fathers after mother and baby had returned home:

All help was focused on the mother and baby. The father's needs were not addressed or, perhaps, even noticed. They were seen as the 'supporters' and as such adopted the role society expects – that of being competent in a crisis (Tolston, 1977). All seven fathers talked of returning to work and trying to search for normality and keep a sense of reality in their lives. (Herbert and Carpenter, 1994: 37–8)

Towers' (2009) research into fathers of children with disabilities incorporated an open question asking for one thing that would have helped them in their fathering role. Common responses emerged about their need to feel included in all aspects of the processes and that appointments should not always be during working hours:

'Recognise that fathers have feelings too and are just as affected by the news of having a child with a disability. That we too, do have our own contribution to make to our child's life. Stop shutting us out and making us feel inadequate and like a bystander in our child's needs', and

'Appointments at more convenient times (i.e. outside work or at beginning or end of the working day rather than in the middle).'

If we acknowledge that mothers and fathers affect their children individually, then it follows that we should support them individually and listen to their views on how we currently involve them. The more involved the father, from the day of conception onwards, the more informed and empowered he can become.

Maternal issues

Quite often, new mothers of babies with special needs are moved to a side ward for 'privacy', theoretically to support sensitivity, but these parents are immediately being segregated from other new mothers who may well be incredibly supportive. While the reasons behind this policy can be appreciated and some mothers may wish to be segregated, each case should be considered individually. A generalised assumption for all is not necessarily helpful. Professionals may avoid conversations with new mothers of children with special needs as they feel uncomfortable and do not know what to say, but this can isolate mothers even further.

Rogers's research included Karen's story whose son has Down's syndrome. They received the initial diagnosis three days after the birth and wanted to leave hospital as soon as possible, and before the conclusive diagnosis was available, stating that: 'either I take him within twenty-four hours or I leave him here and don't take him home at all' (2007: 138). Subsequently, while awaiting the final test results, she could only cope by denying the possibility that the baby may have Down's syndrome, highlighting the emotional rollercoaster that some mothers experience at this time.

If professionals can begin to at least acknowledge some of the difficulties experienced, then perhaps we can support parents positively at this time. Any professional dealing with this emotive situation must demonstrate empathy, understanding, respect, tact and diplomacy. Professionals must be informed and well trained to deal with questions, whether they relate to the condition, the future, the baby or the parents and their handling of the news. Sensitivity is an essential personal characteristic needed, but is sensitivity a quality that can be taught or learnt?

Parental acceptance of special needs at a later stage

As previously mentioned, many specific conditions and/or complex disabilities will probably have been identified prior to, at or soon after birth. Other special needs may emerge at a later stage or develop gradually over a period of time, raising concerns by parents, family members, friends and/or professionals.

When initial concerns are raised

Parents may observe a gap between the development of their young child and older siblings or friends' children, and raise the issue with the general practitioner (GP) or health visitor (HV). However, in many cases it will be the GP or HV who notices delayed development or specific problems such as hearing impairment. Alternatively, it may be the early years practitioner who identifies difficulties and undertakes a period of observation and assessment to confirm or dispel the concerns before raising the issue with parents.

At this point, we are again faced with discussing concerns with parents in a sensitive and caring manner, and the professional issues raised previously apply equally here. General practitioners and health visitors may be trained to deal with such situations but this may not necessarily be the case for early years practitioners. However, the SENCO should be able to directly or indirectly support discussions with parents.

Parental resistance to acceptance

Having identified a disability or special need, practitioners must be prepared for parental resistance to acceptance for a variety of reasons:

- Parents may be shocked and believe categorically that their child is just a little delayed or lazy and will 'catch up' in time.

- Parents may not be able to fully comprehend the information or appreciate the importance of the issues raised.

- Parents may be fully aware of the issues but be unable to come to terms with the reality of the situation.

At all times, we need to remember that whatever emotions family members are experiencing are completely acceptable and we should ensure they are given sufficient support and advice to enable them to move towards acceptance, but at their own pace. These emotional effects should not be underestimated as for some mothers the diagnosis is simply the beginning of an unplanned for and tremendously difficult period of their lives – a period, which for some, becomes overpowering and all consuming. This is summarised in Rogers's research:

> The parents' narratives reported here have illustrated that loss, denial, shock and disappointment can have a dramatic effect on mental health. But, it is not necessarily a long-term problem if parents feel hate, desperation or despair. All of the above, in turn, affect the family as a whole and often, at crisis points, 'disable' the family unit. Intense feelings of powerlessness and depression 'disabled'

many of my participants at some point in their lives, yet all reorganized and re-evaluated future pathways. (2007: 142)

Preparation for discussion/progress meetings

It is pertinent to prepare for discussion/progress meetings with parents and to attempt to pre-empt difficult situations that may arise. When planning, the following can be used as an aide-mémoire:

- Parents should be informed in advance of:
  - who will attend and why
  - any reports to be discussed
  - possible referrals
  - possible outcomes, which should reduce the uncertainty for parents.
- Evidence from observations should be used to support discussions.
- The child's strengths and weaknesses should be highlighted.
- Parental consent should be gained for any referrals to additional professionals.
- Information discussed should be flexible to accommodate parental reactions.
- Practitioners should put parents at ease within this potentially difficult situation and encourage them to contribute throughout.
- The meeting should conclude with a discussion of plans of action, Individual Education Plans (if appropriate) and details of future meetings.
- Recording is necessary for future reference.

Throughout the meeting, the views and concerns of the parents must be heard, as they know their child best and it must be assured that parents feel able to contribute as equal partners. Parental information and observations should enhance the assessment process by adding another perspective of the child. Combined with information from the attending professionals, the meeting, as a whole, should then be in a position to draw informed conclusions.

Practitioners should remember that the success or failure of such meetings will set the scene for subsequent meetings and discussions. Every attempt should therefore be made to ensure an agreeable outcome or the child's difficulties could be exacerbated by delays in parental consent, withdrawal of the child from the provision or parents' future avoidance of any subsequent conversations, informal or otherwise. Mallet concludes:

> Very often, when your child has 'special' needs (i.e. additional to those generally expected), you have contact with a great number of professionals. It is every parent's experience that some can be enabling and empowering, empathetic and supportive, while others are not. In practice what counts is attitude and the style of working which this leads to. (Mallet, 1997: 30)

Home visits can be extremely informative and work positively for both parents and professionals, but it is acknowledged that they are time-consuming and require cover for members of staff unless they are undertaken 'after hours'. However, the benefits of initial or continuing discussions within the home setting can help to break down potential barriers, allowing parents more freedom of speech, increased time for clarifying issues, a feeling of control within the situation and, with appropriate timing, can include the father. This may mean that professionals should engage in home visits at the beginning or end of the working day to ensure fathers are more likely to be able to attend.

Parental issues through SEN processes

Following initial assessment and/or diagnosis, additional issues concerning parents may emerge, bringing their own difficulties and problems:

- a possible increase over time of the range of professionals inputting with one child and his/her family
- a possible increase in appointments
- reactions from family, friends, neighbours and local placements
- ongoing meetings, discussions, reports and assessments
- a possible placement outside of the immediate neighbourhood
- longer-term effects on individual family members
- the need for information and answers.

For first-hand accounts of the challenges faced within SEN processes, readers are directed to the Contact-a-Family report *Our Family, Our Future* (2009) highlighting the views of 30 families with disabled children. While highlighting a barrage of challenges faced, the accounts also celebrate the achievements and successes of not only the children with disabilities but of the families as units, clearly showing their determination to achieve the best possible outcomes for their children. The report highlights:

> Many talk about the constant battle for support and information, and the bureaucracy they are faced with, which prevents them from enjoying family life. Some of their children have time-limiting conditions and each day spent together is precious, so fighting these battles is all the more frustrating and heartbreaking. (2009: 5)

The Lamb Inquiry offers similar findings:

> [F]or too many parents it represents an unwarranted and unnecessary struggle. For some, what should be easy becomes hard; where there should be support there can be indifference; and when there should be speed there is delay. It is no wonder that confidence breaks down in these circumstances. The system needs to feel more like one where 'everyone is on the same side' as another parents put it, with everyone focusing on the best outcomes for all our children. (DCSF, 2009h: 6)

Finally, O'Connor et al.'s research identified that parents were able to highlight specific improvements that could be made to the existing planning, assessment and provision for their children with special needs 'centred on the relationship between parents and professionals, improved communication between them and access to clear information' (2005: 251).

Practitioners must therefore consider carefully, at all stages, the implications of their comments, discussions, planning and provision on parents and ensure the parents (mother and father) are fully included in all decisions about their own child.

Grandparents

Historically, grandparents have been closely involved with their grandchildren and, although family structures and working patterns have changed, many grandparents still play a major role in the lives of their grandchildren. Today more grandparents support the care of their grandchildren while parents work, and thus take on a greater part in the children's upbringing, spending the most time with them and supporting them through various key changes and stages. As professionals, we may see grandparents more regularly, so we must consider issues pertinent to them as part of our planning and policies.

Initial acceptance of diagnosis

At the time of initial diagnosis, grandparents will share many difficulties and concerns with the parents, but may also experience feelings relating to their concerns for the parent (their child) and the need to be supportive. If grandparents also have difficulties accepting the diagnosis, then further complications may arise.

While considering the effects on grandparents, we must also appreciate the individual family relationships that exist, as it is not always the case that parents and grandparents have a healthy, supportive relationship. In such instances, practitioner involvement must be sensitive and ensure the views and wishes of the parents are respected.

Grandparents and extended family members may unintentionally create additional pressures and concerns for parents, who are dealing with very real problems on a daily basis. Blamires et al. suggest that:

> Further removed from the child than its parents, relatives may not see or may not wish to see the reality of the problems.

> It is not easy to continually point out real difficulties to grandparents anxious to dote over 'perfect' grandchildren, and it is not easy to decide how open to be about difficulties that may only worry relatives who will often then feel powerless to help. (1997: 19)

Siblings

Siblings may share common concerns and difficulties with parents but also deserve individual consideration as they will require different types of support and information.

Problems accepting newborn siblings

When a newborn baby arrives in a family, existing children will face considerable change. Basic changes such as reduced attention from parents may well cause difficulties for older siblings, but can be minimised through careful planning and preparation on behalf of parents and the extended family. Parents generally try to involve children before and after the expected birth to help alleviate potential difficulties. However, if the newborn baby is found to have special needs, circumstances may change further and new and very different issues may arise. A prolonged hospital stay may create a situation where an older sibling has to be cared for by relatives, resulting in several or many moves between houses and interrupted attendance at nursery or school.

The position of a child within a family can also impact on their personality and development. The oldest sibling may be expected to assume the role of temporary carer and supporter to younger siblings, placing additional pressures and responsibilities on their shoulders, whereas a middle child could feel isolated as attentions are focused on the newborn baby and the oldest sibling in his/her new caring role.

The effects may be considerable (positive and negative) depending on the age of the sibling, resulting in:

- jealousy
- aggression
- tantrums
- regression
- lack of cooperation
- consideration
- cooperation
- love.

Key issues for siblings of children with special needs

Carpenter (1997) summarised relevant research at the time which explored the effects on siblings highlighting their complex needs. He identified seven key concerns of siblings of young children with special needs which can be summarised as:

1 A need for age-appropriate *information* about the specific special need.

2 Feelings of *isolation* from a range of sources, including isolation from information that is given to other involved family members and isolation from siblings in other families experiencing similar difficulties and problems.

3 Perceived *guilt* at having caused the special need in some way or, at the time of leaving home themselves, guilt at no longer being able to support parents with the care of their sibling.

4 Feelings of *resentment* as the child with special needs commands more time and attention from parents.

5 Pressure felt to *achieve well,* to somehow make up for the possible reduced levels of expected achievement of the child with special needs.

6 Greater demands to help with the *care* of the child with special needs.

7 Concerns for their own *future* and that of the child with special needs.

Similarly, Dodd's research identified that:

> The current challenge for service planners and practitioners is to translate the growing awareness of the needs of siblings into planning strategies which include supporting sibling initiatives. This will entail providing funding for groupwork and encouraging sensitivity to siblings through service provision and across all agencies who are working with the family and child. Siblings can be on no one's agenda, although their needs might best be met by partnership between parents and the agencies with which they come into contact. (2004: 46)

At the same time, however, siblings of children with special needs may identify very positive outcomes, as empathy and a clear understanding of the issues faced may enhance personality as well as maturity.

Supporting materials

The NAS website offers a range of publications for parents, siblings, family members and professionals alike, including storybooks to inform other children, such as Gorrod's (1997) *My Brother is Different*. Written in simple, age-appropriate language, this book can be used within settings to help raise awareness and understanding with young children, parents and staff. This one example demonstrates the availability of useful resources and information for a wide range of special needs which can be accessed from a range of sources.

Key issues for practitioners

As practitioners, we must therefore address the specific issues relating to siblings through:

- acknowledging and respecting their roles and responsibilities
- ensuring that age-appropriate materials are available to provide information
- creating opportunities for them to meet with other siblings of children with special needs, as well as ensuring they have ample opportunity to meet with their peers
- supporting parents in giving quality time to their children
- ensuring staff are aware of the specific needs of siblings
- including siblings in our discussions and planning.

Case study

Andrew was the first and only child of Ian and Sarah and was diagnosed at birth with Down's syndrome. Immediately, Sarah was moved to a side ward and experienced initial feelings of difference, isolation, anxiety and loss at the same time as an incredible love for her child. Acceptance of Andrew's condition took a little time for both parents. Soon after, owing to their own personalities and characteristics, they determined to provide the best possible opportunities for their son, supporting and helping him to achieve his maximum potential. From an early stage, the extended family accepted the news and worked to support the family as much as possible, despite living over 200 miles away. Friends of the parents were generally accepting but there were those that, over a period of time, withdrew contact.

Regular appointments were soon a feature of the family's life, including consultant paediatrician, GP, HV and portage worker. Ian and Sarah would attend the HV clinic on a regular basis for weight checks and advice and the portage worker attended the house regularly to work with the family, setting weekly tasks for Andrew and Sarah to work on. Immediately, a commitment was needed to be at home for these as well as the HV and GP visits, in addition to driving 15 miles to attend appointments with the consultant paediatrician.

At the age of 2 years, Andrew started part-time attendance at a local early years special unit and at the same time was enrolled in a private nursery school. Hence, more professionals became involved: head of unit, staff at the unit, speech and language therapist, occupational therapist, head of nursery school and nursery staff. At this stage, the head of the special unit became the key worker for Andrew and subsequently coordinated all input and chaired review meetings to which all professionals and Andrew's parents were invited.

At age 2 years and 6 months, Andrew was diagnosed with lymphatic leukaemia and was admitted to hospital. A range of treatments followed including chemotherapy, radiotherapy and intensive drug therapy, and his attendance at the special needs unit and nursery were temporarily halted. Throughout this period, the range of professionals extended to include the local nurse from the Cancer and Leukaemia in Children (CLIC) charitable organisation, the oncology team at the hospital including paediatric oncology consultants, plus the local CLIC support group with which the family became closely linked.

Periods of remission and relapse then followed for several years with intermittent attendance at hospitals and thus non-consistent placement attendance. Andrew's development, in all areas, would progress then regress, resulting in regular amendments to his Individual Education Plans.

Despite all the difficulties incurred, Andrew sustained attendance at the unit for long enough to undergo a statutory assessment of his special needs by the LEA, involving the introduction of an educational psychologist. A Formal Statement was produced just before Andrew's transfer to a local mainstream school at the age of 5 years and 6 months. This one-year delay in school entry was agreed by all parties as most appropriate for Andrew, owing to the time spent in hospital and his illness.

A summary of involved professionals highlights a considerable range, each with their own agenda of meetings, appointments, expectations, support and advice:

Portage worker	Educational psychologist
Head of special needs unit	Early years officer (LEA)
Nursery assistants	Local Down's syndrome group
Head of nursery school	Local CLIC group
Staff at nursery school	GP
Speech and language therapist	HV
Paediatric oncology consultant	Occupational therapist
CLIC nurse	Oncology nurses and doctors
Radiology staff	Paediatric consultant

Hopefully, this illustrative case study highlights some of the key issues raised earlier in the chapter and establishes some considerations for practitioners. The practicalities of managing such a network placed considerable pressure on the parents.

Parental issues arising, that impact on professional practice
- The gathering of information was largely due to the determination of Andrew's parents, but not all parents would do this or be able to do this.

- There were time management factors and the need for transport.

- There were difficulties when Andrew's mother needed to return to work and in finding a childminder who would be able to continue attending appointments.

- Andrew's father was working full-time and was unable to attend every Portage session, which he resented.

- Andrew's father wished to attend all appointments and thus needed an incredibly understanding and sympathetic boss who was amenable to flexibility. Would all employers be as accommodating?

- There was the need to understand and assimilate information imparted at meetings, reviews and informal discussions. Could all parents cope with this?

- There was the need for access to a telephone.

- There was the need for the parents to have the strength to cope with the emotive and traumatic diagnosis of leukaemia.

- Andrew's parents needed to choose a school.

- The family should have the basic rights to be able to continue with a 'normal' family life.

Practitioner issues arising
- Careful and considerate management of the key worker system to take place.

- Regular liaison to occur between all parties, including parents.

- All involved professionals to be sympathetic, understanding and respectful.

- All professionals to understand and respect the roles and responsibilities of the other professionals involved.

- All professionals to ensure that both parents were equally well informed at every stage, especially Andrew's father.

- Professionals to consider the needs of Andrew's extended family members.

Implications for practice

Supporting families is important in our support of the child with special needs. At times, children's needs will change and require differing approaches and, perhaps, different professionals to provide the most appropriate support. Knowledge and understanding of all local support networks, statutory and non-statutory, will be essential.

Individual family members may seek support from different sources or a combination of sources in order to deal with situations, concerns and issues. It may be that a mother will listen to the advice of the consultant paediatrician and then wish to debate the conversation with her closest friend to clarify her thoughts before discussing it with her husband. This may then affect the quality of the information passed on to the father. A parent may ask to bring a friend or family member to meetings and appointments to enable clarity of discussion, raise additional issues and concerns, and ensure accurate recollection afterwards. In the same vein, it may simply be that a friend's physical presence is needed for support. As professionals, we should be prepared to respect, discuss and accommodate, if possible, all parental requests regarding their own support networks involving friends, family members, local community groups, charitable organisations and work colleagues. In addition, the advent of the Internet has provided a plethora of information, including websites created by and intended for parents and other family members as well as those created by charitable organisations, but we should remember that not all parents have access to or use the Internet.

Research assists professionals in understanding parental perspectives and supports the view that we may not always know what families need or what is 'best' for them. We should support and advise in the most appropriate manner, and accept the views and feelings of the parents we work with.

The increase in numbers of children with special needs

At the start of the twenty-first century, the increase in numbers of children with special needs places considerable pressures on early years practitioners. This is partly because of the advancements in medical science and technology over the years and the resultant increases in survival of previously fatal conditions. Sure Start conclude that: 'The increasing survival rates of low birth weight babies has tended to increase the number of children surviving with severe and multiple needs, while improved health care and preventative programmes have led to a corresponding decrease in the numbers of children with mild or moderate disabilities' (2002: 6).

So professionals need to consider that today we need to accommodate an increasing range of special needs than ever before. In my early teaching experience, any children with needs deemed as beyond the capabilities and expectations of mainstream schools were moved to special schools (moderate, severe or emotional and behavioural difficulties (EBD)). However today, with the drive for increased inclusion, practitioners are expected to be able to provide for children with a diverse range of sometimes multiple and complex needs and difficulties. Carpenter (2005: 176–7) suggests that:

> early intervention services can no longer focus solely upon children with traditionally recognised disabilities (such as a visual or hearing impairment or Down's syndrome, but have also to offer support to families of children with special educational needs in emerging categories associated with factors such as low birth weight (Champion, 2005), genetic abnormalities and prenatal abuse (resulting in babies born with substance or alcohol addictions, for example). Some of these children may have obvious difficulties. Whilst others may not, they may have characteristics that predispose them to developing special educational needs (Marlow, Wolke, Bracewell & Samara, 2005; Woodward, Mogridge, Wells & Inder, 2004).

The current educational climate of inclusive provision for all children with special needs also has major implications for practice. There is clearly a need for additional and ongoing training to understand, respect and provide effectively for the individual needs of family members, which in turn will help to support the child. The work of researchers such as Carpenter (2000a, 2005, 2007), Dale (1996), Dodd (2004), Rogers (2007) and Whitaker (2007) must be encouraged and supported to ensure that we understand parental and family perspectives with increasing depth. While the IDP may support the increased knowledge of practitioners, it is yet to be shown that (a) *all* practitioners are engaging with the materials and (b) that improved provision is the outcome.

Early Support and families

The government's Early Support programme came into being in 2003, aiming to offer family-centred support for young children (under 5) and their families. Dovetailing with the Portage programme of home visiting for children with disabilities, Early Support offers a key worker system for those families whose child has more severe and/or complex needs. The key worker can originate from any profession and is selected according to the appropriateness for the family and the child's needs. There is a responsibility for local authorities to ensure that:

> Families caring for a disabled child with high levels of need have a key worker/care manager to oversee and manage the delivery of services from all agencies involved in the care and support of the child and family, and to ensure that the family has access to appropriate services. (DoH, 2004: s. 5.8)

For those children with special needs whose difficulties are not severe and/or complex, a key worker can be a practitioner within the early years or school setting who is familiar with the child and the family and is able to effectively coordinate and manage the coordination of services required to address the child's needs.

Summary

Reflecting on issues surrounding the families of children with special needs has, hopefully, highlighted the need to ensure that all family members are equally well supported. As practitioners, we aim to provide the best, and must therefore continue to explore and research family perspectives to enable appropriate intervention and support. At all times, we should consider:

- the family being central to the child's life
- a child's parents know them best
- family members, immediate and extended, and their impact on the child's life
- how well the family is functioning
- the possible negative and positive effects of individual families on their children
- how best to support each member of the family
- existing support systems within the family
- the relevant legislation and guidance regarding parents, parental partnerships and families of children with special needs
- our own working practices regarding coordination of services and effective multidisciplinary working systems
- the sensitivity of the issues we are dealing with.

Historically, parents have not always been considered as partners in their children's development, care and education, but legislation and guidance now ensure practitioners view the family as central to every child's life. Through careful and sensitive consideration of individual needs, views and feelings, we can empower family members and address their needs more effectively.

Throughout our planning, policy making and practice, we must consider and address, to the best of our ability, the needs of each family member. While the child must always be the key focus of our work, family members must always be considered, which will enhance our work with the child and help him/her to work towards achieving his/her full potential. As Carpenter so aptly states:

All family members – brothers, sisters, grandparents, significant others – need to feel acknowledged and valued through this process. Inclusivity is the key to work with families in this millennium. (2005: 180)

Key issues

- The importance of family members must be acknowledged.
- Policies and practices should reflect the needs of family members.
- Practitioners should be familiar with local statutory, private and voluntary supporting agencies.

Points for reflection

- If you assess staff awareness levels of family issues raised in this chapter, what benefits might this bring?
- How are you and your setting supporting the needs of family members?
- How are you and your setting employing the key worker system, and ensuring its effectiveness?

Suggested further reading

Department for Children, Schools and Families (2009h) *Lamb Inquiry: Special Educational Needs and Parental Confidence.* Available at: www.dcsf.gov.uk/lambinquiry/

Towers, C. (2009) *Recognising Fathers: A National Survey of Fathers who Have a Child with a Disability.* Available at: www.learningdisabilities.org.uk/our-work/family-support/fathers/

You can explore the wealth of materials available on the Early Support website, available at: www.dcsf.gov.uk/everychildmatters/healthandwellbeing/ahdc/earlysupport/resources/esresources/

You can also explore the wealth of materials available on the Every Disabled Child Matters website, available at: www.ncb.org.uk/edcm/home.aspx

3

Partnerships with parents

Chapter objectives

To develop awareness of:
- the purposes and benefits of effective partnerships with parents
- the characteristics of effective partnerships
- elements of good practice.

Introduction

As we have seen in Chapter 1, the amount of legislation, policies and strategies emerging from the government has been fairly incessant from the year 2000 and virtually all of this will have made reference to the importance of partnerships with parents. Yet parent partnerships are generally discussed in terms of how parents are their child's primary educator and that effective partnerships are essential, with little specific guidance as to how we, as practitioners, should ensure our partnerships are truly effective and meet the needs of both mothers and fathers, and work to improve the outcomes for their child.

Partnerships with parents do not naturally evolve, and early years workers should never presume to have empathy with, or understand, all parents. At best we can respect, listen and use the systems in place to support parents, ensuring both mothers and fathers have total understanding of everything that occurs, are aware of their rights and feel able to contribute at all stages.

Partnerships should ideally comprise an equal balance between practitioners and parents, with both parties working towards the most appropriate outcomes to support children with special needs in achieving their full potential. Robson (1989: 126) explored equality within partnerships, highlighting:

> A successful partnership is based on equality, whereby each partner recognises and benefits from the talents, skills, expertise and knowledge of the other. At times one partner may adopt a relatively passive role, in other situations a more active role.

More recently, the Lamb Inquiry (DCSF, 2009h), exploring parental confidence in SEN systems, highlighted that parents predominantly wanted a system that worked for them and their child:

> Parents have told us that *good, honest and open* communication is one of the important components of building confidence and good relationships. Face-to-face communication with parents, treating them as equal partners with expertise in the children's needs is crucial to establishing and sustaining confidence. Where things go wrong, the root causes can often be traced to poor communication between school, local authority and parent.

He continues:

> In the most successful schools the effective engagement of parents has had a profound impact on children's progress and the confidence between the school and parent. Parents need to be listened to more and brought into a partnership with statutory bodies in a more meaningful way. (DCSF, 2009h: 3)

All practitioners and strategic leaders would do well to take note of these key messages when reviewing current parent partnership policies.

Parental involvement or partnership?

It may be suggested that in early years settings, parents are generally welcome to visit, discuss their children's progress and participate in a range of activities within the group. This can be beneficial for all parties involved, particularly children, as the skills and expertise of parents can be used within the group to enhance existing practice and parents can equally learn new ideas from experienced practitioners. However, on school entry the involvement of parents may diminish to invitations to assemblies, listening to children read and helping with fund-raising activities. As children then progress to the junior and secondary phases, parental involvement diminishes yet further, creating a distance. Thus, parental involvement and participation are susceptible to change as children progress through the educational phases. Rennie (1996: 197) identifies five distinct stages as a developmental progression of parental involvement that are still as useful today and which could be utilised for the progress of planning and policy-making processes:

1 Confidence building for all involved.

2 Awareness raising and starting participation.

3 Real involvement.

4 Parent–teacher partnership.

5 Parents as co-educators.

As parents approach early years settings for the first time, there already exists a common ground between them. They all have children of similar ages, are about to embark on attendance, have spent the previous few years nurturing and developing their children to the best of their ability and wish for their children to succeed. This common ground presents a bond between parents that can be positively used by the setting to the benefit of all, sharing experiences, discussing common problems and capitalising on personal skills. It is a starting point from which outstanding achievements can be realised if fostered within an ethos of positive and equal partnership.

For most children, the preceding years will have been spent at home with a parent/carer so the introduction to an early years setting can be traumatic. This is not only for the children but also the parents and, if the youngest child in the family is embarking on attendance, then it may be even harder for the parent/carer to accept. The feelings of no longer being needed to support the child in the same way can have severe effects and, while all parents want to see their child settle in happily and confidently, there can be a sense of ironic disappointment if the child does just that. For the child with special needs, the transfer to an early years setting may be more problematic and requires sensitive handling as the parent/carer may feel even more protective and find it much harder to transfer their child's care to others. It is therefore important that practitioners plan the induction process thoroughly in an attempt to eliminate, or at least diminish, possible anxieties. Familiarity with the child and his/her family can ease this process considerably, particularly if it is achieved via a combination of home visits and visits to the setting. Issues of concern, procedures, policies and information sharing can all be explored in a more informal manner prior to admission, and this will hopefully be seen as a two-way process.

The parent/carer has the most concise knowledge about the child, including his/her likes and dislikes, progress to date, appointments attended, referrals made, reports written and friends. This can all be used to support the child's transition through the induction process and in future planning.

Practitioners should recognise and respect the depth and breadth of learning that parents have already undertaken with their children, which can be underestimated and undervalued. Parents have a tendency to see the early education of their children as 'nothing special' or describe it as 'what parents do', but parents are responsible for supporting their child's development and skill learning such as walking, talking, toilet training, social skills, self-help skills, behaviour and playing. This prior learning, albeit unstructured and unplanned, has nevertheless taken place within the home and the parents should accept full credit for this. A key issue to be considered is involvement versus partnership. Involvement infers that parents would participate in some activities within the setting, whereas partnership implies equality, respect and involvement in every aspect of the setting's work from the management group, through planning and delivering the curriculum to working alongside and with practitioners on an equal footing. Langston (2003: 55) considers that:

> true partnership demands as much of one partner as the other and implies that each partner has equal rights and responsibilities. To work in partnership then, is both time consuming and demanding, and can only really emerge over time, when parents and practitioners understand each other's roles, respect one another's rights and individuality, trust one another, and feel confident.

Parental issues affecting partnership

Many issues, such as low self-esteem, hours of employment, social deprivation and poverty, and feelings of inadequacy, can affect the level and quality of parental involvement and any of the issues may present one or more barriers to meaningful participation.

Time can also be a critical factor, even for those parents who do not work during the day, as they may wish to support partnerships with several settings attended by their children or they may experience childcare difficulties for younger children. Any parents who do not appear to be very involved with our settings should not, therefore, be assumed to lack interest or desire to participate. It will be our responsibility to respond to their needs and to remove barriers.

Quality of partnership

If, as practitioners, we strive to accommodate all parents in a meaningful way, we will also share the rewards, but true partnership will very much depend on the quality of the relationships and the perceived benefits to all parties. Inviting parents into the staffroom of a setting to repair damaged equipment may be of little benefit and cannot be described as an effective partnership. Parental and professional roles should support each other in a 'complementary' manner as Beveridge comments:

> The concept of partnership is based on the recognition that parents and teachers have complementary contributions to make to children's education. Accordingly, it is central to the notion of partnership that schools should demonstrate that they not only listen to, but also value, parents' perspectives. Many teachers aim to do this, but it must be acknowledged that the parental experience of contact with the school can be far removed from the partnership ideal. (Beveridge, 1997: 56)

Dale (1996: 2) also raises the issue of the quality of partnership: 'the term "partnership" does not tell us a great deal about the extent of the cooperation and reciprocity between two or more partners, except to suggest that there is some form of mutual cooperation and influence'. As a simple example, a bilingual child may enter an early years setting. Although a non-English speaker, his/her mother can be encouraged to attend sessions to watch and participate, as she feels able. Initially, she may choose to stay in the background, helping with the setting up of activities, making drinks and washing up but, hopefully, over a period of time, she can be encouraged to participate further. Eventually, her English should begin to develop and her confidence should be enhanced. In time, she may feel more able to support the learning of staff and children alike by introducing new activities related to cooking, traditional stories, dress and religious festivals from her own country and culture, as well as adding to more general topic-based work. Opportunities could arise for the mother to participate in adult education classes, help in a crèche and have regular contact with a range of outside professionals. With increased involvement and understanding of how the setting works, she could be elected to the management group and become a full working partner of the setting. From this scenario everyone benefits, but only if the setting is committed to working with parents. Draper and Duffy support this view, concluding that:

> For many staff the opportunity to work in partnership adds a new dimension to their work. Practitioners can assume their experience of family life is the way it is and working with parents from diverse communities widens their views on families and family life. Differences can be shared, respected and explored. Home life provides many opportunities for learning the setting can build on. (Draper and Duffy, 2001: 149)

Partnerships with the parents of children with special needs may be compromised by the existence of special schools and units that prohibit or limit regular face-to-face contact with parents. At their most basic level, partnerships begin with the establishing of relationships, but these take time and effort to plan and develop. In a mainstream setting, parents will arrive on a more frequent and regular basis where meaningful interaction can develop naturally. If, however, your child is transported several or many miles away to attend a special facility, then this interaction is immediately compromised. If parents do not have transport then regular contact is further compromised. Thus, it may be suggested that for special schools and units, parental partnerships may need considerably more effort in planning and maintaining. However, the fact that parents are not in regular contact with a setting does not mean that practitioners should not make the effort to establish effective partnerships, as supported by Hurst:

> This does not prevent them from taking seriously parents' need to be kept informed and to have regular contact with the practitioner responsible for their children. It is the awareness of parents' needs and the willingness to be adaptable in developing ways of meeting these needs which are the most important. (Hurst, 1997: 108)

Yet despite all the guidance and advice regarding parental partnerships, there is plenty of evidence to suggest that provision is not truly engaging with parents in the ways they desire. Russell suggests that: '... a recent study by the Rathbone Society (2001) found that many parents of children with SEN in mainstream schools lack the knowledge and information to become fully involved in their child's ongoing assessment' (2003: 147). So clearly, much still needs to be done to ensure an effective and equal partnership with all families.

Home–school liaison teachers and family centres

During the 1960s and 1970s, there emerged an increased understanding of the influences of a range of factors on children's social development and, as a result, a greater awareness of social deprivation. In several counties, new roles emerged to address these needs, such as home–school liaison teachers. More family centres were established, some funded by education departments and some by social services departments, to address the effects of social deprivation in specific localities and/or 'educational priority areas'.

Home–school liaison teachers were generally assigned to an infant/primary school and/or a family centre. Their roles included the breaking down of barriers between schools and families, encouraging attendance at early years settings, supporting local pre-school providers, responding directly to the needs of the families and working closely with other agencies. Owing to the localities in which they worked, generally areas of poor housing, high unemployment and with very young parents, much of their work involved children and families with special needs, in the broadest sense. Therefore, special needs input, educational or otherwise, became a key feature of their work. In many instances, the home–school liaison teacher acted as a mediator or enabler between the families and the systems and processes in place to help them, but invariably non-educational issues such as claiming appropriate child benefits would emerge. If, as in Chapter 2, we acknowledge the effects of the family on the child, then to enable a parent to resolve financial difficulties would reduce stress and pressure, and ultimately benefit the child. At such times, the practitioner could advise and support, introducing the family to the appropriate department or agency that could best respond to their difficulties. Owing to budgetary restraints, many of these roles were discontinued during the late 1980s or practitioners were absorbed within family centres. While many would reflect positively on the successes of these roles, an alternative viewpoint is offered by Edwards and Knight:

> It could be said that the attempts of the 1970s at encouraging parental involvement because of perceived deficits in the home environment rested on a set of assumptions about the supremacy of middle-class attitudes and values. An unkinder view would be the suggestion that early years practitioners as a group were struggling to be recognised as professionals and were therefore willing to take on parental involvement schemes ... (Edwards and Knight, 1994: 113)

However, having experienced at first hand such work in the 1970s and 1980s, I would raise several issues to establish debate. First, I would agree that early years professionals were, and still are to a degree, fighting a battle to gain respect for the value and importance of their work, along with an acknowledgement of their expertise, knowledge and skills. This battle has been long-standing and will probably continue into the future, although it is hoped that government initiatives will help raise the profile of practitioners, as early years work is not the 'easy option' that some may suggest. Secondly, I consider that some excellent home–school partnerships were established at that time which still thrive today.

Characteristics of positive partnerships

So what are the key features and characteristics of positive partnerships? When defining principles of nursery education,

Goodall suggests that quality provision should include:

> A partnership which:
> - Acknowledges, celebrates and capitalises on parent or carer involvement, as the child's first educator;
> - Is flexible, negotiated and responsive to the needs of individual parents and their families;
> - Provides opportunities whereby nursery colleagues offer parents or carers a range of options;
> - Is centred upon their own child, themselves, their families and their community;
> - Allows them to become active partners in their child's education. (Goodall, 1997: 163)

These principles, while aimed at general nursery education, can equally be applied as a basis for good practice in any early years setting to the benefit of every child, whether he/she has special needs or not.

Focusing more on the early years, the Early Support training materials (Davis and Meltzer, 2007) offer the following as the:

> Characteristics of an effective partnership:
> - Working closely together with active participation and involvement
> - Sharing power with parents leading
> - Complementary expertise
> - Agreeing aims and process
> - Negotiation
> - Mutual trust and respect
> - Openness and honesty
> - Clear communication. (2007: 11)

Further, the parental partnership policy of the National Association for Special Educational Needs (n.d.a) highlights the key principles of effective partnership working:

> - Respecting parental rights
> - Acknowledging parental responsibilities
> - Acknowledging parents as equal partners to ensure parity in partnerships
> - Need to empower parents
> - Clear and effective communication
> - Recognising and addressing the support needs of the parents
> - Recognising the individuality and diversity of parents.

If we want partnerships with parents to be effective, supportive and of benefit to all parties, it is clear that we must view our work with parents as equal and complementary. We should welcome parents into our settings and ensure that our working practices respect the knowledge, skills and expertise that parents can share with us. A child is known best to his/her parents, and their first-hand knowledge can benefit our work and, thus, the child. If a child is interested and motivated, he/she will be more likely to achieve success.

There is a wealth of research available highlighting the positive outcomes of effective parental partnerships. One such example is the study of Mortimore et al. (1988) identifying factors affecting school effectiveness. Although the study is now quite dated, the principles are still relevant today. Improved educational outcomes were used as a marker of school effectiveness, with the research concluding that increased parental links and interaction within the school helped to increase academic achievements and thus enhance overall school effectiveness. More up-to-date texts upholding the importance and need for effective partnerships with parents include Jones (2004), Miller et al. (2005), Tassoni (2003), Weinberger et al. (2005) and Whalley (2007).

Throughout identification, assessment and reviewing of special needs provision, parents have a right and a duty to participate fully, but they can only do this if they are given the appropriate information about the people, systems and processes they are engaging with and if professionals truly listen to them. Whitaker's research (2007) explored issues for parents of children with autistic spectrum disorders in mainstream schools and found that parental partnerships were the source of many parents' dissatisfaction:

> Predictably, parents placed a high value on the willingness of school staff to listen to and take seriously any concerns that they may have about their child's experiences and progress. Conversely, perceived failure to take parental concerns seriously was a powerful cause of dissatisfaction – particularly where parents felt they were seen as needlessly 'fussy'. (2007: 175)

If the early years setting promotes positive partnerships from the outset, then parents and practitioners will be familiar with the stages of assessment and monitoring systems in place. Relevant information will have been shared with parents, their views considered and valued, and they would be fully aware of any action that was to be taken. Within a mutually supportive environment, parents would be aware of their rights and be confident to share in planning and provision. So the characteristics of effective partnerships could be suggested as:

- approachability, care and concern
- channels for two-way communication
- clarity and style of communication
- helping parents see what they may contribute

- providing opportunities for those contributions
- providing encouragement and support (adapted from Wolfendale, 1997: 64–7).

In addition, I would suggest:
- providing accessible information
- keeping parents informed and updated
- empowering parents
- equality, trust and respect.

Positive outcomes for practitioners

A feeling of mutual trust and respect should enhance practitioner confidence. Knowing that with input from parents we are maximising the learning opportunities for the child, and thus improving learning outcomes, should support staff motivation. When practitioners work alongside parents in a setting, they will be confident that parents understand the way in which they work and the pressures they may be under. This greater understanding could help when practitioners are discussing issues with the wider parental audience, as parents who have supported the work of the setting will have a greater awareness of the day-to-day reality.

Shared responsibilities in the setting can also help to alleviate practitioner workload, as long as each role is carefully planned and parents are well prepared. Parents are not replacement practitioners but can support and enhance the work of the practitioner, and the selection of tasks undertaken by the parents will reflect the practitioner's views on control, balance of power and the parent's capabilities. Working alongside practitioners often enables more informal discussions to emerge, which may be of significant importance, so hopefully, with an open, honest, equal and respectful partnership, the benefits will be clearly visible for both parents and professionals alike.

Practitioners should gain increased knowledge about the children from the parents, which will inform planning. A child's likes and dislikes, fears and worries, strengths and weaknesses may be viewed differently by parents and practitioners, so the sharing of information can only be beneficial.

Positive outcomes for parents

Through observing practitioners, parents may gain an improved understanding of the importance of providing appropriate activities, positive role models and supporting children's learning, which could lead to improved support within the home and, thus, improved learning outcomes for the children. Playing a greater part in their child's learning and development should also increase parental confidence.

If we believe that all parents are eager to see their children progress and develop, then it follows that to have played a greater part in that progress will be incredibly motivating. Parents can feel proud of their input in the setting and the direct help and support they are giving both practitioners and children, including their own child. As a result, self-confidence should be raised, and parental development and learning will have taken place which can only benefit everyone involved.

Positive outcomes for children

Arguably, the children will benefit most from effective partnerships, as they will feel part of a supportive network free of tensions between home and setting. Miller et al. (2005: 48) consider that: 'The central question that should be asked of any partnership arrangement is – to what extent is it directly or indirectly benefiting the children?' Children are sensitive to conflict around them which can place them in a compromising position and indirectly affect their learning. In a simple example, a child who is naturally very fond of the practitioner could be upset overhearing his/her parents in conflict with the practitioner. The child may be uncomfortable within the setting or even refuse to attend or conversely be uncomfortable at home. The child's security could be severely compromised and, as young children need consistency and security, this will have a negative effect.

Enhanced learning opportunities may emerge within the home situation, reinforcing the learning within the setting and, in some cases, parents will be enabled to participate more actively at home because of their enhanced confidence and their observations of setting activities. An effective parental partnership system should therefore lead to improved educational outcomes and achievement, and all parties will reap the benefits and rewards.

When focusing on children with special needs, parental partnerships may present more obstacles but the benefits, especially to the children, cannot be stressed more, as suggested by Drifte (2001: 24): 'it is for the benefit of all concerned, but most particularly the children, that a sound and positive working relationship between home and educational setting is established and maintained'.

Levels of partnership

Hopefully, the days are gone when practitioners were viewed as the 'expert professionals' that made all the decisions. Historically, there followed a period when parents were encouraged to play a greater part in their child's education and care, and we are continuing to move towards more empowering partnerships – in fact, all the government guidance and legislation places great emphasis on effective parental partnerships.

However, there are still some parents who feel intimidated or uncomfortable interacting with professionals, for a wide variety of reasons. It may be that their own negative school experiences compromise their ability to work with professionals or that they still view practitioners as 'the experts', with whom they could not enter into purposeful discussions. Wolfendale (1989: 17) concluded: 'One of the most common reasons given by parents for not being involved in their child's pre-school centre is lack of confidence in the face of professional expertise'. For those parents who do not readily engage with the setting, there is all the more need for practitioners to strive to overcome any barriers and begin to build and develop a long-term relationship. Equally, it should not be assumed that any barriers lie within the family as it could well be our systems, services, provision and/or the way we pass information to parents that may be the reason for their reluctance to participate at any level.

As previously mentioned, parental involvement within early years settings can be tremendously varied, ranging from attending concerts to full and total participation in the daily working life of the setting. As required by current legislation and guidance, all settings must identify the ways in which they involve parents. In addition, practitioners should ensure this is a process which supports real partnership and is not just a policy response to government requirements. For a full and meaningful partnership to exist, there should be equality between the parties, with the balance of power being equal.

Both parties must therefore feel that their input is valued. At the stage of initial diagnosis of special needs, parents may need time to adjust and be unable to be effective partners, but with support and encouragement it should be anticipated that parents will be enabled and empowered to take a more active and equal role as time progresses.

While the philosophy and nature of early years settings often lend themselves more readily to parental involvement, settings invariably *expect* a level of participation from parents, which is clearly stated within the policy documents and information given to parents. This is possibly linked to the equality between parents and professionals in this phase, where many groups will have parental input on committees and the daily workings of the group will be open to all for scrutiny and discussion. As a rule, pre-school settings are less formal and have greater flexibility to accommodate visitors and parents. However, in some settings there still exists a certain level of professional control over the domain and, thus, power is reluctantly shared. In addition, planning, recording and delivering the Early Years Foundation Stage and/or the National Curriculum places considerable pressures on practitioners, who may argue that there simply is not enough time to become involved in parental partnership schemes requiring additional time, organisation and planning. So perhaps the level of parental participation is directly linked to the equality or inequality of power within the setting.

Hopefully, the days when schools had signs barring entrance to parents are gone, but as Rennie (1996) concluded, while many schools have disposed of such prohibitive notices, they maintain the philosophy, and some may feel this still occurs today.

Legislation and guidance

In relation to children with special needs, the legislation and guidance that has evolved over the years has continued to emphasise parental rights, children's rights and the need for effective parental partnerships, although Paige-Smith (1997: 41) sees: 'education policy and practice restricting the rights of parents to participate in decision-making'.

The Warnock Report (DES, 1978) offered a complete chapter on parental partnerships and parental rights, with regard to children with special needs, emphasising the need for positive and equal partnerships with schools. The subsequent Education Act 1981 and circular 1/83 encouraged parental input in assessment processes and gave significant legal rights to parents. While the formal assessment process was introduced, it did not offer parents the right of redress if dissatisfied with any decisions or statements made relating to their child, unless there were factual errors. This was later addressed when SEN tribunals were introduced.

Although the 1981 Education Act reformulated special needs provision, the limitations of the Act were soon realised. As a result, a range of parental voluntary support groups emerged to campaign for continued improvements and to support parents in the short term. One such organisation, Network 81, was established by two parents following the difficulties they had experienced with their own child's education. They were aware of their right to be involved in decision making but found it hard to fight against a system that presented continuous bureaucratic obstacles to their input in the processes.

The Code of Practice (DfEE, 1994) outlined the key responsibilities of the role of SENCO and offered a basic principle relating to parental partnerships: 'Partnership between parents, pupils, schools, LEAs and other agencies is important' (1994: 1.2). The Code continued (ss 2:28–2:33) to outline requirements of providers, including registered early years providers, relating to parental partnership covering the areas of:

- SEN information needed for parents

- arrangements needed to ensure effective partnerships

- means of ensuring accessibility to information.

The Code of Practice introduced Individual Education Plans as a detailed working record of provision made to date and planned for the future. This was a result of significant parental lobbying following the 1981 Act as it was felt that such a record should be a shared document between practitioners and parents, giving parents the opportunity to see the targets that were being set for their child and to give them a say in the planning of those targets.

Within the revised Code of Practice (DfES, 2001c) came a requirement for LEAs to have in place Parent Partnership Schemes and to extend the remit of partnerships, as Emad (2000: 49) confirms: 'An important shift in the revised code of practice is the proposal to offer partnership services to all parents of children with SEN, not just those who have a statement or who are undergoing statutory assessment'.

The Children Act 1989 (DoH, 1991) also made reference to parental participation and partnerships by highlighting the rights and responsibilities of parents and emphasising the need to take into account the child's wishes and feelings in any decision-making processes. The area of pupil participation in decision making is further highlighted within the Code of Practice (DfES, 2001d). The revised Children Act (DfES, 2004b) has an underlying principle of 'the importance of parent and carers in improving the well-being of children' (ACE, 2005a: 15).

The fact that a whole chapter in the SEN Code of Practice (DfES, 2001c) is devoted to this area highlights the importance that is now placed on partnerships, which are seen as enabling and 'empowering' parents. The ethos of a shared responsibility is made clear:

> The work of the professionals can be more effective when parents are involved and account taken of their wishes, feelings and perspectives on their children's development. This is particularly so when a child has special educational needs. All parents of children with special educational needs should be treated as partners. (2001c: s. 2.2)

The Code continues to identify the responsibilities of LEAs and settings, plus the need for settings to involve parents fully from the initial identification of a child's difficulties, through Early Years Action and Early Years Action Plus. However, if all settings have effective parental partnerships in place, then the transition to discussing a child's specific difficulties should be made easier, as mutual respect, understanding and the sharing of information would already occur. Two-way communication should therefore be seen as a key feature of effective partnerships.

The Every Child Matters framework (DfES, 2003a) aims to secure improved outcomes for all children, young people and their families, and considers that everyone's 'voice' must be heard in planning and delivering the considerable changes that are currently taking place, including the voice of parents. Emanating from ECM, *Next Steps for Early Learning and Childcare* (DCSF, 2007e) clearly acknowledges the importance and value of parental partnerships stated within the EYFS (DCSF, 2008d):

> At its heart is the principle of parents and practitioners working together, with providers expected to maintain a regular flow of information to and from parents about their child's development. (2007e: 22)

Specifically relating to children with special needs and disabilities, Aiming High for Disabled Children is the government's drive and commitment to improve the lives of all children and young people with special needs and disabilities as well as their families. Following a review of services, the strategy was launched with the report *Aiming High for Disabled Children: Better Support for Families* (HM Treasury with DfES, 2007) which identified a £340 million commitment to improving services 'to ensure that disabled children and their families are enabled and empowered to make a full contribution to the society of which they are a part' (2007: 9). The key principle underpinning this report is the empowerment of parents so they are confident to make informed decisions and be key players in the design and delivery of services for their child. In 2009, we saw the *Aiming High for Disabled Children: Best Practice to Common Practice* document as part of the government's ongoing desire to 'enhance equality and opportunity'. Of the four themes explored, parental partnership is evident: '... working with parents and disabled children and young people to ensure their voices permeate all that we do' (DCSF, 2009g: 2).

In a range of activities to develop these strategic aims, the DCSF has appointed the Together for Disabled Children partnership to support the short breaks programmes and parent participation forums nationally (TfDC, 2008). Already, they suggest that significant progress has been achieved:

> Parent groups in 97% of English local authority areas have now been allocated funding to help them have a say in planning and shaping disabled children's services.
>
> In just two months parents with disabled children in 145 of the 150 local authority areas were successful in bidding for grants to help them get involved in local decision making.
>
> Over the next year a further £1.5 million is available to parent groups to develop participation activity across England, as part of the Aiming High for Disabled Children (AHDC) programme. (TfDC, 2008)

In addition, one of the recent documents emerging from within the Children's Plan is *Your Child, Your Schools, Our Future: Building a 21st Century Schools System* (DCSF, 2009c), which places partnerships with parents as crucial to all future developments, stating that:

> Parents make a critical contribution to their children's success at school and it is important that they have a strong voice at all levels of the system. Local authorities are responsible for ensuring there is a pattern of high-quality provision to meet local demands and aspirations. (2009c: 11–12)

In 2008, the government revised their information booklet for parents, *Special Educational Needs (SEN): A Guide for Parents and Carers* (DCSF, 2008i), which is available online to download or order in a range of languages and aims to guide parents through the SEN process, clearly identifying when and how early years settings and/or schools should intervene and how parents can and should be involved. However, in my current position I am working with many parents of children with SEN who are not aware of the existence of the guide, so this is a cause for concern.

Families of children with SEN in each local authority should be supported by a Parent Partnerships Service (PPS) which strives to ensure parents are provided with relevant and accessible information, help and support at all stages of the SEN process. It will be the SENCO's responsibility to ensure that all parents are informed about this service and that contact is enabled as early as is practicable (Drifte, 2010).

What is abundantly clear is that working with parents is seen as fundamental to the success of all children, but what is now needed is a review and evaluation of each setting's working practices to ensure that each and every parent (including fathers) is given every opportunity to be an active and equal partner in their child's learning and development. So self-assessment in this area is essential if we appreciate the benefits for all parties of successful and meaningful partnerships with parents.

Parental involvement in observation, assessment and reviewing progress

When practitioners are observing children, owing to initial concerns over possible difficulties the child may be experiencing, it is important that parents are fully informed. It may be that once the concern has been discussed parents can offer explanations, such as bereavement in the family or family tensions. If observations follow, then parents should be informed and involved at every stage. If mutual understanding exists at this point then, hopefully, any further action needed will be entered into in a framework of respect, with both parents and practitioners sharing the same goal.

If the child makes only limited or no progress, then Early Years Action would be entered into and, again, parents should be full participants in any discussions and decision making that emerge: 'Settings should make sure that parents are as fully involved as possible with their child's education and should always be fully informed about how the setting is seeking to meet their child's needs' (DfES, 2001c: s. 4.24).

Parents can support the work of the practitioner by working at home with the child to ensure consistency of approach between home and setting, and to support their child's progress. If further intervention is required through Early Years Action Plus and statutory assessment, then parents should again remain as partners throughout. For our youngest children, the Early Years Foundation Stage (QCA, 2008a) demands effective parent partnerships, not just for children with SEN but for all children, stating that all early years settings should include parents' views and information in their ongoing assessment processes.

Factors supporting positive partnerships

Having effective policies in place to support our work with parents and children with special needs is a key element of our work. So how can we ensure that policies respond to the needs of all parties and satisfy legislative requirements?

Policies

All registered providers, that is, all maintained schools and all registered early years providers, must have in place SEN policies regarding existing parental partnerships. Some LEAs may have outline policy documents available that can be accessed and adapted for individual settings. The LEA parent partnership officer, early years officers and/or early years advisory teams would also be useful contacts for support and advice when drafting policies. There seems little benefit in reinventing the wheel when a host of documentation already exists that can readily be adapted.

Settings should include parents in the planning and reviewing of partnership policies to ensure that parental perspectives are considered fully and included. Practitioners should strive to create policies that empower parents and practitioners alike, to support the work of the setting, the parents and the child. If parents are not asked to contribute to the creation of our policies, how can we ensure we are responding directly to their needs, having taken into account their views?

Creating or evaluating policies

When formulating or reformulating policies, all participating personnel should be involved to ensure every perspective is explored and to avoid making presumptions on behalf of unrepresented parties. The SENCO would take the lead, with his/her role ensuring: 'there is effective communication with parents, a shared dialogue in all matters impacting on their child and to involve them generally in their child's holistic development' (Sure Start, 2003: 13). Regarding policy creation, Smith recommends the following questions as a basic guideline for planning SEN policies which ensure parental partnership:

- How can we ensure that information relating to special needs reaches the parents who need it?
- Do parents feel that they can approach the school at any time if they have a concern?
- Do parents know who to contact about special needs?

- What channels do we use for communicating between home and school?
- How do we communicate with parents if we have a concern about their child?
- Do we have effective methods of gathering information from parents?
- Are parents actively involved in IEPs?
- Are review meetings organised in a way which supports parental contribution? (1996: 52)

The responses to these questions should give clear indications of existing gaps and ensure all relevant areas for consideration have been explored purposefully. At this point, policies can be developed and planning for partnerships set up. All relevant parties should be totally committed to partnership and be motivated to employ their utmost to ensure success, as any resistance or concern about issues may compromise success before any partnership is established.

If policies are already in place then regular reviews are pertinent, again ensuring all parties are involved. Views regarding current policies can be invited and used as a basis for discussion to identify problems, concerns and ways forward. If possible or practical, a worthwhile exercise could be to create a simple questionnaire for completion by staff and parents alike as this gives everyone the opportunity to reflect individually or with colleagues or friends and offer constructive comments in an anonymous manner which may encourage improved outcomes. The results or findings could then be circulated to all who participated and used as a basis for further discussions. If we do not seek parental views and respond to them, we are presuming we know their views and are excluding them from the process.

Reviewing existing policies

As a setting, it would be worth exploring precisely what information, support and participation is needed for parents and, conversely, what information, support and participation is needed from parents, perhaps through a questionnaire and follow-up discussion forums. Discussions could include areas such as information, mutual support, participation opportunities, skill sharing, parenting issues and teaching. It will be important to gather the views of fathers in each of these activities. The use of questionnaires is supported by OFSTED (2008) who suggest that:

> Providers actively encourage parents to contribute ideas and opinions on the setting, for example by using questionnaires. Parents' views are then used to inform the provider's plans for improvement. In some cases parents are involved in the management of the setting. (2008: 22)

Information

Information will pass between the two parties for mutual benefit, and obviously in the interests of the children. Settings should reflect on how information is shared regarding:

- the curriculum

- assessment and record-keeping systems

- planning

- identification of special needs

- monitoring progress

- the graduated response

- other local providers

- interagency working.

It may be useful for a member of staff or parent to collate such information as it emerges into a resource file that is readily accessible to all interested parties for reference and to support discussions. Conversely, staff can benefit from parental information about their children, the locality and the availability of resources that could prove useful to other parents. A noticeboard for open use by parents and staff alike can be a useful method of sharing information that encourages parents into the setting. Newsletters which encourage parental input are also a useful tool, especially if parents do not visit the setting regularly, and can be more meaningful if they are compiled by the parents themselves.

Mutual support

Simply offering parents a meeting place can encourage beneficial supportive discussions and the sharing of ideas. Parents of children with special needs may feel more comfortable talking to another parent who may share an understanding of the issues causing concern. Sharing common ground can be tremendously supportive and may help alleviate feelings of isolation and difference. Ideas, suggestions and sources of support could be shared and strong bonds formed that can enhance self-confidence for all parties, ultimately benefiting the children. Of particular interest may be consideration of a 'dads' forum' or 'dads and children' activities. Staff could also be involved in these meetings, if invited.

Participation opportunities

All parties need to be aware of existing participation opportunities and the readiness to welcome any new initiatives that may be suggested. Practitioners must also be ready to justify the existing range, or limitations, of participation as there may be parents who have experiences in other settings or new ideas that they wish to have considered. An open, encouraging environment will ensure that parents will be listened to and that their ideas will be welcomed. Parents will often come prepared to suggest an initiative, having clearly thought it through in advance and having some or many of the required resources in hand. With minor effort on behalf of the setting, a very positive, parent-led initiative could emerge.

Skill sharing

Parents, staff and practitioners can all benefit from the sharing of knowledge, expertise and skills so parents, staff and combined training sessions can be established, with all parties being encouraged to share skills. A whole range of sessions could be arranged on such aspects as behaviour management, immunisations, safety in the home, cooking with children, cooking from around the world, dealing with bureaucracy and purposeful play.

Skill sharing could also extend to parents' skills being used within the setting, from gardening expertise to fluency in a foreign language. Parent-to-parent skill sharing could evolve with parents establishing babysitting circles, social visits and so on. A vast range of opportunities exists.

Teaching

Parents can become real partners in the learning that takes place within the setting or within the home if they are involved in the planning as well as the delivery of that learning. Through a two-way interchange of ideas, practitioners and parents can support the child's progress together. Problems can arise when there is clearly a lack of interaction between home and school, which can result in a child's needs being compromised.

Issues compromising partnerships

There is a range of issues that may compromise or inhibit effective parent partnerships that all settings should be aware of and work to resolve. Debating these issues and any others that may emerge should enable a clarification of possible ways forward and would certainly benefit all as an awareness-raising exercise. Policy documents could then be developed, including existing practices and an action plan for the future.

Practitioners should accept that not all parents will be keen and enthusiastic to enter a partnership but may feel nervous, lacking in confidence or even be antagonistic, but all will have a strong emotional commitment to their child. Reports exist to suggest two distinct types of parents of children with special needs – those who are involved and those who are reluctant (Blamires et al., 1997). The initial and early contacts with parents are therefore vital to the future of the partnership, and practitioners should attempt to support all parents in becoming active and involved partners. The attitudes of professionals towards individual parents can significantly impact on the success or otherwise of any fruitful partnerships. Negative attitudes can be related to general negativity towards the inclusion of children with special needs and/or negativity towards specific parents, for any number of reasons. Where such attitudes exist, it will be the responsibility of the management team to make changes, perhaps via training as negativity can only spell disaster for the young children at the centre of the provision.

Legislation and bureaucracy can also create tensions for parents, so the LEA as well as the individual setting should strive to ease the situation through giving support and information to all parents, but especially those parents of children with SEN. Guides to LEA special needs provision should be readily accessible to all parents and practitioners, and it would be helpful to involve parents in the design and format of such information as it needs to be constructive, easy to understand and in the parents' home language. All parents should also be directed to the government's guide: *Special Educational Needs: A Guide for Parents and Carers* (DCSF, 2008i).

Local education authorities and individual settings must have clear policies and guidelines available to parents, as well as having policies for resolving conflict situations, but must also accept that not all parents wish to engage with our work. Ward (2009) considers that:

> Two factors seem to be fundamental in effectively engaging with parents, firstly, the accessibility of the service and secondly, internal barriers. The service you offer should take the families as a starting point both figuratively and literally. This means offering more flexible services, for example including detached work at times which suit the families and in ways they find appropriate. It also means that your dialogue with them has to be based on the interests they identify and the problems they wish to address. At the same time you have to be

mindful of how families may perceive you and your setting, including potentially negative past experiences and current cultural or religious considerations
which may need to be sensitively addressed before parents can engage with
you. (2009: 71)

What we need to ensure is that issues compromising partnerships
with parents are not brushed to one side, nor should we make
assumptions about some parents' apparent lack of desire to engage
with us. What we must do is to identify these issues and find ways to
address them, which will benefit the parents, the setting and, most
importantly, the children.

In working practice

If we are committed to working with parents, we must acknowledge
the benefits, examine our own working practices and recognise that
this area of work does not simply happen but that we need to plan,
establish and monitor partnerships to ensure positive outcomes for
all involved parties.

When preparing to welcome new children into our settings, parents
should be given information regarding:

- the setting and the policies of the setting
- how practitioners will plan for, monitor and review their child
- which professionals will be involved
- which professionals may be involved in the future
- the roles and responsibilities of professionals
- the requirements of the SEN Code of Practice (DfES, 2001c)
- how parents can support the work of the setting
- what information will be required from parents
- how we see partnership as crucial.

Once children are established within the setting, we should continue
to ensure that parents are active participants in their child's progress
through informing them regularly of the child's activities, successes,
concerns, any changes that may be occurring in the planning and
implementing of provision, and how they can help within the home
situation. Equally, parents should feel able to inform the setting of
activities, successes, concerns and changes. Parents should feel that
they are not only involved with their child's setting but are real and

active partners, taking a shared responsibility, an area that Ofsted will explore and assess as part of the inspection process of every early years provider and setting.

☐ Summary

If the children we work with are to be given the best opportunities to reach their full potential, then practitioners need to work together with parents and other professionals to ensure that this becomes a reality. We cannot do this without parental support, nor should we wish to. If we accept the benefits of effective parental partnerships, then it follows that we should establish, monitor and review our working practices to reflect this philosophy. As a starting point, we should assess:

- how welcoming our setting is to *all* parents and children (including fathers)
- how involved we want parents to become
- how well we include fathers
- our induction and settling-in procedures
- the parental partnership policy
- our information-sharing processes
- whether parents understand the roles and responsibilities of all those involved with their child
- how involved parents are in decision making
- the information that we expect parents to share with us
- the information we expect to share with parents
- the record-keeping systems
- how well staff members deal with parents
- whether staff members are always available to discuss issues with parents
- whether there is somewhere for such discussions to take place
- how we expect parents to work with their child in the home
- how aware parents are of supporting agencies
- how well parents are prepared for and supported in review meetings.

While not an exhaustive list, an exploration of these issues would be a useful starting point for reflection on current practices and moving towards improved practices. Dale concludes:

> What makes it so hard to evaluate is that the real cost can only be assessed through establishing the cost of its absence: of families who are frustrated and dissatisfied and fail to be helped by the services on offer and therefore perceive themselves as unsupported. Partnership

practice has a price – but can we as a society afford or justify the alternative? (Dale, 1996: 307)

Similarly, Wall (2005) emphasises the importance of this work:

> Every new guidance document or law that emerges is sure to make reference to our having effective partnerships with parents and our work in this area will be scrutinized in our inspections. We could pay lip service to these requirements but if we appreciate the benefits to all parties, and especially the children, then we should be prepared to examine our practices and address any areas that fall short of our ideal. (2005: 44)

 Key issues

- Parents should be respected and have their feelings and contributions valued.
- Practitioners should acknowledge the benefits of effective, meaningful partnerships.
- Practitioners should work towards empowering parents.
- Practitioners should review existing partnership policies and ensure that practices reflect policies.
- Partnerships cannot be assumed; they need to be planned, established and reviewed regularly.
- The success or failure of partnerships will depend on the quality of the relationships and the equality within those relationships.

Points for reflection

- Should settings review all aspects of their parent partnership work to identify issues and find ways to overcome them?
- Consider using a questionnaire to explore parents' views of how well your partnership is working from their perspective.
- What are the benefits of settings particularly exploring the ways in which they engage with fathers?

Suggested further reading

Department for Children, Schools and Families (2008i) *Special Educational Needs (SEN): A Guide for Parents and Carers.* Available at: www.teachernet. gov.uk/wholeschool/sen/parentcarers/

Whalley, M. (2007) *Involving Parents in their Children's Learning*, 2nd edn. London: Paul Chapman Publishing.

Wheeler, H. and Connor, J. (2009) *Parents, Early Years and Learning, Parents as Partners in the Early Years Foundation Stage: Principles into Practice.* London: NCB.

4

Responding to the affective needs of young children

Chapter objectives

To develop awareness of:

- the importance of working on 'the self' for adults and children
- the need to consider all factors that can influence children's development and learning
- the need for professionals to consider their own impact on children's development and learning.

Introduction

Research evidence clearly identifies links between low self-esteem, social, emotional and behavioural problems, learning difficulties and academic achievement, therefore it is essential that all early years practitioners acknowledge and address the affective needs of individual children, alongside any additional difficulties displayed. Charlton and Jones highlighted the importance of this area:

> Whether or not time is allocated to work on children's affective functioning too often depends on adventitious encounters with teachers who have been converted to the need to address such areas. It is time – as a profession – that we all recognised, for example, the need to give adequate time to 'working on the self'. It is iniquitous for us not to undertake this task. As educators, are we called upon to educate the 'whole' child? If not, who looks after the neglected parts? (Charlton and Jones, 1990: 149)

A range of potential causal factors exists, including those within the setting and home, and to provide effectively these should all be considered. If a child is experiencing affective problems, then until these are addressed it may be futile attempting to provide learning opportunities related to the curriculum as his/her ability to access opportunities may be impaired. It is also important to acknowledge the role practitioners can play in compounding or supporting a child's affective development and for practitioners to be prepared to critically analyse their own practices.

Through an examination of research and theory, this chapter will highlight some key issues and suggest ways in which practitioners can support the 'whole child' through an exploration of affective development. Social, emotional and behavioural development will be explored, as will the importance of the self-concept. In addition, as many more early years settings are dealing with children experiencing behaviour difficulties, practitioners will be guided through the processes of observation, planning an intervention and evaluating the effectiveness of that intervention, combined with practical strategies for use within any early years setting.

Definitions and terminology

A range of factors can affect our current and future performances, including levels of self-concept, confidence, ability to succeed and learn, motivation, support and encouragement, emotions and social competence. It is these areas that relate to affective development.

If we consistently meet failure then we are less likely to risk trying new challenges for fear of further failure(s). If we are confident about ourselves as individuals and learners, and have learnt that taking some calculated or informed risks can be beneficial, then we are more likely to succeed. All these factors are interrelated and affect a child's development.

Children with special needs may already find success more difficult to achieve or may have difficulties with issues of confidence and/or self-concept related to their individual needs. Therefore, while it is essential to address affective development with all young children, those with special needs may need additional and individualised consideration, but the key principles apply to all children.

Until quite recently, affective development has not been evident within curriculum documents and guidance but, as suggested, if these are overlooked it may be pointless working on a curriculum as the child's abilities to access that curriculum may be severely compromised. Practitioners should therefore acknowledge the affective needs of young children and respond to them appropriately, thus enabling successful and confident individuals and learners who can maximise the potential of the learning opportunities presented to them. Within the Early Years Foundation Stage (DCSF, 2008j), six areas of learning and development are identified that need to be incorporated into regular planning to ensure all children are receiving a broad and balanced curriculum in their youngest and most crucial years:

- Personal, social and emotional development

- Communication, language and literacy

- Problem solving, reasoning and numeracy

- Knowledge and understanding of the world

- Physical development

- Creative development.

To succeed, children need to be motivated to learn and confident to try, so practitioners need to consider areas of affective development at least as much as the EYFS areas of learning if they wish to ensure success for each and every child. This is reinforced in the EYFS documentation (DCSF) which states that:

> Meeting the individual needs of all children lies at the heart of the EYFS. Practitioners should deliver personalized learning, development and care to help children to get the best possible start in life. (2008k: 6)

It is therefore clear that we must consider children as individuals and 'personalised' learning is the way forward. It also follows that to consider the six curriculum areas without reflecting on the child's affective needs will at best be fruitless and at worst detrimental to the child's likelihood of success.

Legislation and guidance

Within the Code of Practice (DfES), children with behavioural, emotional and social development problems are highlighted as possibly needing additional support:

> Children and young people who demonstrate features of emotional and behavioural difficulties, who are withdrawn or isolated, disruptive and disturbing,

hyperactive and lack concentration; those with immature social skills; and those presenting challenging behaviours arising from other complex special needs, may require help or counselling. (2001c: s. 7.6)

The Code continues to suggest specific types of support or help that may be needed which would be incorporated within the processes of Early Years Action and Early Years Action Plus as outlined within the Code.

As part of the development of the early years and primary curricula, the government published the Social and Emotional Aspects of Learning (SEAL) programme to focus specifically on improving outcomes for children in the areas of personal, social and emotional learning and development. The programme is firmly based on research findings which highlighted:

> The key benefits of working on social, emotional and behavioural skills include:
> - Greater educational and work success
> - Improvements in behaviour
> - Increased inclusion
> - Improved learning
> - Greater social cohesion, increase in social capital
> - Improvements to mental health. (Primary National Strategy, 2005: 48–50)

To support practitioners, the SEAL guidance for early years practitioners emerged in 2008 emphasising the importance of working on this area in our settings as: 'Early PSED has a huge impact on later well-being, learning, achievement and economic circumstances' (DCSF, 2008l: 5). The guidance supports practitioners in developing their practice and is part of a range of supporting materials and resources available online.

SEAL itself is defined as:

> a whole school programme that supports schools and plans to help children and young people develop social and emotional skills. These skills are the building blocks to learning, behaviour, well-being and attendance. The skills are grouped into five aspects of learning: self-awareness, motivation, managing feelings, empathy and social skills. All these skills are emphasized within the EYFS … (2008l: 10)

Within the Early Years Foundation Stage, we know that all registered settings have a responsibility to provide for children's personal, social and emotional development as a key part of the curriculum. The EYFS guidance informs us that:

> Children must be provided with experiences and support which will help them to develop a positive sense of themselves and of others; respect for others; social skills; and a positive disposition to learn. Practitioners must ensure support for

children's social emotional well-being to help them to know themselves and what they can do. (DCSF, 2008k: 24)

The guidance then directs practitioners to focus on the following areas for each child which will be used to observe, record and inform planning:

- Dispositions and attitudes
- Self-confidence and self-esteem
- Making relationships
- Behaviour and self-control
- Self-care
- Sense of community.

From an international perspective the United Nations Convention on the Rights of the Child (DCSF) also reflects the need to respond to children's affective development within its definition of education that should be available to all children. Article 29 highlights that:

the education of the child shall be directed to:
- The development of the child's personality, talents and mental and physical abilities to their fullest potential;
- The development of respect for human rights and fundamental freedoms, and for the principles enshrined in the Charter of the United Nations;
- The development of respect for the child's parents, his or her own cultural identity, language and values, for the national values of the country in which the child is living, the country from which he or she may originate, and the civilisations different from his or her own;
- The preparation of the child for a responsible life in a free society, in the spirit of understanding, peace, tolerance, equality of sexes and friendship among all peoples, ethnic, national and religious groups and persons of indigenous origin;
- The development of respect for the natural environment. (DCSF, 2009k)

If, as early years practitioners, we aim to develop young children to their maximum potential then, clearly, we have a responsibility to address their affective development as well as the more commonly highlighted curriculum areas such as language, literacy and numeracy. The links between the areas cannot be overlooked and yet training courses, books and journals still tend to separate academic development from affective development, highlighting special needs, behavioural difficulties or affective development as separate. It could be argued that sufficient evidence now exists to combine all areas within educational training and provision as inclusive, as supported by the current climate, which would have the benefit of acknowledging the interrelationship between them and thus breaking down the perceived division. This philosophy would add further support to providing personalised learning in a holistic manner, taking into account all influencing factors including affective development.

Personal, social and emotional development

The importance of this area of development has now been established and is highlighted in current legislation and guidance so practitioners need to consider and understand the social and emotional development of young children in order to respond appropriately. Harnett provides a useful summary of research in this area:

> The importance of developing children in this area is well documented from Piaget (1896–1980, quoted in Barnes, 1997) through to writers such as Rogers (1983) and the High Scope Educational Research Foundation (Hohmann and Weikart, 1995). Reports such as Plowden (1967) and Gulbenkian (1982) also highlighted the need for children to have a broad and balanced curriculum that developed the whole child. This has been further refined within the Early Learning Goals by providing explicit guidance on the opportunities that enhance this area of learning. (Harnett, 2002: 62)

To be able to provide for children's needs, practitioners need to understand development in each of the specified areas but, at the same time, acknowledge the interaction across and between them. Bertram and Pascal identify five key messages relating to this area:

- Children's overall development is fundamentally affected by their relationships and feelings.

- Children's sense of self and their ability to form relationships with others is substantially shaped by their early interactions with others.

- The emotional life of the young child underpins the way they explore and make sense of the world.

- The social and emotional life of the child is culturally embedded.

- Children's identities are shaped by the nature of their interactions with different culture. (2010: 75)

Social development

According to Beaver et al., the process of socialisation enables children to:

> learn the way of life, the language and behaviour that is acceptable and appropriate to the society in which they live. This is their culture. The process of

socialisation involves children learning from the experiences and relationships they have during childhood. (1999: 226)

Beginning with primary socialisation in the child's home environment, this is later extended to secondary socialisation, where children learn that different expectations exist in different situations. As children progress through the stages of social development, they learn to adapt behaviour according to the context they are in, being able to change to satisfy the rules of the grouping, so a child may behave appropriately at the early years setting but not at home, or vice versa. This is perhaps because the rules, structure, reinforcement strategies and routines in each are different, so they become skilled at adaptating, as long as they are confident within themselves and clearly understand the rules of each environment. The way these skills are learnt will partly depend on the learning style of the child, partly on his/her background and culture and how these skills are passed on. Examples of ways in which young children learn social skills would include:

- observing, copying and imitating adults and children around them

- stories and role play

- being positively rewarded for acceptable and appropriate behaviour within any environment.

Social development will also depend greatly on the family, the culture of the family and other outside influences on the child. In the primary socialisation phase, the key influencing factors will include the parents, siblings, additional carers (for example, early years practitioners), neighbours and other close family members. In the secondary socialisation stage, influences would extend to include the local community, television, video and computer, storybooks and peer group. Children clearly need opportunities to develop their social skills within both of these stages to develop appropriately. Any missing elements may have a lasting effect on the child and create difficulties for him/her when entering new and unfamiliar situations. David suggests:

> Resilient people tend to have, or have had, at least one person in their life to whom they feel they (and what they do) matter. Staff in ECEC settings sometimes need to help children integrate into the group and they need to be aware of how friendships can help children cope with transitions. Most important, babies and young children need to experience unconditional acceptance, continuity of relationships – these can be with several people – and to bask in interactions and play with those who love them. (2009: 88)

Stages of social development

From birth, babies tend to demonstrate social development through:

- reactions and reflexes, such as sucking and gripping
- being content cuddled up to a parent or close family member
- indicating distress when hungry or in pain
- an increasing awareness of surroundings.

By the age of 6 months, tremendous progress has already been made as demonstrated by:

- laughing, smiling and interacting with their environment
- participating in simple games such as 'peepo'
- amusing themselves for short periods
- appearing eager when a known person approaches them
- showing a preference for certain people
- stopping crying when responded to
- holding and exploring objects (usually by mouthing).

By the age of 2 years, we can see rapid changes demonstrated through:

- being responsive to a wider range of emotions
- acquiring increased language and communication skills
- being very independent and, on occasions, uncooperative
- finding it difficult to share and wait for a turn
- being able to wait for something but preferring an immediate response
- being able to display love and affection
- playing alongside other children
- joining in with simple repetitive songs and rhymes.

By the age of 6 or 7 years, children demonstrate their social skills through being able to:

- cooperate well with adults and children
- be rebellious and aggressive, miserable and/or sulky

- feel devastated when their best friend deserts them
- be aware of gender differences
- be generally self-confident with people
- persevere with an activity
- be greatly influenced by peers
- be very self-critical.

The rapidity of development indicated in the first seven years of life will hopefully alert practitioners to the importance of supporting development during the early years. In general, most of the activities and learning experiences presented within early years settings will naturally enhance children's social development but, rather than allowing this to happen of its own accord, careful planning and personalised learning opportunities should always be considered. This is especially pertinent when supporting children who have difficulties with sharing and/or turn taking, are shy or withdrawn, are overconfident and may always need to be in control of a situation, have special needs, behavioural difficulties or have simply lacked prior social development opportunities. Any child who has experienced emotional, social and/or behavioural difficulties will probably need additional support in developing additional skills appropriately.

As previously highlighted, a child's culture will generally be developed within the home and family, where customs, traditions and values will be handed down through generations, but practitioners have a responsibility to be aware of and understand these cultural differences that will be tremendously important to children. Within our inclusive, multicultural settings, we can inadvertently create significant problems for a child through ignorance of the facts relating to his/her culture and/or religion. Practitioners should be aware of the possibility that the ethos and practices within the setting may not be concordant with the family and their local community as their values may be different. This is not necessarily a problem as both can be proud of their values and customs, which should be celebrated, and the children will all benefit from experiencing equally valid, situational values.

Representational images of a cross-section of children should be displayed within the setting to highlight the sameness as opposed to highlighting the differences between children. Books and resources should also move away from the stereotypical images that were evident only a generation or two ago. This will support positive images of society in general to be generated among the children, staff and all others entering the setting. Similar issues can arise from gender stereotyping which should be avoided in early years settings. Children's awareness of differences, whether regarding gender or any other issue, can be established surprisingly early and we need to be sensitive to this. Often the influences of parents and/or older siblings can have detrimental effects on younger children who are not concerned about any differences between people. Young children play with whoever they choose and are not generally prohibited by any stereotypical images, but other influences can create situations that practitioners should be aware of and be ready to respond to. For example, if a young boy is playing hospitals with his peers and wants to take the role of a nurse, he may be inhibited by other children suggesting that this is a girl's role. Lack of awareness that men can and do train as nurses can affect children's play in a negative manner.

The issue of gender is often compounded by the few qualified male early years practitioners and, thus, a lack of positive male role models. Work in the early years and caring for young children is still predominantly viewed as a female domain, and recent experiences have indicated that male students following courses in early years or early childhood studies have to be highly committed and motivated as they tend to take some friendly but pointed gender-stereotypical comments when socialising with their peers. However, in a society where there is an increase in the numbers of children being brought up by single mothers and an increase in the number of 'house fathers', perhaps there is a greater need for an increase in numbers of male early years workers to balance out the role models. Hopefully, the Children's Workforce Strategy (DfES, 2005a) will continue to support development in this area through increased recruitment of men into the early years, although it should be clarified that without significant changes in areas such as low pay, this is unlikely to happen. The House of Commons *Education and Employment First Report* (2001, s. 29) reported that:

> According to the National Early Years Network, 'the issues around the gender balance within the workforce in the early education field need urgent attention'. Men have an important role to play in the care, education and support of young children and their families with potentially far-reaching consequences for children's healthy and balanced intellectual and emotional development.

It is not always appropriate to treat all children the same owing to cultural differences which deserve respect and understanding. It is more important to be aware of multicultural issues in a sensitive manner that is not judgemental, but respectful and valuing. Diversity within our early years settings is positive and, if supported appropriately, will enhance the development of understanding of all the children, and possibly parents and staff as well. Diversity should be celebrated as it will enhance social development for parents, practitioners and children alike.

Emotional development

We are all aware of the effects our emotions can have on our ability to perform successfully in our everyday lives, from a short-term panic situation to a longer-term emotional difficulty. The effects can be devastating. If we then consider children's emotional development, it should be clear that we should support their gradual development of emotions and emotional understanding while acknowledging that on occasions they, too, will need additional short- or longer-term help.

Our emotions develop from very basic emotions expressed at a young age (for example, anger, love, happiness, distress) to much subtler forms of emotion expressed as adults (for example, pride, jealousy, envy, sympathy, embarrassment). For healthy maturity, children need emotional support and understanding throughout childhood.

At birth, babies clearly demonstrate very basic emotions in as much as they can be happy and content or fractious and distressed, but from these early days we see continued development in their abilities to demonstrate emotional expression and understanding. Barnes (1995) describes the research of Haviland and Lelwica in examining the display of emotions between 10-week-old babies and their mothers expressing facial happiness, sadness and anger, concluding that:

> Analysis of video recordings taken of the babies showed that they reacted in distinct ways to each of the displays, but they were not simply copying their mother's expression. They did respond to their mother's happy display with a happy face, but the angry face resulted in either an angry expression or stillness, and the sad display generated an increase in mouthing, chewing and sucking behaviour. (Barnes, 1995: 143)

From the very early attachments to significant others (usually parents/carers), children's emotional development begins. Miller et al. (2005: 166) suggest that:

> Attachments and trust are vital in setting the foundations for healthy emotional development. Making a child feel loved, wanted, valued and cared for provides a safe and supportive environment, from which they can explore the world. This opportunity to explore independently in a secure environment is the beginning of children seeing themselves as separate from their parents.

In the first year of a baby's life, the mother will begin to discriminate between a range of emotions expressed by her baby, and the baby, in turn, will become more able to respond to emotional signals from the mother's face and use that information to inform their own emotions. By 18 months, toddlers begin to have an image of their 'self' in relation to others and begin to verbalise their feelings/emotions, but by 3 or 4 years of age children can manipulate their emotions, confident that a desired response will follow, thus they have learnt to use their emotions in a controlling manner. They also have an understanding of the feelings, emotions and desires of others and are beginning to be aware of and understand another person's perspective.

As children mature, there is an expectation that they will (or should) be able to control their emotions relating to culturally and socially accepted norms and values. However, this does not mean we should discourage children from acknowledging and expressing their emotions. With increased age also comes the ability to experience more complex emotions such as jealousy and embarrassment, and practitioners will be able to identify children who are more sensitive to such emotions. The inability to share as a toddler is more a response to the child's perceived need for an object than a jealous emotive response. Jealousy develops at a later stage.

Young children rely heavily on a firm and secure base in which they develop confidence to build strong emotions. This is further extended by the child's need to continue their strong attachments with one or more carers. Again, practitioners will need to be sensitive to children who do not appear to have experienced this firm foundation and have not developed strong attachments as they may need additional support. Such issues were highlighted in the research of Lafrenière and Sroufe, and Waters, Wippman and Sroufe, summarised by Keenan:

> Further research showed that these same benefits associated with a secure attachment relationship held into the preschool years, with preschool teachers rating securely attached children as less aggressive toward their peers, less dependent on help from the teacher and more competent than insecurely attached children. (Keenan, 2002: 189)

Such research also highlights the importance of acknowledging the relevant areas of development to support later progress and abilities to maximise on the learning experiences offered. Considerable research has been undertaken exploring the qualities of effective schools that support children experiencing difficulties of a social, emotional and/or behavioural nature. Many of these are as relevant to early years settings. Long and Fogell suggest that:

Schools have a central role to play in supporting all children through adverse and difficult events. Our task in school is to make a difference where we can make a difference. It is not always possible or appropriate for a class teacher to work with children's families. We do not have the power to change their home circumstances but we can ensure that the school environment is emotionally supportive for all children and especially those who are most vulnerable. (Long and Fogell, 1999: 26)

David (2009) sees emotional development as critical to future success:

[E]motionally sensitive parents and carers who encourage young children to explore and enjoy 'their world' find these children take greater pleasure in goal-directed task persistence, and as a result are socially and cognitively more competent in later life, whereas babies whose key adults constantly fail to support them can develop 'learned helplessness'. So we can conclude that emotional well-being is the bedrock on which all later development depends. (2009: 82)

Practitioners should therefore ensure that factors within settings support the emotional development of all individual children.

Social, emotional and/or behavioural difficulties

When a child is experiencing difficulties, practitioners should assess whether these are short- or long-term difficulties, and plan accordingly. In the case of a child who has rarely left his/her parents from birth and has had limited contact with adults or children from outside his/her home environment, practitioners should rightfully expect some adjustment difficulties on entering the pre-school setting and separating from parents. This may be short-lived or may continue over a period of time and require more purposeful planning. We cannot expect children to settle quickly, as for some the stages between entering the group and becoming a fully active participant may take time. Planning and support will help this child considerably and, if recorded, may help the child if similar difficulties arise later. Each child must be treated as an individual and his/her personality, characteristics and prior experiences should be fully explored to account for any factors that may be affecting current performance levels. Discussions with parents should help practitioner understanding of the issues. There is much evidence available indicating links between social, emotional and/or behavioural difficulties with learning difficulties and cognitive development, and early intervention is necessary to ameliorate later problems. If learning difficulties exist, whether at the pre-school or later stages, then behaviour problems may follow. Repeated failure to achieve success may result in avoidance tactics and may manifest as withdrawal or task avoidance through inappropriate and unacceptable behaviours.

What can settings and practitioners do?

The following are some practical suggestions for settings to consider:

- awareness and knowledge of the need to address affective development
- caring and sensitive staff who value and respect children and parents
- a positive ethos of the setting
- appropriate interactions with children, acknowledging children's likes/dislikes, culture, special needs, gender and identity
- appropriate learning opportunities that offer success and support confidence and self-esteem
- positive reward systems
- allowing children to express feelings and emotions
- supporting children to make decisions and gain independence
- planning to include the EYFS requirements for personal, social and emotional development
- individualised planning for children needing specific help
- effective parental partnerships
- the ability to listen to children.

The EYFS guides us in effective practice suggesting three key areas that need to be addressed:

Positive Relationships:
- Form warm, caring attachments with the children
- Establish constructive relationships with parents
- Find opportunities to give encouragement to children
- Plan for opportunities for children to play and learn, sometimes alone and sometimes in groups.

Enabling Environments:
- Ensure each child has a key person
- Make sure there is time and space for children to concentrate on activities and experiences to develop their own interests
- Provide positive images that challenge children's thinking and help them to embrace difference
- Establish opportunities for play and learning that acknowledges children's particular religious beliefs and cultural backgrounds
- Support the development of independence skills.

Learning and Development:

- Plan activities that promote emotional, moral, spiritual and social development
- Provide opportunities that help children to develop autonomy and a disposition to learn
- Give support and a structured approach to vulnerable children and those with particular behavioural or communication difficulties. (DCSF, 2008k: 24–5)

When children are demonstrating distress, perhaps caused by a current issue within the home such as parental separation, practitioners need to be aware of the situation in order to support the child. The distress may manifest in a variety of ways but the underlying issues should be examined before any action is taken. It will compound the child's problems if settings deal more firmly with the child to reduce the unwanted behaviours presented, when the child clearly needs support dealing with distress. We must address the causes not just the symptoms.

Causal factors

Some factors that can positively or negatively impact on children's affective development have already been highlighted but it will be pertinent to present them together to clarify understanding.

Within the home

- Poverty and deprivation.
- Poor housing causing stress and anxiety.
- Poor parenting skills – too restrictive, protective, lenient, lacking structure and routine, lacking quality family time, lack of or too severe behaviour management – often the result of poor parenting in their own childhood and the cycle being repeated.
- Parenting style that lacks love and security, often due to parental lack of self-esteem and confidence.
- Negative parenting that reduces confidence and self-esteem.
- Poor diet and standards of hygiene.
- Child abuse – physical, sexual, emotional or neglectful (all forms of abuse generally have an emotionally abusing effect).
- Alcohol and/or drug abuse by parents.
- Poor attachments.

- Parental separation, bereavement or other loss.
- Unrealistic expectations of parents.

Within the setting

Many factors within settings have already been indicated but a few suggestions are offered here that will support children's affective development:

- Positive use of the key worker system.
- Effective planning, evaluation and monitoring of curriculum (hidden and prescribed).
- High and consistent levels of organisation within classroom/activity room.
- Resources which are readily accessible to the children.
- Effective observation and assessment processes.
- A supportive and positive ethos.
- Structured day and individual lessons/working times.
- Clear guidelines and rules.
- Positive staff attitudes.
- Well-motivated staff.
- An ethos of individualised and holistic planning.
- Meaningful policies.
- Positive parental partnerships.

Practitioner

- Good knowledge base of child development.
- Knowledge and understanding of responding to individual needs in a holistic philosophy.
- Familiarity with current legislation and guidance (particularly regarding the Early Years Foundation Stage and special needs provision).
- Effective planning, record keeping and time management.
- Good organisational skills.

- Appropriate tasks presented for child's current level of performance.
- Not overreliant on standardised worksheets.
- Good classroom management skills.
- High but realistic expectations of him/herself, staff and children.
- Encouraging and motivating qualities.
- Effective management of behaviour.
- Use of positive reinforcement strategies for all children.
- Ability to undertake observations that inform planning.
- Ability to plan SMART targets which are appropriate for individual needs.
- Inclusive practices.
- Ability to recognise when additional training is required.
- Awareness of gender and multicultural issues.

An illustrative example

The ability of practitioners to be critically reflective of their own practices is not always easy but, if confident with colleagues, then peer appraisal or review processes can support this. In my own experience, I bravely decided to reflect on the positive verbal feedback I gave children in a reception class. At the time, I would have fiercely defended my positive interactions with the children and I thought the exercise would support my views. My nursery nurse noted at random intervals for half an hour at a time, over a month, whether my comments were negative or positive and I confess to being appalled at the outcomes. Despite my positive views of my verbal feedback, the negative statements I uttered totalled 68 per cent and the positive 32 per cent. Interestingly, the observations were classified into academic reinforcement and behaviour reinforcement, and the outcomes indicated that the majority of my positive comments were directed towards academic issues and the negatives towards behaviour issues. Overall, my feedback regarding behaviour also far outweighed my feedback on academic work (see Figure 4.1).

It was evident that a review of my verbal interactions was necessary, and over the next few weeks I focused strongly on positive verbal reinforcement, especially of behaviour, as my negative comments were actually rewarding and encouraging unacceptable behaviours. Through a system of ignoring minor behaviour issues and consistently praising acceptable behaviours, the balance of my verbal inter-actions changed.

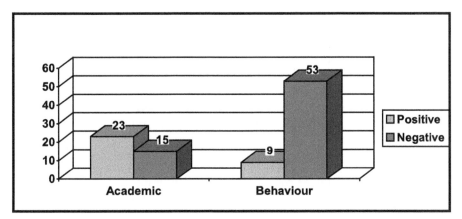

Figure 4.1 Positive and negative teacher feedback

Perhaps the most interesting outcome of the exercise was that the children's behaviour, in general, improved considerably, so although this had not been the intention it became a very pleasing outcome. This example highlights three important issues:

- The practitioner (myself) was negatively rewarding unacceptable behaviours.

- The practitioner's verbal interactions have a powerful effect in improving children's behaviour.

- There is value in examining practitioner practices through action research.

Self-concept

Definitions

Practitioners will be well aware of the importance of enhancing self-esteem but may have limited knowledge of self-concept development and the powerful effects the self-concept can have on very young children. Wall (1996: 82) suggested: 'A child's self-concept is crucial to a positive outlook and progress towards his/her full potential and a range of factors can create a positive or negative self-concept'.

The self-concept is developed through feedback from significant others in our lives, such as parents, siblings, extended family, teachers/practitioners and peers. The level of self-concept is directly related to both self-image and ideal self in that high self-esteem occurs when self-image and ideal self are both positive and you view yourself as near to your ideal self. Low self-esteem occurs when self-image and ideal self are distanced from each other and your ideal self differs considerably from your self-image. The ideal self is therefore very powerful. It may also be that as adults in a professional capacity we can feel motivated, confident and successful, and thus have high levels of self-esteem, while outside work we may feel socially inadequate and therefore have a reduced level of self-esteem. The effects of self-concept cannot be overlooked. Charlton and David offer a helpful summary:

> The self-concept is formed by a process of socialisation by interaction with others and as a result of the feedback of that interaction. 'You are a good boy'; 'You are clever'; 'You are not as good as your sister'. We learn of ourselves by comparison, by competition and by selection processes. The self-concept is related to social skill and like social skill is learned. Failure of social competence leads to rejection, social isolation and subsequently to the formation of poor self-concept. (1990: 109)

Regarding young children, Cousins (2006) summarised that:

> Young children rely on good feelings to help them grow in confidence and emotional stature. Self-esteem for them is a mixture of feeling happy, confident, secure, important and feeling they fit in. A child develops the feelings that make up his self-esteem from the responses and interventions by people, mainly adults, round about him. To build up a child's self-esteem nursery staff need to help a child feel OK in his surroundings, to feel accepted, valued, happy and confident. This aim must inform the staff attitude, the nursery philosophy and the organisation's policies, so that staff know how to respond to effect the best outcome for the child's self-esteem.

An illustrative example

A 3-year-old girl from a deprived household may present at nursery as dirty and unkempt, not wearing fashionable clothes and, as hygiene standards at home are poor, may have an unpleasant odour. In my experience, despite many positive characteristics and qualities, she may find it very difficult to make friends and socialise, thus it would be difficult for her to become a full participant of the group. Invitations to play, have tea or attend parties outside the nursery may be limited or non-existent and children may be told by their parents that they are to stay away from her within the nursery. Within the setting, children may choose not to sit next to her and, sadly, their naive comments may be very blunt and hurtful. The effects on this little girl could include:

- social difficulties

- emotional difficulties

- poor self-image

- unrealistic ideal self

- low self-esteem

- low self-concept

- lack of motivation.

Considerable support will be needed for her affective development as well as for any additional difficulties that may arise, such as withdrawal, task avoidance, behavioural issues and problems accessing the curriculum because of the affective difficulties.

Mortimer (2001) summarised the characteristics of children with high and low self-esteem. Children with low self-esteem may:

- avoid new tasks

- need reassurance, as they may feel unwanted, unloved or worthless

- feel emotionless or indifferent to emotions

- be quick to respond to frustration and/or failure

- have little faith or belief in themselves

- resist or ignore being corrected or reprimanded

- have a tendency to display physical/emotional aggression and/or bullying behaviour

- resist decision-making situations

- have difficulties with learning.

Conversely, children with high self-esteem may:

- be confident and independent

- be able to take responsibility

- cope well with frustration and/or failure

- greet new tasks with eagerness and motivation

- acknowledge and understand their own emotions

- help and support others

- accept being corrected or reprimanded

- be aware of their own strengths and weaknesses.

Locus of control

Allied to self-concept theory is locus of control theory, developed from Rotter's (1966) social learning theory. Locus of control relates to the way in which we see success or failure and where the responsibility for that success or failure lies, either within our control or from outside our control. If a young boy achieves success and believes this is because of his hard work and effort, then he will have an internal locus of control as he accepts responsibility for the outcomes. However, if he feels his success was because of his brother's help, this is external locus of control as the success is not perceived as his own. The same locus of control concept relates equally to failure.

A child's locus of control can therefore affect his/her expectations and future performance either negatively or positively. Some children, usually with internal locus of control, will be able to accept some failures, learn from the experiences and move forwards. Therefore, failure is not necessarily a negative issue; it is the way the child deals with it that is important. Generally speaking, very young children begin with an external locus of control but as they mature it is hoped that with appropriate learning experiences and support they will develop an internal locus of control. Lambley (1993: 88) suggests that: 'It has been shown that the self-concept, self-expectation and locus of control beliefs often determine pupils' responses to, and achievements in, the learning situation. The investigation of these factors has highlighted the close relationship between affective and cognitive performance'.

Factors affecting self-esteem

As mentioned previously, significant others play a vital role in the development of a child's self-esteem and if practitioners are promoting positive self-concept development, but the opposite is happening at home, then the child's difficulties will be compounded. It will be a constant battle of one step forwards and two steps back, but is nevertheless worth persisting with.

A range of additional factors also affects a child's self-concept including:

- levels of motivation
- positive experiences of learning
- feeling valued and respected
- levels of confidence

- positive feedback for effort as well as achievement

- security and love

- practitioner awareness of affective development

- consistent structure and routine

- clear and realistic expectations of parents, practitioners and the child him/herself

- social and emotional difficulties

- stress.

Enhancing the self-concept

Practitioners should remember that the classroom and/or the practitioner can affect children's self-concepts positively or negatively. All interactions and learning opportunities presented to the children will have an effect and it is the practitioner's responsibility to ensure these experiences are positive. A useful resource is the book by Canfield and Wells (1976), offering 100 ways to enhance self-esteem.

Enhancing the self-concept in the classroom/activity room
- Systems of rewarding children for effort as well as achievement.

- Systems of effective target-setting.

- Clear rules agreed between practitioners and children.

- A supportive system in which adults accept the blame for children's failures, as the situations may have arisen through inappropriate tasks/mismatch of curriculum.

- An environment in which all individuals are valued and respected.

- An environment in which children's experiences, likes/dislikes, preferred activities, learning styles, background and culture are known and valued.

- Well-organised resources that are accessible to children.

- An ethos that offers security and encourages confidence and independence.

Practitioner qualities
- Having knowledge of children's affective development.

- Being supportive, motivating, encouraging and sensitive.

- Planning for individual needs.
- Setting challenging but achievable targets.
- Having positive classroom management skills.
- Making time to listen to children.
- Valuing and respecting individual children, parents and staff.
- Using positive reinforcement strategies effectively.
- Praising effort as well as achievement.
- Having effective, practical and meaningful recording systems.
- Encouraging peer support and understanding.

Self-concept of adults

Adults within the setting, both staff and parents, should not be over-looked when considering strategies for enhancing self-concept. It is a fact that many of us find it hard to accept praise and will often brush aside comments or devalue an achievement into something less praiseworthy. However, all adults, like children, need support, encouragement, sensitivity and motivation to feel positive about themselves as professionals as well as from a personal perspective. It is important that we demonstrate the same levels of consideration to all adults we work with, which will help enhance their own self-concept as well as supporting their motivation and, in turn, benefit the children.

Behaviour

Babies are not born behaving inappropriately but as they grow they develop behaviours and strategies as responses to experiences. It there-fore follows that the child within an early years setting who displays unacceptable behaviours is not a 'problem child'; it is the learned behaviour that is the problem. These behaviours can be interpreted as appropriate or inappropriate. In a simple yet quite common example, a toddler wanting a biscuit and wanting it now (as they invariably do) may have learnt the following behaviour pattern:

1　Ask or point, to indicate desire for a biscuit (possibly perceived as a need rather than a desire).

2　If request rejected by adult, persist by repeating request.

3　Continue to persist if unsuccessful, tugging at the adult in the hope they will concede.

4 If this fails, begin whimpering and repeat 'please' constantly.

Possible outcomes: the adult, especially if under pressure, may concede and despite having refused the toddler several times, give the biscuit, or the adult will distract the child or remain firm and no biscuit will be given. Whichever outcome occurs, the child will have learnt a useful and valuable lesson for the future. Either, if you persist and whimper you will gain control and win, or it is pointless persisting. The adult's response to this common occurrence may well set the scene for future encounters.

If we accept that behaviours are learned from significant others, then it follows that behaviour should be defined according to the values and cultures of a child's home environment. Practitioners should reflect on this aspect when responding to behaviours, as they may consider a specific behaviour unacceptable by their standards and values that may be highly acceptable within the culture of the home.

Learning behaviours

If behaviours include all our actions, physical, expressive and verbal, then practitioners will need to explore how exhibited behaviours have been learnt and which variables and causal factors are involved.

Young children learn behaviours in much the same way as they develop any other skill, through processes of observing, imitating and experimenting and, as they mature, different variables will emerge that will lead to further changes. Once children enter the pre-school and primary phases of education, the importance of the peer group will begin to affect change, while the parents and significant others will still have an important influencing role. When children advance to the secondary phase then the effects of the peer group, combined with the onset of puberty, may well become the stronger forces affecting behaviour.

For the significant others in the lives of very young children, the following features would be influential in encouraging positive behaviour:

- consistency of approach
- clear boundaries, rules and expectations
- positive modelling of acceptable behaviours
- strong and positive attachments

- encouraging confidence and independence

- rewarding acceptable behaviours.

Labelling

In situations where children enter an early years setting and are described by parents and/or other professionals as having behaviour problems, practitioners should be aware of the possible debilitating effects of labelling. Settings should ensure that all adults interacting with the children, whether staff or voluntary helpers, do not allow labels to affect the way they work with the children. Practitioners may inadvertently place unrealistic expectations on the child or simply assume that they will demonstrate unacceptable behaviours and wait for it to happen. If adults expect a child to behave inappropriately, then their verbal interactions, gestures and body language may actively encourage such behaviours. If the setting employs positive reinforcement strategies that are different from the child's previous environment(s), then this alone may bring about positive change over time. Labelling also infers the child is a problem, which we know is not the case. Practitioners should observe, assess and monitor all children and make informed decisions on the basis of the evidence collated, and not make assumptions. Clearly, we need to look beyond any labels, to the child, in a personalised and holistic manner. This approach is far more likely to incur success and is good early years practice.

Causal factors

As with social and emotional difficulties, any child exhibiting unacceptable behaviours should be discussed with parents and staff to agree possible strategies, but before this stage all possible causal factors should be explored. The same range of factors previously explored under social and emotional difficulties should be examined. These can be found in greater detail earlier in this chapter, but cover the areas of:

- the setting

- the home environment

- the practitioner.

If no satisfactory explanations for the current behaviours emerge then observations should take place to establish precisely which behaviours are occurring, how often they occur and how these impact on the child's learning and/or that of other children within the setting.

Observations

Initially, staff should use observation techniques to establish the precise behaviours that are causing difficulties and these should be cited in clear and observable terms. 'He/she is aggressive' tells us little about a child's current behaviours, and what is deemed aggressive to one adult may be acceptable to another. 'He/she pushes other children away from desired toys at least six times per three-hour session' describes precisely what is happening and how often it occurs, indicating the level of the problem.

The most appropriate observational method must then be selected (see Chapter 5) and several baseline observations completed to indicate the level or frequency of the behaviour. When dealing with unacceptable behaviours, it is also beneficial to note the ABC of the behaviour (see Figure 4.2), as it may be the antecedents (A) that are causing the behaviour (B) or the consequence (C) that is rewarding and encouraging the behaviour. For example, if a child receives adult attention each time he/she pushes other children but does not receive adult attention when behaving appropriately, then the adult attention (the consequence) will negatively reward the unwanted behaviour and the child is likely to repeat it. All children (and most adults) like attention and negative attention is better than no attention to some young children, as this may be the only sort of attention they generally receive. On the other hand, if a child snatches a piece of equipment from a second child and the second child reacts negatively creating adult attention, it is the first child's behaviour (antecedent) that needs support not the latter.

Reverting to the example of the child that pushes others away from a desired toy or piece of equipment, baseline observation (see Figure 4.3) would clarify the extent of the problem and on the basis of this information, combined with knowledge of the child and input from the parents, appropriate strategies could be devised to form an intervention plan. If observations are repeated after a period of time, the results will hopefully show a reduction in the behaviour when compared with the baseline. This evidence will form the basis of any discussions and become a part of the child's records. These would be recorded alongside targets in the form of an IEP or Individual Behaviour Plan (IBP) and would become a working document for future recording. A timescale would be set for the intervention stage and then an evaluation would occur. If successful, the strategies could be gradually withdrawn or, if unsuccessful, then revised strategies would need to be prepared.

Figure 4.2 The ABC of behaviour

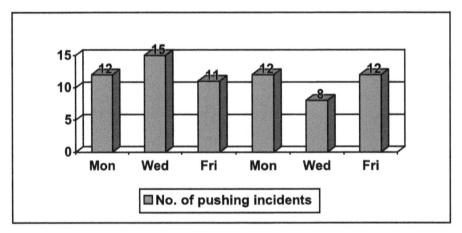

Figure 4.3 Baseline record of number of times child X pushes another child to gain equipment

Any intervention should be in place for at least three or four weeks before any decisions are made regarding the outcomes, as changes rarely occur overnight. It is also worthy of note that if a child is displaying several or many unacceptable behaviours then these should be prioritised and interventions planned for only one at a time. When planning and evaluating the success, or otherwise, of an intervention, practitioners should ensure they have taken into account the possible influences of the home, setting and practitioner, and have not simply focused on the behaviour itself. We need to remember that the behaviour could be a direct result of our own inappropriate task setting or inappropriate feedback. All possible causes must be examined.

If the intervention was unsuccessful and the staff feel that specialist support is needed, the incoming professional will have excellent records through which he/she can identify precisely what the difficulties are and what strategies have been implemented. This will not only save time but will present the staff as competent and thorough in its efforts to support the difficulties.

Monitoring and evaluation will be implicit throughout interventions with recording undertaken throughout the process, guided by the requirements within the Code of Practice (DfES, 2001c).

Positive reinforcement

Intervention strategies will generally include an element of positive reinforcement which requires praise and reward for acceptable behaviours (or the lack of unacceptable behaviours) combined with the avoidance of negative reinforcement. Earlier in this chapter, my own experience of verbal interactions in an early years setting was a clear example of inadvertently negatively rewarding undesirable behaviours and not rewarding desirable behaviours enough. In addition, there was an imbalance between my reinforcement of academic achievement and behaviour.

Reinforcements do not need to be costly, rather comprising a selection of verbal feedback, use of stickers, drawn pictures or time spent at a favoured activity. It could be that a child always wishes to sit on an adult's lap for circle time activities, so this would be an appropriate reward for that child. Verbal reinforcement should be event specific and child specific to be of real value. To keep repeating 'Well done' throughout the day becomes meaningless, whereas 'Well done, Ben, you have coloured that really carefully' is specific to a child and identifies which behaviour you are rewarding.

When using reinforcement as part of an intervention programme, practitioners should be vigilant to catch the child when displaying the desired behaviour, or when not displaying the undesired behaviour. Little and often will reap rewards. With some children, it may appear difficult to find acceptable behaviours to reward, but they can be found. Any reinforcement system should be shared with parents and extended within the home whenever possible to increase the likelihood of success.

Summary of behavioural intervention

The process can be summarised as follows:

1 Identify, discuss and record behaviours causing concern.

2 Plan and undertake baseline assessments.

3 Examine antecedents, behaviours and consequences.

4 Examine factors within the setting, home and practitioner.

5 Clearly define and record unacceptable behaviours.

6 Discuss with staff and parents, recording outcomes.

7 Prioritise behaviours.

 8 Decide on appropriate observational method(s).

 9 Implement strategies through IBP, including time limits and SMART (specific, measurable, achievable, relevant and time bound) targets.

10 Monitor and record progress.

11 Evaluate and record the process.

12 Decide on and record the next steps.

Throughout the process, discussions with parents and relevant professionals will be ongoing.

Summary

Throughout this chapter, the value and importance of considering the affective development of *all* children, not just those with special needs, has been emphasised. For children with special needs, the fact that they experience difficulties which they may well be aware of makes it all the more important to examine their affective development. Social, emotional and behavioural difficulties are now included within our early years guidance (EYFS and SEAL), so practitioners have a responsibility to address these areas.

Practitioners should have specific knowledge and skills of average developmental patterns as well as how to provide when difficulties arise, and this may have ramifications for future training needs.

There is an identified need, supported by research, to reflect on a range of possible causal factors including the setting, home and practitioner practices, but at the same time the excellent work already taking place should be acknowledged and celebrated. Issues surrounding personal, social, emotional and behavioural difficulties cannot be overlooked if we aim to provide effectively for the whole child, and practitioners should ensure that provision for these areas of development is included within their planning. Interventions should be planned and evaluated with parental involvement central throughout the process. Self-concept enhancement, of children and adults, should also be an integral part of our work, and excellent practices can be seen in evidence nationwide.

This chapter has barely touched on this important area but, hopefully, has given the reader food for thought, reflection and some ideas for future use as we cannot overlook provision to support children in these aspects of their learning and development.

Key issues

- Practitioner knowledge and skills in the area of affective development are essential.
- Consideration should be given to personal, social, emotional, behavioural and self-concept development.
- Factors within the setting, home and practitioner should be examined.
- Any interventions should be carefully planned, recorded, implemented and evaluated.
- Parental involvement is essential.

Points for reflection

- Should staff knowledge of these areas be reviewed and appropriate training sought if needed?
- By focusing on one or two children and noting down all the possible influencing factors on his/her progress, consider how you currently utilise this information in your planning.
- What benefits might reflecting on the self-esteem of individual staff members in a setting bring? If more is done to ensure every staff member feels respected, valued and motivated, how will this help young children's learning and development?

Suggested further reading

Cousins, J. (2006) 'Self-esteem in young children', *Early Years Update.* July. Available at: www.teachingexpertise.com/articles/self-esteem-in-young-children-1119

Department for Children, Schools and Families (2008l) *Social and Emotional Aspects of Development: Guidance for Practitioners Working in the Early Years Foundation Stage.* Available at: www.publications.everychildmatters.gov.uk/default.aspx?PageFunction=productdetails&PageMode=publications&ProductId=DCSF-00707-2008&

Long, R. and Fogell, J. (1999) *Supporting Pupils with Emotional Difficulties: Creating a Caring Environment for All.* London: David Fulton.

Roberts, R. (2010) *Wellbeing from Birth.* London: Sage.

5

Observation and assessment

Chapter objectives

To develop awareness of:

- statutory responsibilities within this area of work
- methods of observation and assessment in the early years
- the principles of effective observation and assessment.

Introduction

As part of the ongoing recording and monitoring system within early years settings, the usefulness and power of observation and assessment should be acknowledged as crucial to effective planning as together they can:

- inform planning
- inform understanding of a child's current competence levels
- support reflection on the appropriateness of provision
- enable the sharing of information with other parties
- enable assessment of specific children, groups, interactions, the learning environment and staff.

The Early Years Foundation Stage guidance (DCSF, 2008k) and Code of Practice (DfES, 2001c) acknowledge the value and need for observation and assessment, placing requirements on all early years practitioners to ensure these are a part of the teaching and learning process: 'Through observing children and by making notes when necessary, practitioners can make professional judgments about children's achievements and decide on the next steps in learning' (DCSF, 2008k: 22).

In order to identify a child's current competence levels, we rely on observation of skills mastered, which then informs our future planning. For children experiencing difficulties, we should strive towards early identification, diagnosis of specific difficulties and the introduction of appropriate intervention strategies. None of these can take place without prior observation and assessment of the current situation.

Observation and assessment processes can also be used to identify the effectiveness of the setting, specific areas of the setting, specific activities and the practitioner. Arguably, to see the children progress and be happy is every practitioner's ultimate aim and one that gives us tremendous satisfaction and reward. We therefore need to be prepared to examine our own practices closely to ensure we are supporting and not inadvertently compounding children's difficulties.

Purposeful observation offers benefits to practitioners, parents and children, and is a positive way of responding to the needs of all children, not just those experiencing difficulties, and my own experience supports this view. However, for those children experiencing difficulties, we should ensure that we focus on assessing the child and not the difficulties. In the case of a child with cerebral palsy, for example, while practitioners need to understand cerebral palsy, they should focus on the child's current skills, strengths, weaknesses, likes and dislikes which will inform planning. The condition is secondary. With each child, we are thus increasing our knowledge and considering each child as individual and unique.

We usually observe children when they are involved in their everyday activities, but there may be occasions when we need to set up specific activities to explore a precise skill – however we look at it, observation and assessment should take place in every early years setting.

Children's rights, legislation and guidance

The Warnock Report (DES, 1978) emphasised the importance of effective assessment through initial, more informal, assessments through to the stages preceding formal assessment and the production of a statement of special educational needs. Early identification of special educational needs was also deemed essential, and within the report observations were clearly shown to support this process. The Education Act (DES, 1981) adopted many of the Warnock Report's recommendations and thus continued to support early identification and provision, informed by ongoing observation and assessments.

Children's rights

The United Nations Convention on the Rights of the Child acknowledged the rights of all children to education which should be free in the primary phase. It continued to state that:

> The education of the child shall be directed to:
> (a) The development of the child's personality, talents and mental and physical abilities to their fullest potential;
> (b) The development of respect for human rights and fundamental freedoms;
> (c) The development of respect for the child's parents, his or her own cultural identity, language and values, for the national values of the country in which the child is living, the country from which he or she may originate, and for civilizations different from his or her own;
> (d) The preparation of the child for responsible life in a free society;
> (e) The development of respect for the natural environment. (DCSF, 2009k: 9)

While it may not be explicit in the Convention, it could be argued that to provide such an education, it would be necessary to establish observation and assessment to ensure individual development to the fullest potential.

Listening to the child

The Children Acts (1989, 2004) and the Childcare Act (2006) support the importance of listening to the child, which is also echoed in the Code of Practice (DfES, 2001c). This is an important consideration as it is often presumed that very young children, and specifically those with special needs, are incapable of contributing to discussions regarding their education and learning, when in reality they have valid opinions which can inform parents, practitioners and practice. If children are capable of contributing to the process of assessment, then their views should be valued and respected. The Code of Practice also echoes the importance and value of consulting with children, concluding that:

> Ascertaining the child's views may not always be easy. Very young children and those with severe communication difficulties, for example, may present a significant challenge for education, health and other professionals. But the principle of seeking and taking into account the ascertainable views of the child or young person is an important one. (DfES, 2001c: s. 3.3)

Back in the 1940s, Susan Isaacs emphasised the importance of listening to children's views and since then there has been a steady flow of increased support for this philosophy. The view is further supported in the UNCRC, article 12, ensuring that we should:

> Assure to the child who is capable of forming his or her own opinion the right to express these views freely in all matters affecting the child, the views of the child being given due weight in accordance with the age and maturity of the child. (DCSF, 2009l: 4)

The *Listening to Young Children* project work led by Clark and Moss (2001, 2005) introduced the Mosaic approach which considers all young children as competent and skilful and utilises a range of methods to ensure the voices of our youngest children are heard and that their views are incorporated into any decision making about their lives. The child's voice will therefore be an important part of the information-gathering processes we all use to inform our planning. Within the Mosaic approach, the views of the child, the parents, the practitioners and other professionals are evaluated and combined with information gathered from observations. In combination, we have a much fuller picture of the whole child. Listening to children's views and taking them into account in our decision making has now become central in governmental policies and frameworks for early years.

Practitioner requirements

The *Curriculum Guidance for the Foundation Stage* (QCA, 2000) recognised the importance of observation and assessment in relation to effective teaching and learning in early years settings, along with the current EYFS which offers us the *Observation, Assessment and Planning Cycle* (DCSF, 2007f: 5), confirming that observation leads us to assessment of current abilities and therefore future planning to move the child to the next step. So practitioners should identify current performance levels in order to plan the next steps to ensure progression for all children but we should not be focusing solely on identifying weaknesses and/or difficulties (the deficit model of provision).

With particular reference to children with special needs, observation and assessment will be a part of our everyday work at each stage of provision. When initial concerns are raised, observation can help to clarify thinking and identify specific areas of difficulties as well as strengths, which can both be used to inform subsequent planning. At the stages of Early Years Action and Early Years Action Plus (DfES, 2001c), observation will continue to play an important role, ensuring progression and monitoring the effectiveness of subsequent interventions.

Observations and assessments for children with special needs

As the regular observation and assessment of all children in our care is expected, we may wish to consider how this would be different for children with special needs and/or disabilities. I would suggest that the cycle of observation, leading to assessment and informing planning is indicative of good practice and that this should be no different for children with special needs (see Figure 5.1).

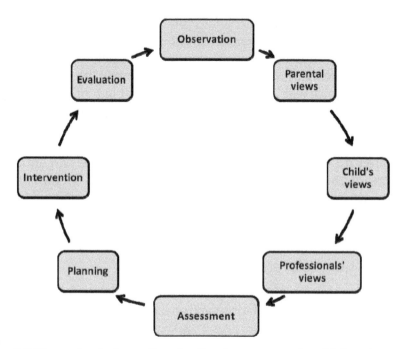

Figure 5.1 The cycle of observation, leading to assessment and informing planning

However, we still need to assess, through observation, how a child is currently functioning and use this information to inform our planning. Whether the child's starting point is above or below the majority of children is irrelevant. If our support and provision progresses through the stages of Early Action, Early Action Plus, School Action and School Action Plus, outcomes and interventions will rely heavily on the observational processes built into the setting's practices. If a statement of special educational need follows, then observation and assessment will continue to play a major role in the work of practitioners. At annual review meetings, a range of assessment outcomes will be discussed as objective evidence of progress made and further areas to work on can be identified and planned. So clearly observation and information gathering are evident at every stage of these processes.

The abilities required to be an effective observer are not necessarily inherent and training should be available to practitioners covering:

- purposes and values of observation and assessment
- principles of observation and assessment
- the range of observational methods available
- considerations required prior to observing
- adapting teaching, individual education plans and planning as a result of observations
- the need to involve parents and children.

The need for and requirements regarding observation and assessment are now clear, but a more detailed examination of some of the above areas will deepen understanding and awareness.

Purposes and value of observation and assessment

Within the working day, it is often difficult for practitioners to be able to stand back and observe a child or a group, as sufficient numbers of adults need to be present to ensure that the observer can be freed from their responsibilities and so focus entirely on the observational process. Perhaps as practitioners our greatest reward is to watch children playing and learning from what interests them and marvel at their enthusiasm and natural curiosity, but through careful and systematic observation we can ensure we maximise the potential of the learning environment for all children and thus maximise their progress. Nutbrown and Carter conclude that:

> Watching young children can open our eyes to their astonishing capacity to learn, and make us marvel at their powers to think, to do, to communicate and to create. As well as being in awe at young children's capacities, early childhood practitioners must understand, really understand, what they see when they observe. (2010: 111)

If a child begins at an early years setting with identified special needs, then practitioners will need to communicate with parents to establish which professionals have been involved to date, gather information from any previous assessments and/or reports, plus, perhaps most importantly, the nature of the child's difficulties and the implications for the child within the setting. Ideally, this should take place during a home visit when the parent(s) and child are in their own environment, which would be reassuring and hopefully give the child confidence in the situation with a professional or, as for many families, yet another professional. Alternatively, if professionals are working more effectively together, then practitioners would already have access to such information which will be supplemented by parental information.

With all the information to hand, practitioners can begin to plan appropriate learning experiences for the child and, as their knowledge of the child increases, more effective planning will follow.

As previously mentioned, *observations can help to clarify a child's current levels of performance and skills mastered,* but it should be remembered that if interventions and provision are to be amended in the light of observations then practitioners should not assume that if a child has not mastered a skill then he/she is incapable of doing so. We must check that:

- the task is child appropriate (exactly at the right level to move the child forwards, thus stretching his/her knowledge and skills but without the risk of failure)

- it capitalises on the child's interests

- as practitioners we are supportive and encouraging

- difficulties such as a child's emotional development and/or self-concept are not prohibiting the child from accessing the task

- the room encourages success for that individual child

- our classroom management skills are effective.

Perhaps this may seem an impossible task, but it could make the difference between success and failure for many children. Therefore, the skills of the observer, combined with their knowledge of the child and the setting, will be paramount.

Observations can be shared with parents to discuss progress made and to consider parental observations from outside the setting. A child may demonstrate skills at home, but not in the setting, for a variety of reasons, including self-confidence. This information will help the practitioner to create a 'holistic' picture of the child. In addition, parents and practitioners can work together to maximise progress. A child whose grandfather is seriously ill in hospital may be distressed with stories about doctors and/or role play, but with practitioner understanding his needs can be supported.

Observational outcomes will also be shared with a range of supporting agencies working with the child and the family. At progress review meetings or annual reviews for statements, evidence from all parties will be needed to inform further decision making. Observational evidence will support this process with clear indicators of progress made, which when combined with reports from the child's parents and other professionals will allow the holistic picture to emerge, informing decisions and planning.

Observations can be undertaken on:

- individual children – focusing on one or more specific areas of development or progress, for example, social interactions

- groups of children – to focus on one or more area, for example, abilities to share and take turns

- the whole group – to assess whether all children have mastered one skill, for example, jumping with two feet together

- an area of the room – to assess whether the area is well used, appropriately used and what interactions occur there

- a practitioner – to assess an area of professional skill, for example, appropriateness of interactions with the children.

Thus, the purposes and values of observation and assessment can be summarised as to:

- develop our own understanding of children's current competence levels (to assist with individual planning)

- reflect on the appropriateness of provision (tasks securing failure for some children, mismatch of curriculum)

- inform planning (organisation of room, session)

- inform others (parents/carers, outside professionals, staff)

- assess interactions (adult–child, child–child, adult–adult, child–adult)

- assess specific events (behaviour, speech and language, physical development, social interactions, and so on)

- assess staff (performance, interactions with children, supporting children with activities, and so on).

Information gathered can then be used in our monitoring, evaluations and future planning, as Woods summarises:

> With the insight from the observations we are better equipped to:
> - devise optimum environments to promote the holistic development of each child and respond to his/her needs;

- take appropriate action if any aspect of a child's development, behaviour, health or well-being causes us concern and does not appear to be within the range typical for his/her age;
- interact more sensitively with children and form happy relationships with them;
- monitor, evaluate and improve the provision we make for children, i.e. the care we give, the curriculum we devise and the outcomes we achieve. (Woods, 1998: 16)

Principles of observation and assessment

The principles of effective and purposeful observation and assessment processes are interlinked with their purpose. If we have a clear understanding of the purpose of our intended observations, then this will be our guiding principle.

Before undertaking observations, practitioners should ensure they have reflected on ethical issues such as gaining permission from the child's parents and considering the responsibilities of the observer. Any parent has a right to refuse permission but this will be unlikely if the purposes and potential benefits are explained thoroughly, as most parents will be supportive of initiatives that will encourage progress. The responsibilities of the observer would include consideration of the safety of the children, confidentiality, appropriate behaviour and, perhaps most importantly, entering the process with an open mind. If practitioners have preconceived ideas and/or expectations of the outcomes, then there is the risk that outcomes will be affected, or worse, invalid.

The principles for observing and assessing can be summarised as the need for practitioners to:

- be clear on the need for and purpose of assessing
- ensure the appropriateness for the child
- ensure the process is meaningful
- consider ethical issues
- ensure the validity of outcomes
- use appropriate observational methods for the child and the setting
- consider the timing of the observation as children can perform differently in mornings to afternoons, and Mondays to Fridays
- ensure adequate staffing to free the observer from additional responsibilities if necessary

- be clear on how the outcomes will be disseminated, and to whom.

Perhaps the key to effective assessment is an understanding of the observational process as a whole, with thorough planning being central. Practitioners will need to work through the following stages:

1 Decide on the need and purpose.

2 Plan the process.

3 Be clear on ethical issues.

4 Begin assessment.

5 Reflect on outcomes.

6 Decide ways forward.

7 Adjust planning appropriately.

8 Monitor progress.

The effectiveness of the process will depend on careful planning and implementation, resulting in outcomes that positively inform future practices to the benefit of the child(ren), practitioners and parents alike.

Methods of assessment 1 – observations

For most practitioners, observation is a feature of everyday working life and many can be found with a notebook and pen close to hand to jot down unplanned observations that can be added to normal recording systems at a later time. However, as previously discussed, specific observations should be planned. Prior to beginning the observation, practitioners should work through the stages outlined in the previous section and decide on the most appropriate observational method. It will also be helpful to produce a cover sheet including such details as:

- child's name and age
- date
- name of observer
- the specific setting or area of setting
- permissions gained
- aims and purpose of observation
- start and finish times.

Using a cover sheet attached to records of observations can be added to a child's general records/profile as evidence to staff, parents and outside professionals of actions undertaken by the setting to evaluate an individual child's performance. When working with children with special needs, records are crucial to enable access to the information for all parties. When seeking the support and advice of outside professionals, such evidence will prove accessible and useful.

Time sampling

The observer makes a note of the child's actions and interactions at regular intervals over a set period of time. If concerned about the amount of time a child spends at the sand tray, the time-sampling approach will enable collation of evidence. It may be that the child is observed every ten minutes throughout a session of three hours, on a Tuesday morning and a Thursday afternoon, giving over 36 recorded entries during the period. At each ten-minute interval, the observer will note exactly where the child is in the room, or simply place a tick or cross on the record sheet to indicate whether he/she is at the sand tray or not. The outcomes of such an observation will clarify to the staff (and others) the amount of time spent at sand play and action can be considered. Perhaps removing the sand tray from the activities available to the children two or three days a week will encourage increased involvement in alternative activities. So, through this relatively straightforward approach, the child's opportunities, and thus potential, can be extended. If staff are also concerned about the child's interactions with others, then the process can record with whom he/she is interacting and the nature of interactions.

Time sampling is also useful to investigate aspects of the learning environment. For example, staff may be concerned about the lack of use made of the book corner and a time-sampling approach can be used to note if there are children using the book corner, or not, at preset intervals. If results indicate that the book corner is used for a minimal amount of time, then staff can devise ways to encourage greater usage. Similarly, if the quality of language used in the book corner is a concern, then this can be recorded at the same time intervals.

In summary, time sampling produces a snapshot of a child's behaviour (academic or social) or of a specific activity or area of the room. From the findings, changes can be planned and implemented to lead to improvements.

Event/frequency sampling

Event or frequency sampling is useful when practitioners wish to clarify their understanding of a specific event as it records the frequency of that event. As an example, if we are observing a child's unacceptable behaviour, for example, hitting another child, the information can be used as a baseline. A programme or strategies can be implemented to reduce this behaviour and possibly encourage an alternative behaviour. At a later date, the observations can be repeated, hopefully to highlight the improvement in behaviours demonstrated and the success of the intervention. Recording can take the form of a simple tick sheet to indicate the number of times the behaviour occurs, or more details can be included, such as time of day, antecedents, consequences, whether an adult was present and so on. Additional information will enable more individualised strategies to be introduced. For example, if the child only hits one other child when that child interferes with his/her play, practitioners would need to consider which child the strategies should be aimed at. Results of the initial observation can be presented within a report as a simple table of 'scores' or as a graph or chart (Figure 5.2).

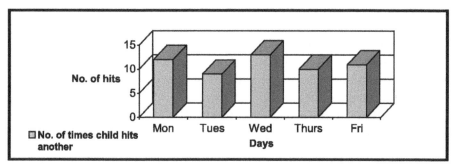

Figure 5.2 Baseline observations

When strategies have been implemented, graphical representation clearly summarises the process, as in Figure 5.3, where the first week was the period of baseline measurement and during the second and third weeks the intervention strategies were in place. The outcome is that the number of times the child hit another is successfully being reduced.

An illustrative example

The results of such observations can inform practice greatly, as in my own experience a child's hitting out and anger was observed by event sampling, but in addition to recording the number of times the child hit out at another the antecedents were noted. It became clear that the child reacted this way when the group was asked to tidy up and he was in the middle of a task or project, such as building with bricks and another child began clearing his project away. The strategy that supported this child was to speak to him five minutes before tidying up time and decide on how to store or protect his work until later, if it was not finished. Incidents of hitting out and anger reduced dramatically. A significant discovery was made through the observational process and the learning environment was successfully adapted to suit his individual needs with very little effort from anyone.

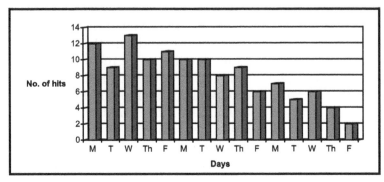

Figure 5.3 Baseline and intervention observations

Time sampling and event sampling are both relatively straightforward to undertake and give precise data to work with, however finding the time to complete observations within a busy setting may not be so easy, as additional staff may be needed to cover. In addition, it is not easy to remain detached from the children and focus solely on the observations in hand, and the children themselves may make this difficult by constantly asking you to help or support them, as you would usually do during the session. Children are not used to staff members sitting at the perimeter of the room and writing, instead of playing and working with them.

Focused or target child observations

A full, detailed written record of a child's movements during a predetermined time can offer practitioners a full account of:

- which specific activities the child has selected
- which area(s) of the learning environment he/she has been working in
- with whom he/she has interacted
- with whom he/she has spoken
- evidence of expressive language used.

While observing a child in this way, it is useful to have a watch to hand and to note the time at frequent intervals, clarifying the exact time spent at each activity. To ease notation, codes can be evolved which should be written on the record sheet for clarity of understanding by others. Possible codes could include:

TC = target child	A1, A2, A3 ... = adults
B1, B2, B3 ... = other boys	AC = art corner
G1, G2, G3 ... = other girls	HC = home corner
ST = sand tray	CP = cooperative play
BP = brick play	SP = solitary play
BC = book corner	PP = parallel play

As a result of the observations, strategies can be implemented to promote changes for the child, the practitioners and/or the setting.

An illustrative example

Through the process of focused observation, minor changes were made to the learning environment and planning for Adam, who was 3 years and 6 months old. Adam was generally perceived to be lacking in application to tasks other than cars, lorries and train play, and had a tendency to run from one end of the room to the other, regardless of who or what was blocking his way. He had been referred to an early years special needs unit as the local pre-school group could not cope with his 'disruptive behaviour'. While these behaviours could be deemed age appropriate for a 2-year-old, they were clearly impeding his opportunities to access the learning environment in a meaningful way. The observation over a 45-minute period was repeated three times during one week and identified the following key issues:

- Adam spent his time flitting between activities, but rarely settled to any activity for more than three/four minutes at a time. (This could also be represented in graphical form – see Figures 5.4 and 5.5.)

- Adam did not once walk around the room – each time he got up to move elsewhere, he ran.

- Adam mostly avoided all table-top activities such as puzzles, sharing or turn-taking games, cutting and sticking, art, colouring or writing-based activities.

- Adam resisted attempts by adults to participate in table-top activities.

- At any time that Adam remained at a table-top activity, he needed immediate success or he was unable to cope and would leave the table.

- Adam needed to be in control of any activity he was involved in and did not appear to be aware of interrupting other children's play and sometimes annoying others.

- Adam's speech and language skills were advanced for his age.

Through these and subsequent observations designed to focus more specifically on certain aspects of Adam's performance, the following key issues were highlighted:

- Adam did not have the necessary skills to participate successfully in the table-top activities.

- Adam's social skills were delayed or he was demonstrating inappropriate social skills.

- Adam felt a need to run between activities.

- Adam particularly enjoyed activities involving a range of vehicles.

- Adam demonstrated good imaginative skills in his vehicle play.

- Adam demonstrated good creative skills in his building with bricks or Duplo – but these mostly centred on roads, rails, tunnels and bridges.

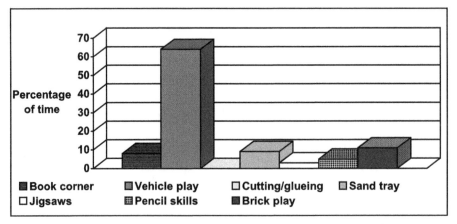

Figure 5.4 Baseline observations – percentage of time spent at each activity

As a result, the staff discussed Adam's progress with his parents to suggest possible ways forward. The following strategies were employed:

- The layout of tables in the room was changed to limit free running space.

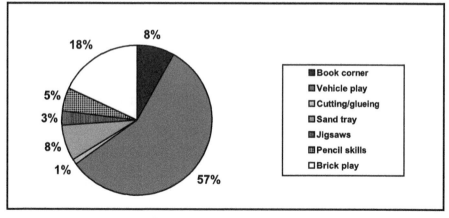

Figure 5.5 Baseline observations – percentage of time spent at each activity

- Whole-group and small-group activities were planned into the curriculum around a theme of 'fast and slow vehicles'. This had a dual purpose of capitalising on Adam's love of vehicles and also extending his learning.

- One-to-one activities were planned and introduced to help develop Adam's skills required for the successful completion of table-top activities, such as turn taking, sharing, achieving success and patience. This was supported by increased praise as positive reward.

- Role plays and stories were used to develop Adam's awareness of appropriate and inappropriate social interactions, with adults and Adam's peers acting as positive role models.

Adam's behaviour and progress within the group situation improved consistently and in some areas surpassed expectations. It became apparent to the staff that he had somehow 'missed' some stages of skill development and simply needed to be shown these and have them explained to him. For example, it was soon clear that rather than not having the patience to complete a jigsaw, he simply did not know how to tackle it. The steps needed to complete a jigsaw were introduced to Adam in small stages to ensure success, and within weeks he advanced from six-piece jigsaws to 50+ pieces – a very pleasing outcome for staff and Adam's parents alike.

It was the carefully planned and instigated process of observation that enabled this structured response to Adam's individual needs, yet many of the activities implemented were also of benefit to the other children in the group. Through the sharing of information with parents at every stage of the process, changes were also implemented within the home. The information gathered was further shared with

Adam's health visitor at his progress review meeting, so all parties involved were informed and able to support the process.

Sociograms

Continuing to assess Adam, a sociogram could have been used to develop greater understanding of Adam's social interactions. A record would have been established and observations carried out for a set period of time to note, for example, who he shared time with, the nature of the interactions and what verbal interactions took place. Again, this could be represented graphically if desired and even reflect gender relationships or type of play Adam was involved in (Figure 5.6). While a sociogram can clearly focus on one particular area of development, practitioners should note that children's friendships and favoured playmates can fluctuate on a fairly regular basis, and this should be reflected in any interpretation of the data.

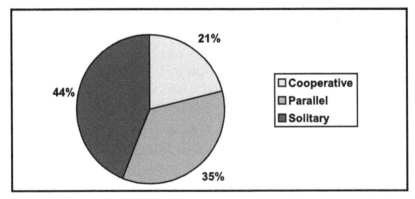

Figure 5.6 Types of play

Movement/tracking charts

Such charts are a rapid method of noting a child's movements during a set period. Starting with a basic sketch of the room layout, arrows and times can be added to indicate a child's movements between activities so that conclusions can be drawn about how many activities are approached and the length of time spent at each. If subsequent movement charts are taken at different times of the day and week, then a fuller picture will emerge, but as can be seen in Figure 5.7, the mass of arrows can be very difficult to interpret easily and if the times were added on to this chart it could appear even more muddled. If we reflect on Adam (previously highlighted) and his difficulty with rapid and brief times spent at activities, the chart would have been very confusing. In addition, the same information can be elicited from a target child/focused observation.

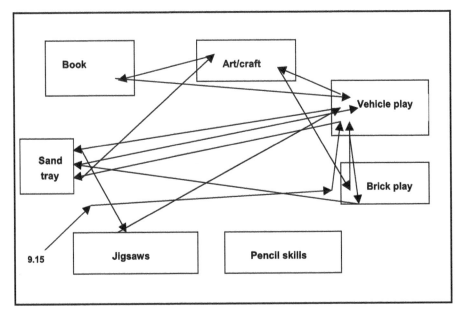

Figure 5.7 Movement sample chart

Methods of assessment 2 – checklists and questionnaires

Checklists are often the preferred choice of early years practitioners and are viewed by some as easier to implement and interpret. However, certain issues should be reflected upon before relying on checklists alone.

First, checklists only offer a snapshot of what a child can do, on that day and at that particular time, and tend to note achieved milestones. So, for those children with complex special needs, by nature of the large gaps, they equally represent the skills a child has not mastered. If the checklists do not cover, for example, every physical skill, then only those checked can be commented on. A checklist may indicate that a child can hop, jump, run and catch a large ball at two metres but may not show whether the child can pedal a tricycle. Caution should therefore be employed in the interpretation of outcomes if a thorough understanding of a child's development is required as opposed to a snapshot.

Second, checklists are created around a sequential approach to development and assume that all children will proceed through the defined stages in much the same systematic order. Practitioners working with any young children will be aware that not all children progress in this way. However, despite reservations, developmental checklists are used within many early years settings and do have some usefulness, for example in baseline assessments.

Usually presented in tabular form, checklists are generally easy to interpret and therefore accessible to all, but they can also be represented pictorially so the children themselves can be involved in recording their own progress (see Figures 5.8 and 5.9).

NAME	Hops X4	Jumps from 50 cm	Climbs 6 steps		
Ian			√		
Mark	e	√	√		
Michael		√	√		
Kate		e	√		
Tracy	e	√	√		
Samantha		√	√		
Rowan	e	e	√		

Figure 5.8 An example of a tabular checklist (e = emerging skill)

Strategies needed to support children who need to develop particular skills further can be devised and implemented using the evidence from the checklists which can be updated regularly as part of an ongoing monitoring process.

Some local authorities may have their own checklists, either self-created or taken from a standardised checklist, for use within all registered settings or within special needs settings. Portage workers base all their work on the portage developmental checklists (Bluma et al., 1976) covering all skill areas and breaking down tasks into achievable steps to ensure success. Health visitors and speech and language therapists will use their own specific checklists or screening tools to monitor children's progress. Mortimer (2000) devised the Playladders checklists, originally created for use in early years settings and using existing checklists as a foundation. They are designed to avoid the developmental checklist approach in favour of approaching observation and assessment from the realities of children's activities. Mortimer summarises the process:

> Early years educators are encouraged to play alongside the child as part of their regular activities within a group of children. By observing how a child is playing, it becomes easy to visualize and record the stage on the playladder later, once the children have left. Play thus proceeds uninterrupted by the assessment and recording. Once the play behaviour is recorded on the checklist, a 'next step on the ladder' is suggested, and this new skill can be encouraged or taught at a future play session. (Mortimer, 2001: 125)

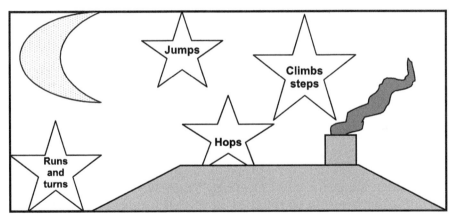

Figure 5.9 An example of a pictorial checklist

Mortimer's particular approach fits in well with the Foundation Stage's breaking down of steps into achievable targets to ensure success for all children.

Methods of assessment 3 – observing through play

Much debating continues around the difference between play and learning, but current thinking supports the view that learning through play, with appropriate support or 'scaffolding' by adults, is an ongoing process in which all young children participate, be it the baby who places everything into his/her mouth as part of early discovery, or the child who struggles to build a bridge to pass trains under and, through a process of elimination combined with trial and error, learns about shape, size, balance and develops fine motor skills. If we therefore accept that much learning transpires from play situations, then it seems sensible to find ways of recording evidence through observing children at play.

One of the problems with observing play is objectivity. As adults, we may assume we understand what a child is doing and learning in a play situation, but it may be difficult to assess progress and record it in a meaningful manner. Moyles's suggestion back in 1989 is still relevant today:

> The problem appears to be that human beings are all unique and all perceive situations in different ways, depending upon their own experiences, expectation, attitudes and values and, therefore, interpretation of what individuals observe and what they assess as progress will be different from person to person as we each operate our own selection systems. (Moyles, 1989: 101)

Perhaps the key is to be clear on our intended learning outcomes for play-based activities and from this we should be able to identify if outcomes have been met or not, thus informing future planning. If, for example, a setting is working within a theme or topic entitled 'Travel', then activities will have been planned and early learning goals identified. There will be a range of learning objectives the topic will support and, once these have been identified, outcomes can be matched against them. Record sheets can be devised to note the learning objectives and evidence of the children's outcomes that can then inform future planning. Observational methods can be selected according to their appropriateness for the task.

Practitioners support a child's learning through skilfully intervening to encourage progression to the next stage of learning. This lies within a Vygotskian philosophy that suggests children have a 'zone of proximal development' indicating their learning potential, with adult support. It should be remembered that practitioners, often feeling pressured by legislation and requirements, may feel inclined to direct or lead children's play, learning, progress and development too much by telling them what to do next or informing them how to overcome obstacles they are facing without giving them the time and opportunity to discover solutions for themselves. Perhaps more useful and practical learning will take place through a child's own process of trial and error and elimination. Identifying the problem and trying to discover ways around it can often produce more lasting knowledge and skills.

Practitioners can play alongside a child and use the Playladders approach to recording, or take notes throughout the period, which can be transcribed in more detail later if required. Alternatively, an adult can observe a child playing with an adult and make detailed observations. Sometimes this approach has the benefit of enabling greater objectivity and can highlight issues surrounding the practitioner and his/her approach, as well as the child's development. Subsequent observational records can then be shared with parents and other practitioners at progress review meetings. In addition, discussions after the observation could highlight different adult interpretations of the same event.

Methods of assessment 4 – involving the children

As the need to hear the child's voice has become more prominent, we must avoid the assumption that very young children are not mature enough, knowledgeable or verbally capable of contributing to our observations and assessments. It must also be acknowledged that there are discrete differences between listening to and truly hearing and understanding what a child is saying. The Code of Practice (DfES) clearly highlights the importance of involving children in decision-making processes at every stage:

> [The children] should, where possible, participate in all the decision-making processes that occur in education including the setting of learning targets and contributing to IEPs, discussion about choice of schools, contributing to the assessment of their needs and to the annual review and transition processes. (2001c: s. 3.2)

For very young children with special needs, difficulties may occur owing to limited verbal and/or recording skills, but ways can be developed to enable and empower children. Knowing a child's likes and dislikes can enable more successful progress through heightened motivation for the child to participate, so it would be of greater use to plan activities that the child would prefer in order to achieve targets, than to continually present them with tasks they do not particularly enjoy. As we saw earlier, Adam's likes and dislikes were identified and used successfully within future planning, benefiting all the children in his setting.

For very young children, likes and dislikes can be discovered through simple pictorial records, which can be added to the child's records and shared with parents and other practitioners. Simple drawings or photographs of a range of common activities can be presented alongside three faces – one happy, one indifferent and one sad. The activity can be discussed with the child and then he/she could colour in the appropriate face to indicate preferences. To ensure understanding, an adult could complete a similar chart alongside the child, making sure that the child is not simply copying the adult's selections. With the advent of information technology (IT) and the extensive IT skills of many practitioners, the production of such charts would be straightforward, but children are generally quite happy with an adult's attempts at drawing, however limited and inaccurate they may be. If practitioners do not feel able to produce a recording sheet, then there may be a parent or friend of the setting who will help. It should not, however, be forgotten that children have a tendency to want to please the adult and may give the responses they think the adult wants to hear.

Young children can also be involved in progress recording through progress books, collecting and presenting evidence of their work in portfolios, responding to interviews (to identify their likes, dislikes, views) and through the self-completion of charts as previously described. In my own experience, sticker books (made from sugar paper) were a successful way of involving children as they helped to make their own book and they were allowed to enter at least one smile each time they attended, with an adult adding the reason for this success. When supporting children with behavioural, social, emotional and/or self-esteem difficulties, many smiles were added on a daily basis to celebrate achievements (no matter how small) and to encourage continued progress and effort.

Using digital records has become common practice, whereby young children are given access to digital cameras to record their favoured, or less favoured, activities. They can also record their successes and retain images of building creations, art and craft work, even shapes and colours. These offer a useful tool to open discussions with the child, even if they cannot verbalise their responses as they can point to the pictures in answer to carefully selected questions.

Circle time can be a valuable tool to facilitate listening to others, and even children with limited or no communication skills or withdrawn children can still participate, albeit in a different way. If appropriate, the practitioner can tell the group what the child has achieved and how much effort they have made. This way, all children can be positively rewarded through the respect of being heard and their efforts being acknowledged and valued.

Methods of assessment 5 – children's behaviour

Children demonstrating unacceptable behaviours can be supported through observation and appropriate interventions but, firstly, we should remember that children develop and learn inappropriate behaviours, they are not born with them, and, secondly, the behaviours are the problem and not the child. If a child is persistently told he/she is naughty or unkind, then the self-fulfilling prophecy will allow that child to remain naughty or unkind, and it may well be that the negative adult responses received are exactly the reinforcement necessary for the child to continue demonstrating the same behaviours.

In my own experience, I have received many children into settings with 'behavioural problems'. If we are not careful, the label awarded the child along with practitioner expectations can severely compromise our responses to the child. If we believe the child will 'be a handful', 'be difficult' and 'achieve little', then our provision may well reflect this. Through detailed observations over a period of time, intervention strategies can be designed and put in place to reduce the unacceptable behaviours and increase acceptable behaviours. It may be that a combination of event sampling, time sampling and target-child observations are completed to give a detailed overview of the child's current difficulties and the issues surrounding them. The outcomes could highlight problems with practitioners, the setting, the tasks and/or the behaviours, and each should be carefully reflected upon before intervention strategies are devised. In addition, the child should be considered within the wider context and all the possible causal factors affecting the behaviours identified, even if some may be beyond our control.

Links between behavioural difficulties, academic achievement and low self-concept have been highlighted consistently over several decades, as summarised by Lambley:

> Pupils who lack success in learning often react to failure by non-involvement strategies. Their withdrawal of effort can show in various forms: total lack of motivation and retreat into dullness and laziness; avoidance strategies (such as distraction, fidgeting, day-dreaming) or resistance to the learning task expressed in actions such as antagonistic and aggressive behaviour. (Lambley, 1993: 86)

Practitioners should be prepared to examine all possible causal factors including their own practices and appropriateness of the tasks offered to the child to support any child experiencing behaviour difficulties. Observation will play a key role in this process.

Profiling

Profiles of young children and their progress are commonplace in early years settings. Each child will have individual records kept including:

- basic information and details

- entry profile

- previous involvement with other professionals

- intervention strategies employed

- stages of Early Years Action or Early Years Action Plus

- parental information gathered

- records of progress review meetings.

In addition, evidence of work undertaken and progress made will generally be kept, linked to the early learning goals, which may include photographic, video or audiotape records.

Many early years settings will undertake a home visit before a child begins attendance, during which the parent will be asked basic information about their child. This should include the child's fears, self-confidence, likes and dislikes, and self-help skills, which will help the practitioner to prepare for the child's entry, thus making the transition as smooth as possible for the parent(s) as well as the child. For children with special needs, the information would extend to cover previous assessments or referrals and details relating to any particular areas of difficulty and the specific implications this may have for the setting, child or the planning of activities. This will be the start of the child's profile of development.

As time progresses, the profile will naturally increase considerably in size, but will contain a thorough and detailed catalogue of past, current and future progress made, and all plans and strategies that have been implemented. In today's climate of inclusive 'educare', practitioners who have identified a child as experiencing difficulties will use the profile to inform any outside professional who may become involved. This will be a complete and informative record on which to base discussions. When discussing progress or issues with parents, having the child's work as evidence should support clearer understanding.

The EYFS profile and assessment

Within the EYFS, there is a requirement to complete an EYFS profile for every child in the last school term of the year when the child reaches 5 years of age. The profile aims to:

> provide year 1 teachers with reliable and accurate information about each child's level of development as they reach the end of the EYFS, enabling the teacher to plan an effective, responsive and appropriate curriculum that will meet all children's needs. (DCSF, 2008m)

Along with the *EYFS Profile Handbook* (QCA, 2008b), practitioners can access an online version of the profile which can be downloaded on to their own system for completion for the children in their care (Suffolk LA/DCSF, 2009). Each child's progress will be recorded against 13 assessment scales and within each of these there will be a 9-scale points system. Points 1–3 suggest a child who is still working towards the early learning goals in that area; points 4–8 highlight a child who is meeting the early learning goals; and point 9 suggests the child is exceeding the expectations of the early learning goals. These are summarised in the handbook as:

> There are 13 scales, based on the early learning goals and divided between the six areas of development and learning. The scales are:
>
> Personal, social and emotional development:
>
> 1. Dispositions and attitudes (DA)
> 2. Social development (SD)

   3.   Emotional development (ED)

Communication, language and literacy:

   4.   Language for communication and thinking (LCT)

   5.   Linking sounds and letters (LSL)

   6.   Reading (R)

   7.   Writing (W)

Problem solving, reasoning and numeracy

   8.   Numbers as labels and for counting (NLC)

   9.   Calculating (C)

  10. Shape, space and measures (SSM)

  11. Knowledge and understanding of the world (KUW)

  12. Physical development (P)

  13. Creative development (CD). (QCA, 2008b: 24)

Using their knowledge of the child and their observations as a base, practitioners must complete one record for each child they have who is moving from the EYFS to Key Stage 1 of the National Curriculum and, as previously identified, this is to inform future teachers of the child's current competencies.

However, it could be argued that such a profile for a child with significant difficulties will simply highlight what they cannot do rather than suggest their successes. For parents, this may be difficult to accept as once again their child is being viewed within a deficit model. This concern extends to the potential negative impact of assessment for children with special needs within a system that places children in relation to national targets and league tables, as summarised by NASEN:

> Moreover, there are dangers that the current pressure to rank children, schools and other establishments against national norms may take insufficient account of *relative* achievement and progress, and may subject some young people and parents to processes that are degrading or discouraging. (NASEN, 2000a)

To support assessment for children who are not achieving at the expected levels, the P Scales were introduced, primarily for use with children aged 5 years and over who are working at below the criteria for assessment at level 1 of the National Curriculum:

> The P scales are differentiated performance criteria. They outline attainment for pupils working below level 1 of the national curriculum and describe some of the important skills, knowledge and understanding that pupils may gain from the programmes of study and the national curriculum.
>
> There are P scales for each subject in the national curriculum and for religious education. The P scales use eight performance levels to illustrate the learning that leads to national curriculum level 1.
>
> • Levels P1 to P3 show the earliest levels of general attainment with subject-focused examples.
>
> • Levels P4 to P8 show subject-related attainment. (QCDA, 2009)

So completing statutory assessment within the EYFS is not straight-forward and training will be needed for relevant staff, but these can only be completed successfully if practitioners are regularly under-taking observations which help them to build up the picture of the whole child. The *Progress Matters* guidance (DCSF, 2009l) identifies the areas that need to be explored to ensure full understanding of the child is achieved, and these areas closely link with those identified earlier in this chapter:

- What do parents and carers tell you about their child?

- What play choices does the child make?

- What is the child really interested in?

- How are the child's views sought?

- How does the child interact with other children and adults?

- How does the child respond to different situations and routines?

- What can the child do now?

- What is the child trying to do next?

- How does the child like to learn?

- What can professional partners contribute to the picture?

(Adapted from DCSF, 2009l: 5)

Summary

The purposes and values of effective observations as part of an ongoing assessment process have been highlighted, indicating that all practitioners have a duty and responsibility to monitor the progress of each child in a way that is accessible to parents, children and other professionals and the *Progress Matters* document (DCSF, 2009l) supports this. A range of observational methods has been offered for consideration, with clear guidelines as to the practical and ethical issues that must be taken into account before embark-ing upon any such process. Effective observation will greatly inform practice and ultimately benefit the child, ensuring that the plans and interventions that follow have been informed through an examination of a range of information relating to the child's current levels of performance and considering all factors that may com-pound or enhance future progress. Macintyre highlights the crucial role of the early years practitioner:

> Detailed observations of early years practitioners who have watched the child in different settings and used the competences of the peer group of children as 'comparisons' and the expertise of colleagues as

sounding boards are key assessments in making decisions. Practitioners must have the confidence to make their observations known. (2006: 59–60)

Practitioners with a thorough knowledge of child development should undertake child observations and assessments to monitor progress. If children are experiencing difficulties, or additional difficulties, then observations will support early identification and appropriate intervention. If a practitioner needs to refer a child to an outside professional, or discuss progress with parents, then evidence of observations and assessments undertaken will support those discussions.

It should be remembered that observations must be based around the child, within the child's world, and take into account all possible influencing factors on the child's progress and development. The more natural the observational setting, the more natural the responses of the child are likely to be. Effective observations and assessments should continue as an ongoing, cyclical process to ensure the most appropriate provision is made available to our youngest, and perhaps most vulnerable, children. If early identification is viewed as essential, then observations and assessments should be deemed equally as essential.

Key issues

- Observations and assessments are a part of everyday working practice.
- Practitioners will need a thorough knowledge of child development and observational methods to undertake and evaluate observations.
- Observations should have a clear purpose, be manageable and inform planning.
- Children and parents should be involved in the process.

Points for reflection

- How confident of their skills for observation and assessment are each of the staff in the setting? Is further training required?
- How do you interpret children's play? Compare your observation with the observation of a colleague of the same play activity and discuss the outcomes.
- How well do parents/carers understand your assessment processes?
- How do children contribute to their own assessments?

Suggested further reading

Hutchin, V. (2010) 'Meeting individual needs', in T. Bruce (ed.) *Early Childhood: A Guide for Students*, 2nd edn. London: Sage.

Nutbrown, C. and Carter, C. (2010) 'The tools of assessment: watching and learning', in G. Pugh and B. Duffy (eds) *Contemporary Issues in the Early Years*, 5th edn. London: Sage.

Qualifications and Curriculum Authority (QCA) (2008b) *Early Years Foundation Stage Profile Handbook*. London: QCA/DCFS. Available at: www.testsandexams.qcda.gov.uk/17852.aspx

6

Programmes of intervention

> ## Chapter objectives:
>
> To develop awareness of:
>
> - the importance of early intervention and effective programmes of intervention
> - effective use of IEPs
> - case studies of speech and language difficulties and autistic spectrum disorders (ASDs).

Introduction

In the preceding chapter, we considered the need for regular observations and assessments within our work with children with special needs. To be meaningful, observations need to inform our planning and any intervention programmes or strategies we put in place to support progress.

It is now widely acknowledged that early intervention is essential to ensure all children are given opportunities to achieve their full potential and this was embedded in the *Removing Barriers to Achievement* report (DfES, 2004c):

> Early intervention is the cornerstone of our strategy. Every Child Matters recognised the lasting benefits of early identification – providing a sound foundation for future learning and development. (p. 9)

In this chapter, a range of intervention programmes that could be used in early years settings to respond to the identified needs of a child or children are examined. Programmes and suggestions for supporting children with speech and language difficulties and children with ASDs are explored as exemplars to demonstrate how and why programmes could be individually tailored to meet specific needs. This is achieved partly through description and partly through case studies.

Definitions

An intervention is any interaction between two people to bring about change and, therefore, early years practitioners undertake interventions each time they are working with children. Interventions may be short, medium or long term and will be planned carefully to ensure effectiveness and appropriateness. In the scenario where children enter a new setting, some may find parental separation distressing. The supportiveness of staff and encouragement to participate in the range of activities available will be planned in the adult's mind before action is taken. Even if it is not planned in a formal way, through normal recording systems, this support is nevertheless an intervention strategy. At the other end of the scale, we could consider a child with severe autism who has long-term and very specific needs. Interventions for this child will be discussed in advance and committed to paper through short-, medium- and long-term goals and plans, which will form the child's IEP. These will be monitored and reviewed regularly, with parental and outside professional input, along with the child's views informing discussions, which are all supported by our ongoing observations and assessments. Any interventions will have considered the needs of the child, all the factors impacting on the child and the best use of resources (human, time and equipment) to encourage progress. One-to-one adult support will not always be necessary but will be considered as part of the planning process. As the Code of Practice (DfES, 2001c: s. 4.26) suggests: 'The key lies in effective individualised arrangements for learning and teaching'.

Effective interventions

Key features

As previously outlined, interventions are part of a cyclical process and cannot exist on their own (see Figure 6.1).

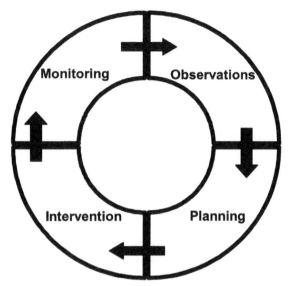

Figure 6.1 Intervention as part of a cyclical process

In today's inclusive climate, all practitioners will be working towards providing appropriate opportunities for all children within their setting, so adapting tasks to suit individual needs is an integral aspect of the practitioner's role. Considering children with special needs as somehow different from this can exclude them and is not, therefore, inclusive. However, the cycle of intervention highlighted here is one that is appropriate for all children, regardless of whether they have identified needs or difficulties, as good early years practice is good special needs practice.

To ensure our intervention is effective, practitioners need to be clear as to their intentions and should therefore consider the following questions:

- Why is intervention necessary?
- What are we aiming to achieve?
- How will we measure success or effectiveness?
- How will this be planned and executed?
- Is this a short-, medium- or long-term intervention?
- How will the intervention and outcomes be recorded and where?
- Who will need to be informed?

With the new child who is experiencing difficulties separating from his/her parent, the intervention will hopefully be relatively short term and will need little prior planning and organisation, nevertheless there is a need to record the events in the child's profile or records as this difficulty in adapting to a new situation may be indicative of other social and/or emotional difficulties. In the future, if subsequent difficulties arise, say at the transition to primary school, the information recorded may be pertinent and help practitioners and parents to understand the new situation and thus inform any subsequent interventions.

As practitioners need to be accountable to parents, other professionals and the government (local and national), the recording of any interventions to show effectiveness (or otherwise) is a requirement, not simply a suggestion. Through consistent monitoring and evaluation of intervention strategies employed, practitioners will be able to satisfy these requirements, which will be indicative of the effects of the interventions used.

Legislation and guidance

The inclusive schooling statutory guidance offered the following structure for practitioners implicitly acknowledging the role of effective observation and intervention:

> in planning and teaching the National Curriculum teachers have a responsibility for:
> - setting suitable learning opportunities;
> - responding to pupils' diverse learning needs; and
> - overcoming potential barriers to learning and assessment for individuals and groups of pupils. (DfES, 2001a: 4)

Linked to the Code of Practice (DfES, 2001c), the inclusive schooling document offered guidance for children over statutory school age, but it could be suggested that the guidance is indicative of good practice and is therefore relevant to working in the early years. The graduated response within the Code of Practice also highlights the importance of effective observation, assessment and intervention for children experiencing difficulties. In the same vein, the EYFS (National Strategies, 2007) informs us that:

> Effective assessment involves evaluation or decisions about the child's progress and their learning and development needs and gives us the information we need to plan for the next steps. This is called assessment for learning; it is the formative assessment, based on observations, which informs or guides everyday planning.

Since 2001 and the SEN Code of Practice, legislation and guidance has continued to emerge but with a strong focus of improved outcomes for young children and their families. However, each document makes reference to the common themes of effective practice and provision for children, which naturally includes those with special needs.

Throughout the current legislation and guidance, we are reminded of the cyclical process of observation, planning, intervention and monitoring outlined previously, and the manner in which each element is embedded within the others. These are not separate and discrete but part of the ongoing working practices of early years practitioners. More recently, the government focus of personalised learning and responding to the individual needs of every child have become firmly established.

The features of effective interventions can be summarised as:

• part of an ongoing, cyclical process

• responding appropriately to legislation and guidance

• responding appropriately to individual needs

• having measurable outcomes

• involving and informing parents, children and other professionals.

'Differentiating' the curriculum

When the National Curriculum first entered our schools, we were advised that we could modify or differentiate the curriculum for children with SEN. However, the terms 'modification' and 'differentiation' suggest separateness from the norm and are not therefore terms I would endorse. I prefer the personalised learning approach using the planning cycle already suggested which is suitable for all children and is therefore more inclusive. Using a child's known likes and dislikes, appropriate resources and materials can be incorporated that will motivate the child. In a similar way, knowing a child's preferred learning style can inform planning. In previous chapters, Adam was introduced, whose needs were supported through interventions that reflected each of the above issues, were meaningful and offered him success. Systematic recording at each stage enabled clarity of understanding for all adults within and outside the setting, and transferring details into progress review reports was then a straightforward process. Recording also enabled another adult to continue with the work if Adam's key worker was absent.

Setting appropriate targets or teaching objectives will be essential when differentiating the curriculum for an individual child and, again, these can be shared with and supported by parents. Webster and McConnell offer practical suggestions for working with children with speech and language difficulties and support the importance of clear objectives:

> There are several good reasons to set down a clear profile of teaching objectives. In the first place, there may be many professionals, other than teachers, involved with the child and objectives should be agreed upon through discussion so that targets to aim for are clear to all concerned. Secondly identification of what it is hoped the child will learn provides a framework for evaluating progress over time. (Webster and McConnell, 1987: 164)

Using Adam's situation as an exemplar, the following teaching objectives and strategies were developed to support the development of his jigsaw skills:

Aim: For Adam to complete a six-piece puzzle unaided by half-term.

Strategies:

- To sit with an adult for up to five minutes to work on jigsaws.
- Every positive response to be rewarded verbally by the adult.
- On completion of his time maximum, to be given a sticker.
- The adult to explain each stage prior to commencing.
- Adam to undertake as much of the task as he is able, with the adult withdrawing physical support as his skills develop.
- Adam to share his successes at circle time and take a jigsaw home to work on with his parents.

This step-by-step approach was discussed by staff at a meeting with Adam's parents and they were happy to support the intervention within the home. They also appreciated being involved and were able to transfer the skills they developed into other areas of Adam's learning and development within the home with great success. Their response was very positive for Adam but, perhaps as important, for themselves as they felt supported in their desire to encourage and support their son's progress, and they informed staff that their new-found abilities were useful in so many other areas of home life, thereby improving life for the whole family. They concluded: 'It was so easy once they showed us how to break it down into steps.'

The EYFS practice guidance also supports the personalised learning approach:

> Practitioners should deliver personalised learning, development and care to help children to get the best possible start in life. You must plan for each child's

individual care and learning requirements. The focus should be on removing or helping to counter underachievement and overcoming barriers for children where these already exist. (DCSF, 2008k: 6)

The guidance also highlights the importance of knowing each child to ensure every factor is taken into account when planning activities, thus ensuring the appropriateness of the tasks set and the likely success for the child. It clearly states that:

All effective assessment involves analysing and reviewing what you know about each child's development and learning. You can then make informed decisions about the child's progress and plan next steps to meet their development and learning needs. (DCSF, 2008k: 12)

The EYFS comprises six areas of learning and development which are interrelated and together they: 'make up the skills, knowledge and experiences appropriate for babies and children as they grow, develop and learn' (National Strategies, 2008). Each area of learning is then further broken down into specific aspects, for example:

Personal, social and emotional development comprises:

- dispositions and attitudes

- self-confidence and self-esteem

- making relationships

- behaviour and self-control

- self-care

- a sense of community.

For each of the above the practitioner is guided by the early learning goals according to the child's age: Birth to 11 months, 8–20 months, 16–26 months, 22–36 months, 30–50 months and 40–60 months. However, it must be remembered that practitioners may need to break down stages even further for children with special needs, as their individual requirements may demand more graduated stepping stones to develop some skills. The SEN Toolkit (DfES, 2001d) was produced for use alongside the SEN Code of Practice (DfES, 2001c) and section 5 offers a wealth of accessible information for practitioners regarding managing individual education plans. Included within the Toolkit (DfES, 2001d) is the suggestion of using SMART targets within IEPs. To suggest a target of: 'Adam will improve his ability with jigsaws' is not specific, measurable, achievable, relevant or time bound (SMART). However, the target could be rephrased to satisfy the SMART target criteria: 'By half-term Adam will be able to complete a six-piece jigsaw.' All targets should be formulated as SMART targets.

Individual Education Plans

If a child's difficulties have not responded to initial intervention strategies, then the graduated response outlined within the Code of Practice (DfES, 2001c) will commence with Early Years Action. At this stage, information will be collected from parents, the child and any other professionals involved, including the SENCO, so they will be in an informed position to suggest ways forward. Formalising future plans will involve the creation of an IEP which will be drawn up in accordance with the requirements of the Code of Practice (DfES, 2001c: s. 4.27): 'this (the IEP) should include information about the short-term targets set for the child, the teaching strategies and the provision to be put in place, when the plan is to be reviewed and the outcome of the action taken'.

The IEP will make it clear to all involved exactly how the curriculum will respond to the individual needs of the child, thus being child-led rather than special-needs-led. The SEN Toolkit suggests:

> The IEP should include information about:
> - the short-term targets set for and by the pupil
> - the teaching strategies to be used
> - the provision to be put in place
> - when the plan is reviewed
> - success and/or exit criteria
> - outcomes (to be recorded when IEP is reviewed). (DfES, 2001d: 7)

While there is no set format for IEPs, they should be clear and to the point, and should identify what and how progress is to be achieved. The SEN Code of Practice (DfES, 2001c) and Advisory Centre for Education (ACE, 2005a) clearly set out aspects which should be included. The format can be individual to the setting, created by a group of local settings through the local early years forum or network or set by the LEA. Using the expertise and skills of a greater range of practitioners can save reinventing the wheel and incorporate an increased diversity of experience. In addition, a consistent IEP format would produce consistency for feeder schools. A key issue regarding the management of IEPs is that of being achievable and manageable. They should not become paper exercises that take SENCOs away from their crucial work with the children and staff. The SEN Toolkit suggests:

the procedures for devising IEPs and reviewing them must be manageable. The IEP should be considered within the context of the overall class management of all pupils and staff.

Timeslots for delivery of the IEP should be realistic and integral to classroom and curriculum planning.

All IEPs must be achievable for both the pupil and the teacher. Targets should be in small steps so that success is clearly visible to the pupil, the parents and the teacher. (DfES, 2001d: s. 5, p. 8)

All IEPs should be reviewed 'regularly', identifying the outcomes of the previous IEP and preparing SMART targets for the subsequent IEP, if one is needed. The Advisory Centre for Education (ACE, 2005a) suggests that reviews should occur 'at least three times a year'. They continue to conclude that:

These may not be formal meetings but parents' views should be sought and parents consulted throughout. As with IEPs for children in school, they will focus on three or four key short-term targets and describe provision that is additional to or different from the pre-school's routine differentiated curriculum. (p. 22)

Reverting to Adam, his IEP could be as follows:

Sample Individual Education Plan

Name: Adam
DoB: 03.05.02
IEP no: 1
Stage: Early Years Action
Start date: 15.09.05
Review date: 30.11.05

Nature of difficulties:
1 Runs everywhere
2 Limited concentration and attention span
3 Limited activity range

Targets:
1 Adam will be able to complete a six-piece jigsaw unaided.
2 Adam will be able to sit and focus on a circle time activity for a minimum of five minutes.
3 Adam will not run around the room between the activities.

Methods:
1 Transport and buildings puzzles (4–12 pieces) will be purchased for use with Adam. Each session, Adam will be supported to develop the skills of completing a jigsaw.

2 Positive verbal encouragement will be used at all times.

3 Adam's efforts will be shared with the whole group at circle time.

4 Adam's parents will be shown his successes.

5 Adam will be allowed to take a jigsaw home each time he attends.

6 Rhymes and short stories with clear pictures involving farms, building sites and vehicles will be used often.

7 Adam will sit near the front at storytime to ensure he can see the pictures clearly and that he can see and hear any positive reinforcement (verbal and/or body language) from the adult.

8 The activity room will be reorganised to limit free running spaces.

9 Music and movement times will focus on a topic of fast and slow to emphasise different and appropriate movements at different times.

NB: The IEP could indicate the resources required (human, equipment and time) for each of the tasks.

Parental and child input:

This IEP was prepared and discussed with Adam's parents on 12.09.09 who support the targets and will praise him appropriately to reinforce the praise and encouragement received within the group. They will follow up at home the work with jigsaws and using stories to encourage his attention skills. Adam will be given 'his special time' after he has had his bath but after his younger sibling has gone to bed.

This IEP was discussed with Adam on 06.09.09 who agrees that doing puzzles is now a favourite activity.

Statements of special needs

Statements of special needs follow the process of Statutory Assessment where appropriate, in which the views of all professionals working with the child, along with the parents and the child him/herself, will have submitted their reports, views and opinions on the difficulties experienced, support already in place and detailing the provision required to ensure future progress. If the LEA agrees to assess, they will take into account all relevant information provided and inform the parents of the outcome, all within an agreed timescale. The resulting statement is a binding document which should clearly state the provision required to respond to the child's individual needs. Parents will receive a copy with a letter of explanation which 'should explain the opportunities parents have to express a preference for a school and to negotiate over the contents of the Statement' (ACE, 2005a: 46). Parents do have the right to appeal through the SENDIST.

While the process may appear straightforward, parents who have experienced it may have cause to disagree. Depending on local funding arrangements, either schools or the LEA will be expected to fund the extra provision, but if the school is expected to provide and claims they are doing everything they can, parents' positions can be made very difficult. Similarly, if the parents wish their child to attend a school other than those suggested, particularly if they are out of the county, it may not be easy to secure their wish. If parents nominate a private school or a non-maintained school, then the LEA is not obliged to agree, although they must consider the request. The Independent Panel for Special Education Advice (IPSEA) report highlighted that:

> IPSEA casework has consistently shown that parents are made to feel they are being greedy, over-anxious or unreasonable for requesting assessments for their child, and both LEAs and the Department for Education have been guilty of implying that the issuing of statements is a purely parent-driven phenomenon, owing nothing to the actual needs of individual children in our schools.
>
> So a process designed to ensure needs are met does not always result in positive outcomes. (IPSEA, 2005: 6)

So getting a statement for a child sounds fairly straightforward but the reality is sadly very different for practitioners and, perhaps more importantly, for parents. Sandy Row describes her long and drawn-out 'battle' for her own children in her book *Surviving the Special Educational Needs System: How to be a Velvet Bulldozer* (2005) which clearly demonstrates that for many parents every single stage of the process can become a battle, which has subsequently been highlighted in the Lamb Inquiry (DCSF, 2009h) as the experience of many other parents. Row claims that:

> We couldn't seem to get anyone to do anything to help. I asked people for help but either I was asking the wrong people or I was asking the questions in the wrong way. (Row, 2005: 66)

Specific intervention programmes 1 – speech and language difficulties

Unless specially trained or qualified in the field of speech and language, early years practitioners are not expected to make a diagnosis or devise a specialist programme for a child with speech and language difficulties. If a child requires such specialist support, then the practitioner's role is to enable a referral. If speech and language delay is a concern, the child may be referred for a full hearing assessment at the local hospital. If hearing is cleared and there are no other issues that could be causing the speech and language delay, then a referral to the local speech and language therapist should follow. After an initial assessment, a report is produced and the early years setting is, hopefully, included on the circulation list to receive a copy. If the early years setting is a multi-agency setting, then a speech and language therapist may already be working in the centre, either full-time, part-time or on a visiting basis. In this case, the whole referral process can be dealt with within the setting. It should be noted, how-ever, that the availability and regularity of appointments of speech and language therapists will vary across the country, and sometimes within areas, so it remains a postcode lottery.

The Bercow report (DCSF, 2008f), highlighted in Chapter 1, reviewed provision for children and young people with speech, language and communication needs (SLCN), concluding that improvements were needed in five key areas. His subsequent report, *Better Communication* (DCSF, 2008g), focused on the 40 recommendations and suggested ways in which each should be addressed. The report was clear in identifying that all practitioners need to have knowledge and skills in this area to ensure success for all children with SLCN:

> All professionals working with children should support the development of all children's speech, language and communication skills. Practitioners need an awareness of SCLN so that they can identify them and, if necessary, refer chil-dren for additional support. (2008g: 3)

Also in 2008, we saw the Inclusion Development Programme (IDP) focus on *Supporting Children with Speech, Language and Communication Needs: Guidance for Practitioners in the Early Years Foundation Stage* (DCSF, 2008e). The IDP is part of the governmental strategy to improve practitioners' skills in supporting all children with SEN and each year saw a new focus. However, the guidance handbook and supporting DVD need to be accessed by staff teams as part of their continuing professional development, suggesting that:

> It is the responsibility of leaders and managers to demonstrate their commit-ment to inclusive practice by ensuring that practitioners are given the necessary time to work through the materials as a group and the opportunity to carry out follow-up work in the session. (DCSF, 2008e: 6)

Whether staff do have the time to engage in the materials is therefore up to individual settings so the outcome is likely to be that while some settings engage totally, others will not (for very legitimate reasons) and thus provision will be patchy and a postcode lottery for children and families. This is hardly the outcome we would choose if we wish for improved provision for all children with SCLN nationally.

Definitions and terminology

Early years practitioners should be aware of the following terms as they may appear in speech and therapy reports:

- *Comprehension of speech* – relates to a child's ability to understand language. Some children with speech and language difficulties become experts at lip reading and using clues from the environment as well as visual and body language clues, and may be able to respond appropriately, thus concealing underlying difficulties. Early years practitioners are naturally, and quite rightly, experienced at giving a range of indicative clues when interacting with children.

- *Expressive language* – relates to the ability to use language appropriately in a range of situations.

- *Articulation* – relates to the physical muscle use of the mouth, tongue, teeth, nose and breathing, all of which are necessary to produce sounds.

- *Phonology* – comprises the individual sounds that combine to make words.

- *Syntax* – relates to the combining of words into phrases, and later sentences appropriately.

- *Intonation* – relates to the raising and lowering of voice in different parts of sentences and phrases for emphasis.

The impact of speech and language difficulties

Speech and language skills are a necessary requirement for development in areas of cognitive, social, emotional and self-concept development and are the medium used mostly within early years settings to deliver the curriculum. Without these skills, children's development will be compromised. Some children will be frustrated at their inability or limited ability to communicate as well as their peers and may withdraw within themselves and away from any interactions to avoid further frustration. They may have been repeatedly told they 'don't listen' or 'never listen' so may give up trying. Very young children can at times be very supportive of their peers who are experiencing difficulties but a few may be unkind and insensitive. Such children could be supported in their approaches to others. Levels of frustration may result in unacceptable behaviours within the home and/or setting and it would be futile to spend time focusing on the behaviour difficulties without first attempting to alleviate the underlying cause – the speech and language difficulty. Webster and McConnell (1987: 12) suggest that: 'We should not underestimate the deep and pervasive influence of language difficulties upon the child's development.'

Assessments

A range of assessment materials is available for speech and language therapists to use, and some which early years practitioners can be trained to use, but arguably, the most effective knowledge early years practitioners can have is that of 'normal' language development. With this knowledge and their working experiences, they are generally well placed to identify difficulties, or potential difficulties, and respond appropriately. Closer observations of a child over a period could focus on their social interactions, self-concept development and speech and language skills, with the evidence made available to support referrals if needed.

Intervention strategies within early years settings

Some children experiencing speech and language difficulties will have difficulties in other areas as well, and may require special school provision or language unit provision, either short or long term. However, with the current moves towards inclusive education, most children will remain in their local provision and be ably supported there. If a child is undergoing regular sessions with a speech and language therapist, then working together will enable the early years setting to support the work being done in therapy sessions. It may be that the speech and language therapist will send, via the parents, tasks that can be undertaken within the setting to support the specialised work in the therapy sessions. Coordination in this way, among parents, setting and therapist provides the most comprehensive support for the child. In addition, the speech and language therapist may visit the setting on a regular basis to discuss progress and the next steps with staff. This again is beneficial to all, particularly if the parents are involved. Perhaps the most appropriate suggestion for supporting children with communication difficulties is to encourage and support effective communication skills, not to correct but to model language and to support and minimise the effects of the difficulties on the child. Spenceley (2000: 51) suggests hints and tips for practitioners:

- Speak slowly and clearly.
- Simplify your speech.

- Give instructions in the order in which they are to be carried out.

- Repeat key words and information.

- Expand simple utterances (e.g. child: 'teddy chair'; adult: 'yes, teddy is sitting on the chair').

- Model correct use (e.g. child: 'teddy falled over'; adult: 'yes, teddy fell over'). (Spenceley, 2000: 51)

Once the practitioner knows which specific areas of the child's development require support within the setting, then an IEP can be drawn up to clarify the provision, the arrangements required and the teaching strategies. It may be that the speech and language therapist has recommended work on memory skills, attention skills and free conversation during small-toy play, all of which can readily be supported within the setting. Using the therapist's suggestions, three or four targets can be established and future planning can be adapted to begin supportive work. The IEP will ensure monitoring is consistent and progress review meetings will involve feedback and further discussions between the practitioners, parents and therapist.

Makaton

Makaton is an additional resource available for use with children experiencing communication difficulties. Usually suggested and established by a child's speech and language therapist, training is available in most parts of the country for early years practitioners but, as always, funding may be a barrier for some. Makaton uses a combination of speech and gestures or signs which are further supported by a standard line-drawn picture. The underlying philosophy is that we all use gestures and other visual clues when we communicate, so, for those experiencing difficulties with expressive language, Makaton can give additional support and structure to enable communication without the need to verbalise. However, practitioners themselves do use verbal language to accompany the use of the signs and/or pictures as a model.

In my experience, Makaton enables communication and thus increases self-confidence as it relieves the frustrations of not being able to verbalise and communicate in the same way as others. While some may suggest that replacing verbalisation with signs and pictures removes the need and desire to speak, evidence to date supports the opposite. In my own experience, Makaton relieves the child's frustration and removes the focus on expressive language. Over time, the child's expressive language begins to develop. Makaton can be used easily within any setting and ideally should be introduced within the home situation at the same time, which clearly depends on parental support and willingness to participate.

Words, signs and symbols are introduced in a gradual and progressive manner beginning with the obvious mummy, daddy, drink, biscuit, please and thank you, and subsequently additional words are introduced.

Specific intervention programmes 2 – autistic spectrum disorders

As with communication difficulties, practitioners need to have a sound basic awareness of the effects of autistic spectrum disorders (ASDs) and the implications for the learning environment if they are to provide effectively for young children with ASDs. An understanding of the effects on the individual members of the child's family would also be beneficial. Without this basic knowledge, practitioners can inadvertently severely compound the child's difficulties and in the early days of working with children with autism, I now know that, despite my best efforts, I did not have sufficient knowledge or understanding of ASDs to provide effectively. I would strongly recommend that any early years practitioner who is receiving a child on the autistic spectrum into his/her setting should spend time exploring the National Autistic Society website (www.nas.org.uk) which contains a wealth of accessible, practical and up-to-date information on all aspects of ASDs as well as a useful publications list.

Within an inclusive educational philosophy, combined with the increase in children diagnosed with an ASD, mainstream settings can expect to provide for children with such difficulties. The Code of Practice, for the first time, makes specific reference to autistic spectrum disorders and acknowledges the type of support such children need:

> These children may require some, or all, of the following:
> * flexible teaching arrangements
> * help in acquiring, comprehending and using language
> * help in articulation
> * help in acquiring literacy skills
> * help in using augmentative and alternative means of communication
> * help to use different means of communication confidently and competently for a range of purposes, including formal situations

- help in organising and coordinating oral and written language
- support to compensate for the impact of a communication difficulty on learning in English as an additional language
- help in expressing, comprehending and using their own language, where English is not the first language. (DfES, 2001c: s. 7.56)

In 2002, as a result of the Autism Working Group, the DfES published *Autistic Spectrum Disorders: Good Practice Guidance,* which stated that: 'The government is determined to see improvements in the understanding of autistic spectrum disorders and in the provision that is made for children and adults with the condition and their families' (DfES, 2002: 3). The guidance continues to outline a range of 'pointers' to good practice at school, LEA and national levels.

The IDP also spent 2009/10 focusing on ASDs (DCSF, 2009m) and in the same vein as with the IDP for SCLN, the success (or otherwise) of this will depend on practitioners' access to the materials and resources. The ASD guidance suggests that:

> the difficulties described above (those of ASD) could limit children's access to the EYFS, as most areas of Learning and Development are underpinned by social understanding and communication. The quality of the support that practitioners are able to offer children with autism will determine the extent to which these children are able to make good progress in all areas of Learning and Development. (DCSF, 2009m: 10)

Definitions and terminology

Autism is a lifelong developmental disorder and, although appropriate educational and social provision can lead to improvements, some characteristics will remain throughout the child's life. Primarily, autism affects social, imaginative and communication development but children with autism can have additional learning difficulties, as well as sensory difficulties. Children with autism may appear disinterested in the learning environment and/or the people within it and will have great difficulty establishing friendships, as they do not see a need to interact with others. They will not, in general, be alert and interested in any activity except their own ritualistic behaviours, such as repetitively rolling a train up and down a table for long periods of time.

The three key difficulties associated with ASDs form the triad of impairments (see Figure 6.2).

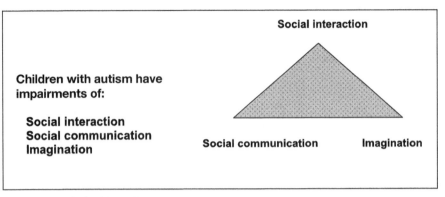

Figure 6.2 Triad of impairments

To provide for children with ASDs, practitioners should attempt to understand the child's view of the world through 'autistic' eyes. We can all acknowledge that children generally develop great curiosity about the world around them, but for children with autism this is not always the case. We cannot presume to bring the child fully into 'our world' as he/she will not understand it, but should consider the need to understand and access the 'autistic world' and with that understanding we can plan and provide appropriate and stimulating activities for the child. The early years setting will simply not make sense to a child with autism, and he/she will not be capable of making sense of it without specific help and support.

The impact of autism

The characteristics of autism have been highlighted but some of the resulting effects on the child in an early years setting (depending on the severity of autism) would be some or all of the following:

- Appears aloof and disinterested.
- Does not interact with others.
- Does not attempt to communicate.
- Does not respond to his/her name or other verbal comments.
- Avoids eye contact.
- Does not sit down for circle time or snack time.
- May place hands over ears.
- May rock back and forth and/or flap hands vigorously.
- May scream.

- Does not demonstrate imaginative skills.

- May stare at lights.

- May demonstrate unusual and obsessive behaviours.

- May not understand a sequence of events or routine easily.

- May be insensitive to pain.

- May be sensitive to sounds, visual stimuli, smells, tastes and textures.

- May resist trying new experiences.

- May become highly distressed at unexpected changes to routine. (Adapted from Wall, 2010)

If we pause to consider the impact of these effects on a child (a) within the early years setting and (b) within the home, we will begin to have an understanding of the impact of autism on the child, the family and, thus, the setting.

Diagnosis and assessments

To diagnose autism is complex and specialised and is not undertaken by early years practitioners. Depending on local arrangements, the clinical psychologist, educational psychologist, consultant paediatrician or a local specialist child development centre or autistic unit undertakes the diagnosis and makes recommendations regarding provision. Early diagnosis is helpful to ensure appropriate support is available as early as possible and any planned interventions can begin.

Assessments informing the diagnosis should be thorough, detailed and of an interagency nature including:

- a detailed history of development

- any relevant medical information

- an evaluation of progress to date from parents and any professionals working with the child and/or family

- assessments of all developmental areas.

Intervention strategies and specific approaches

There is a range of specific intervention approaches available to the practitioner and in my own experience it may be that you choose to use some elements from more than one approach, in an eclectic manner. Some strategies will be common to more than one approach and will suit the practitioner and the needs of the individual child. As a general rule, the following can be used.

General strategies

As a broad general rule, structure within the learning environment will probably support the child with ASD very successfully, helping with understanding, increased learning potential and encouraging independence. Structure can be achieved through:

1   Sticking to routines to ensure consistency.

2   Visual routines: using photographs or simple pictures attached to a board or display. As each task is completed, the child will remove it from the board and place it in the 'finished' box. The child will always know what comes next.

3   Visual labels with accompanying words on all resources and learning materials, which when combined with organisational structure will encourage independence.

4   Work systems where each task to be completed by the child is placed in a tray or basket and placed on the left-hand side of the work table. The child will soon learn to work in this order through the tasks and place them on the right-hand side of the table when completed. This will encourage independent learning. Tasks must be explicit as the child will not be able to assume what you want them to do.

Other strategies

1 Extend imaginative play. If the child with autism is obsessed by trains, vehicles and wheels, you will find there is a tendency to identify any vehicles and circular shaped objects that could rotate, even in materials where you cannot see them. This can be used by modelling and extension of the child's existing and possibly obsessive play routines through initially playing alongside the child (not with the child who may react negatively to your close presence). This could simply be imitating the child's play. As the child allows you to continue, you can demonstrate an extension to the current play routines. Through repeated modelling, the child will hopefully begin to imitate and 'allow' you to become more involved as he/she begins to realise that play and fun can be a shared experience.

2 Be vigilant of potentially unsafe situations and play. A child who

is obsessed with hinges and locks may repeatedly open and shut a door onto the fingers of his/her other hand, apparently oblivious to any pain.

3 Help the child to understand what you are asking by presenting only that which is necessary. A child presented with a table covered in round interconnecting shapes may be overpowered by the visual stimulation of so many and simply leave the table to escape or cover their eyes or ears to block out the sensation. If you are working on connecting three pieces together, then only present three pieces to the child.

4 Offer a quiet area for one-to-one work that is free from stimulation and distraction to enable greater concentration.

5 Talk slowly and in simple language when working near or with the child to offer examples of good language. Repetition of common words and phrases will eventually pay dividends and support communication development.

6 Be aware of the child's possible sensitivity to touch, hearing, taste, smell and sight. Whereas you may naturally offer physical comfort to a child who has fallen over or is distressed, to pick up and hug a child with autism may increase the distress.

7 Have consistent routines within the setting, as children with autism need structure and familiarity more than their peers.

8 If the child will only join in snack time if he/she has the same chair, in the same place (possibly away from the table) and must have the same type of snack and cup, then so be it. The benefits of limited participation in this social activity will allow access to role models of social interaction, social skills and language skills.

9 Exaggerate your use of bodily, facial and hand gestures to encourage awareness and understanding of gestures.

10 Avoid using phrases and idioms, as children with autism understand literal not implied meanings. 'Jump in the bath' means exactly that!

It should be noted that immediate responses and/or progress are unlikely, but for the child with less severe autistic difficulties progress could be more rapid.

Specific approaches
A range of specific approaches or programmes exists to support young children with ASDs, including:

- the Lovaas approach

- Treatment and Education of Autistic and Related Communication Handicapped Children (TEACCH)

- the Picture Exchange Communication System (PECS)

- Makaton

- Structure, Positive (approaches and expectations), Empathy, Low arousal environments and Links with parents (SPELL)

- Auditory Integration Training (AIT)

- the Son Rise programme (Options therapy)

- the Higashi approach (Daily life therapy).

(For information on any of these, readers are directed to Wall, 2010, Chapter 5.)

📁 Case study

Ben was referred to an early years special needs unit by his health visitor and was described as demonstrating 'autistic type behaviours'. He was currently awaiting a full developmental assessment by the consultant paediatrician. A home visit was made at which both parents were present to discuss Ben's individual needs and to identify the key issues from their perspective. They had researched Ben's difficulties, felt sure he was autistic and were able to accept this. The behaviours described certainly fitted within the autistic spectrum. It was agreed that Ben would commence attendance and that the staff would observe and assess him over the first few weeks before meeting again with his parents to discuss their observations and plans for the future. It was hoped that by this time he would have had his appointment with the consultant paediatrician and the report would be able to inform discussions.

The observations and assessments identified the following issues:

- Ben did not interact with adults or children and would remove himself from potentially interactive situations.

- Ben demonstrated obsessive and ritualistic play routines with his tractor, which always had to be within his sight. If he could not see his tractor, he would become distressed.

- While rolling his tractor back and forth along the window sill, he would watch the traffic pass by and became very excited and animated when a fire engine passed.

- Ben would not join the group for snacks or circle time and would become distressed if encouraged.

- Ben could identify rotational qualities in any object and could become fixated with it.
- When Ben picked up something new to him, he would explore it with his hands and mouth for two or three minutes before playing with it or discarding it.
- Ben would spend up to ten minutes flicking through books (from left to right, and turning pages appropriately) looking for tractors. When he found one, he would slide the book along the floor to simulate vehicle movement.
- Ben was oblivious to the usual noises within the room but would become very distressed if a child cried or the fire alarm went off, rocking his body, flapping his hands and shutting his eyes very tightly.
- Ben enjoyed rolling his tractor down the slide but did not want to try himself.

Note: These outcomes are in detail to illustrate points to the reader. Any written records would be more succinct. The observational outcomes were discussed by staff and Ben's parents who felt they summed up Ben accurately. The following strategies were agreed, to be reviewed after six weeks. In addition, a daily diary was passed between parents and staff.

- Ben's key worker was to spend two or three minutes, at least four times each session, playing alongside Ben at the window sill, imitating his play and making comments about the passing traffic. The length and time, frequency and level of interaction were to be adapted according to Ben's responses.
- The key worker was to introduce alternative vehicles into window-sill play and begin rolling vehicles on a table placed by the window.
- On the table would be one or two four-piece jigsaws – one of a tractor and one of a fire engine, plus a book about a farm. At the key worker's discretion, she would complete a jigsaw, describing what she was doing and/or describe the pictures in the book.
- At snack time, the key worker sat at a separate table away from the group with a snack and a drink, plus the same for Ben. Initially, he would be allowed to remove his snack and eat/drink it elsewhere but he would be encouraged to join her.
- For the first six weeks, the unit requested that no fire drills took place on the days Ben attended.

At the review six weeks later, it was noted that Ben would now watch the key worker completing the jigsaws and listen to her talking about the book, although he would not join her at the table. He now played alongside her with the vehicles and occasionally offered her

(Continued)

(Continued)

a specific vehicle to indicate he wanted her to play. Two days before the review, he had shared snack time seated at the table next to his key worker, provided she did not look at him or talk directly to him.

Staff and parents were very pleased with this considerable progress and activities were continued and extended over the coming weeks and months, with short- and long-term targets included in Ben's IEPs. By the end of his second term at the unit, Ben was successfully undertaking one-to-one work with his key worker at a table using a structured teaching approach (as per the TEACCH programme), he was using visual timetables and had begun to communicate using PECS. The same strategies and principles were used within the home situation and regular progress reviews took place involving parents, staff and other professionals.

Elements of effective practice

Hickman and Jones (2005) explored the elements of effective practice and concluded, like myself, that good early years practice is good special needs practice. So effective practitioners will utilise strategies that incorporate the following characteristics:

- the use of structure and routine
- practitioner language
- visual systems
- individualised motivators
- practitioner awareness and knowledge
- appropriate and creative use of support staff
- knowledge of the individual child's perspective and sensibilities
- a recognition of the role of other children and peer relationships
- a recognition of the role of parents
- a commitment to an inclusive philosophy. (Hickman and Jones, 2005: 37)

Individualised or personalised planning and provision, as opposed to special needs planning and provision, is thus the key. In this way, children will be observed and assessed within a holistic philosophy which then informs planning and, hopefully, improved outcomes.

☐ Summary

Throughout this chapter, we have emphasised the need for practitioners to provide appropriately for the individual needs of young children through a cyclical intervention approach incorporating gathering information, observations, planning, interventions and monitoring. Individual Education Plans will clarify the arrangements made and include short- and long-term targets established to ensure progress. These IEPs should be reviewed regularly, and partnerships with parents should be encouraged at each and every stage. The breaking down of tasks into small steps or 'stepping stones' is essential for meaningful task setting that will ensure success and thus progress for the child. The next stage of the process would involve formal assessment, possibly leading to a Statement of SEN.

We have examined scenarios involving provision for children with speech and language difficulties and ASDs in some detail and, through this, the principles of assessing children and formulating targets which directly respond to their individual needs have been emphasised. The case study of Ben does not actually include the word 'autism' in the setting's planning as the condition is not really viewed as the key issue, rather that understanding and responding to Ben's individual needs is the key issue, taking into account his preferences, likes and dislikes. However, it could be suggested that, without a sound understanding of the impact of autism, the targets formulated would not necessarily have been appropriate for him. So, while the possibility of 'autism' was not an issue for the staff, prior knowledge of autism was indeed necessary for Ben's intervention programme.

While a range of approaches has been discussed, it must be clarified that no single approach will necessarily offer all the answers for all children. Practitioners will often use elements from a variety of approaches to provide most effectively for children's individual, and often changing, needs.

⚷ Key issues

- Any intervention should begin at the child's current stage of development and progress in small steps, reflect individual needs and take into account any contributing factors.
- Regular evaluations and monitoring are needed.
- IEPs comprising SMART targets are needed.
- Parental partnerships and interagency working are essential for effective intervention.

~~~ Points for reflection

- Think about the children in your care/setting. Identify a child with SLCN or ASD and consider whether provision addresses each of the areas highlighted in this chapter.

- Discuss how staff feel about supporting children with SCLN and/or ASDs. Identify any training needs.

- Reflect on the effectiveness of intervention systems utilised in your setting.

Suggested further reading

Department for Children, Schools and Families (2008e) *Inclusion Development Programme – Supporting Children with Speech, Language and Communication Needs: Guidance for Practitioners in the Early Years Foundation Stage.* London: DCSF. Also available at: www.nationalstrategies.standards.dcsf.gov.uk/node/161358

Department for Children, Schools and Families (2009m) *Inclusion Development Programme – Supporting Children on the Autism Spectrum: Guidance for Practitioners in the Early Years Foundation Stage.* Available at: www.nationalstrategies.standards.dcsf.gov.uk/node/173893

Wall, K. (2010) *Autism and Early Years Practice*, 2nd edn. London: Sage.

7

Interagency working

Chapter objectives

To develop awareness of:

- historical developments in interagency working
- the need for effective interagency working
- key features of effective practice
- the roles of key professionals
- factors affecting collaboration and ways forward.

Introduction

Now, more than ever before, early years practitioners need to work together with colleagues from other disciplines and agencies to support their work with children and their families. Government legislation and guidance demand improved working across agencies in a proactive and 'seamless' manner and increasingly the importance of this area has been promoted in the considerable range of legislation since 2001. Predominantly emanating from Every Child Matters (DfES, 2003a), the CWDC is now:

> responsible for implementing and supporting the following areas:
> - Information sharing
> - The Common Assessment Framework (CAF)
> - Lead Professional
> - Multi-agency working toolkit. (CWDC, 2009b)

For each of these areas, specific professional guidance is also available for professional guidance (CWDC, 2010a, 2010b, 2010c, 2010d).

However, effective and successful interagency working presents many challenges for practitioners and policy makers at local and national levels.

Awareness and understanding of the roles and responsibilities of colleagues in other agencies is vital if we are to work together effectively, as only then can the knowledge, expertise and skills of each participant (including the parents) be used to full advantage. Pugh suggests:

> the explicitly multi-disciplinary nature of government initiatives in recent years and their focus on co-ordination and integration of early years services require something more than benign co-operation across existing professions. These initiatives require a truly multi-disciplinary response. (2001: 180)

This chapter explores the need for, and benefits of, interagency working, and highlights factors that may enhance or constrain effective practice.

Definitions and models

Terminology has changed considerably over the years and a range of terms is used to describe professionals from different agencies working together. These include multidisciplinary, multiprofessional, multi-agency, interdisciplinary, interagency, transdisciplinary and transagency. At times, these terms have been used interchangeably but the development of each term has been specific to the philosophies of the time.

Multidisciplinary, multiprofessional and multi-agency working

The terms multidisciplinary, multiprofessional and multi-agency are somewhat simplistic as they indicate more than one professional or agency working with a child but do not imply working together across professional boundaries. In the simplest form, each professional provides expertise and the child then moves on to the next professional. Professionals are seen as working in discrete and separate ways and information sharing may be limited.

Interdisciplinary and interagency working

Within the interdisciplinary and interagency model we are progressing from a system in which professionals work in isolation with a child and his/her family to one in which professionals still work in parallel but more cooperation exists. There is an increased acknowledgement of the need for professional skills from a range of theoretical perspectives needing to work together to support the needs of the child. One discipline or professional is seen to be insufficient to provide for all the needs of the family and child but professionals may still be largely dependent on parents passing relevant information from other professionals. At this stage, systems are still working on a skills-based response to needs rather than a child- and family-centred approach, although current initiatives are bringing about more change.

Transdisciplinary and transagency working

The transdisciplinary or transagency approach developed in response to the recognition that areas of child development are inextricably linked and, thus, professionals cannot provide effectively without working across disciplines. This model also encompasses the needs of the family as well as the child as it supports the wide range of factors that can impact on a child's life, so the sharing of information and decision making is deemed fundamental. This model is therefore dependent on professionals implementing a key-worker system whereby one professional will take responsibility for coordinating and managing provision for the child and his/her family. The family needs are thus supported by having only one contact source for information. Case conferences and progress review meetings are also central to this process, with all professionals, the parents and the child (if appropriate) coming together to discuss progress, comment on provision and make plans for the short and long term.

Research indicates that the transdisciplinary model of working is the most effective, supporting current philosophies (Carpenter, 1997; Mortimer, 2001). However, as the SEN Code of Practice (DfES, 2001c) uses the term 'interagency' working, this term will be used throughout this chapter.

Whichever model is adopted, the guidance within the SEN Code of Practice highlights the need to work together:

> Meeting the special educational needs of individual children requires flexible working on the part of the statutory agencies. They need to communicate and agree policies and protocols that ensure there is a 'seamless' service. (DfES, 2001c, s. 10.1)

Historical developments

It is only since the 1970s that interagency work has become established and moved forwards. Possibly the two earliest and most influential documents to support interagency work were the Court Report (Court, 1976) and the Warnock Report (DES, 1978), but since then subsequent legislation and reports have continued to endorse this philosophy (see timeline at the end of Chapter 1). The development of Sure Start Children's Centres was seen as the key mechanism to deliver the ECM agenda and to improve outcomes for young children and their families. Commanding considerable governmental funding, these centres were established as one-stop shops and were initially centred in deprived areas. The aim was to have all the required services under the one roof to ensure all parents and children had easy access to any and all of the services they required. These services were supplemented by outreach workers from across education, health and social work departments who would visit families and encourage them to make use of the local centre and all the services on offer. However, this does assume that all families desired to engage with Children's Centres and those families who had had previous negative experiences of anyone representing a professional would not necessarily automatically begin accessing services.

Initially, family centres, funded either by education or social services, were set up in the 1970s, but the first Sure Start centres were established in the late 1990s and their purpose was to bring together all those professionals working with children and young families to offer the 'seamless' provision that was the vision of the time. Since their inception, Sure Start centres have been well funded and have seen continued periods of growth and expansion. In 2009, the government reported that:

> Children's centres bring together all the different support agencies to offer a wide range of services to meet your and your child's needs, all in one place. They're somewhere your child can make friends and learn as they play. You can get professional advice on health and family matters, learn about training and job opportunities or just socialise with other people. There are more than 3,000 children's centres in England – by 2010 there will be 3,500 so that every community is served by one. (Directgov, 2009)

So as the growth continues, the aim has changed from providing centres in deprived areas to providing centres in every local community.

Within any Children's Centre, a variety of activities will take place with guidance suggesting that:

Children's Centres will be expected to provide the following services to children under 5 and their families: early education integrated with full day care, including early identification of and provision for children with special educational needs and disabilities; parental outreach; family support, including support for parents with special needs; health services; a base for childminders, and a service hub within the community for parents and providers of childcare services; effective links with Jobcentre Plus, local training providers and further and higher education institutions; effective links with Children's Information Services, Neighbourhood Nurseries, Out of School Clubs and Extended Schools; management and workforce training. (TfC, 2006)

Staffing within Children's Centres will vary according to the needs and demands of the local community but will include professionals from a range of backgrounds, each offering their expert support for the young children and families they are working with, but would typically include: centre manager, deputy manager, family support workers, health professionals, parent classes worker, drop-in workers, crèche workers, early years professional(s), qualified teacher(s), administrator, receptionist and social worker (sessional or attached to the centre). Each of these professionals will be able to refer families to other professionals as appropriate, so clearly parents and children have direct access to a vast range of support, all within walking distance of the home.

However, simply by placing a diverse group of professionals into one centre does not, by itself, ensure effective interagency working. Although parents may have access to each professional, interagency working will also require engagement with professionals from outside of the centre, which will need thorough and time-consuming organisation and management. The success of interagency working will depend on the agreed aims and vision of *all* staff members. Rudge (2010: 133) suggests the following as key to a successful Children's Centre, with partnership working as a key element of success: commitment to excellence, partnership working, shared ethos and flexibility.

Progression to date

So, how far have we progressed and to what benefit? From the preceding historical reflection, it would seem that we have consistently moved towards improved interagency working but, in 2002, McConkey reflected on the work of Gulliford since the 1960s and presented quite a damning picture of progression regarding interagency working:

It truly has been a road 'less travelled' as each service system has forged its own highway in trying to reduce the disabling effects of an intellectual impairment and the inevitable social consequences that it brings. Worse still, at times they have worked competitively rather than cooperatively, blaming one another for perceived shortcomings. And perhaps most seriously of all, they have worked in ignorance of one another's values, priorities and achievements. (McConkey, 2002: 3)

At the same time, there are clearly areas where progression has been very positive:

- interagency assessments prior to statementing
- the development of Children's Trusts
- the setting up of more interagency early years centres
- increased interagency training
- the development of the team around the child (TAC).

However, it may also be suggested that there are still key issues to be addressed if we wish to secure continued progression, such as:

- increased understanding and awareness of the roles and responsibilities of other professionals
- expansion of the key worker and lead professional schemes
- joint funding
- joint training
- joint decision making at all levels
- joint policies
- rationalisation of professional differences
- consideration of merging of roles and responsibilities, including shared or joint planning.

While current legislation and guidance indicates that these issues will be addressed, the ways in which this will be achieved are still not clear. Stating that this will happen does not automatically result in the desired outcome, so strategies at local and national levels will need to continue for progression. This view is supported by Milbourne's study (2005: 690): 'However, this study identifies a gap between policy intentions and practice, and significant barriers to effective or collaborative services when examined from the point of view of families.'

The need for interagency working

When children attend our early years settings it is our responsibility to provide appropriate educational, personal and social activities to support their overall development. It is our aim to ensure they all achieve their full potential, but children with special needs and/or special educational needs may require more individualised opportunities. For some children, this will require input from several or many professionals and thus there becomes a need for professionals to work together. David echoed this view in 1994 yet it is still valid today:

> Their (the children's) teachers must often work with other professionals, and volunteers who are in some way connected with children and their families in order to understand children's difficulties, find ways of helping them and help children to learn effectively.

> It must be recognised that teachers of young children are not isolated and autonomous professionals, they work with a range of people who all contribute services for under-fives and their families. (David, 1994: 45)

The following case study highlights several key issues.

Case study

Jodie was referred to a local early years special needs unit at age 3 years and 3 months presenting with developmental delay. The consultant paediatrician's report indicated that Jodie had originally been referred by her health visitor and was particularly delayed in the areas of cognitive and social development. In addition, there were family difficulties in that both her parents were drug and alcohol abusers and had recently parted. There was also a history of domestic violence. Following this, the mother had left her husband and moved from another county to her current address.

As Jodie began to settle within the unit, it became apparent that her difficulties lay predominantly in the areas of social and emotional development, and other difficulties stemmed from these difficulties as well as a lack of appropriate learning opportunities. Once staff encouraged her and showed her how to play, her development took off at a considerable pace. A setback occurred when her father moved back into the house and levels of drug and alcohol abuse rose once again. At this stage, the local supporting agency for drug and alcohol abusers and their families was introduced, offering specialised help to the parents. It was also at this time that the social services department became involved, to support the family and work towards improving the family situation for all members.

Within a year, Jodie was performing age-appropriately in the areas of language and communication, cognitive and creative skills, and at the same time her self-esteem was considerably enhanced.

At all times, the agencies involved maintained regular contact and the head of the early years unit acted as key worker to ensure effective

(Continued)

(Continued)

coordination of services, monitor progress, call regular progress review meetings and act as the one focal point of contact for the family. Outside professionals working with the family used rooms at the unit for meetings with the family. The head of the unit was selected as the key worker because she had most regular contact with the family and had gained their trust.

Key issues from the case study

- Fundamentally, the difficulties experienced by Jodie were attributable to her parents' difficulties and, thus, the home life. This is a clear indication of the effects of the family and environment on a child and his/her development.

- Total respect had to be accorded the parents who were approached in a non-judgemental way.

- As the family had no transport, the local special needs unit became the central focus of provision.

- There was a need for professionals to share information, knowledge and skills to ensure an understanding of roles and responsibilities.

- Without a supportive network of agencies and professionals, Jodie's difficulties would have been exacerbated, as her parents did not consider using pre-school provision until it became a part of their rehabilitation and support programme.

- The range of professionals involved spanned all agencies, including the voluntary sector, and depended on effective interagency collaboration and coordination.

- As the head of the unit had not previously dealt with issues of drug and alcohol dependency, she had to address this lack of knowledge to support the parents and thus, indirectly, Jodie.

This case study shows that professionals from health, social services, education and the voluntary sector, each with their own theoretical frameworks and philosophies, needed to find effective and manageable ways to work together to support the needs of the family.

The case study explored in Chapter 2 required input from a far greater number of professionals, and the coordination of such a large group of professionals is a mammoth task requiring careful planning and management. In any early years setting, there may be many children experiencing difficulties, so the coordination becomes magnified, and it should be remembered that this is only one aspect of the practitioner's (and/or SENCO's) role. Demands are thus considerable.

If we continue to consider the child holistically as a member of our setting, their family, the local community and beyond, we need to work towards the 'seamless' provision of services that is being called for. We must work together in a collaborative manner, sharing expertise, information and skills which need to be managed in a way that addresses the needs of the families. Parents should not be responsible for passing on information from one professional to another; it is the responsibility of the professionals. As Wall concluded:

> effective co-operation and collaboration must exist to provide a clearly defined response to individual needs. For this to be achieved all personnel involved must understand and respect each other's role. While this may seem a tremendous task it must be remembered that teachers have a knowledge of the workings of most of the outside agencies they are likely to deal with, but perhaps a deeper understanding combined with local policies for working together would benefit all. (Wall, 1996: 84)

The need for this area of early years practice to be successful cannot be over emphasised as is evidenced by the tragic incidents of child deaths resultant from poor and ineffective interagency working, such as those of Victoria Climbié and Baby Peter. This view is supported by Johnston and Nahmad-Williams:

> it is essential that we work together effectively, understanding the different roles and responsibilities and how we can facilitate each other as well as support the child. It is when the professionals do not work together effectively or there is a gap in provision and support that children suffer, sometimes disastrously, as in high profile child abuse or child death cases. (2009: 394)

Following the Baby Peter case, the Laming Inquiry highlighted the need for improvements in interagency working as fundamental to future success. Offering 58 recommendations for improvements, the government responded with their Action Plan (DCSF, 2009n) in which interagency working was again deemed as fundamental. However, although these relate to the most extreme and tragic of cases, we should place equal priority to every child and family we work with, whatever the circumstances.

Features of effective practice

Whichever direction our interagency working takes us, we must ensure that the child remains central to everything we do. Remove this focus and success is likely to be limited. As we have already seen, children with special needs and/or disabilities may need to attend multiple appointments with specialist professionals and this will require very careful management. For the family without a car, multiple appointments at specialist centres are immediately problematic. If the family has other children at home and/or at school, then the demands of taking them and fetching them need to be considered, alongside the round of appointments. The more effective the interagency working, the better coordinated the appointments can be, to the benefit of the parents (normally the mother). The number of professionals involved with any one child can be considerable which, in turn, can easily translate to 20 or 30 appointments per year. The stress this brings to the family is unnecessary and could be eased.

So what are the key features of effective interagency working? Gasper (2010) gathered the views of Children's Centre leaders and concluded that the following principles were key:

- Those involved are valued, differing perspectives are respected, and skills, training and experience contribute collectively.
- Change comes from the bottom up rather than top down.
- Services need to be brought into the community rather than the reverse and accessibility improved.
- Services need to be co-located to improve coordination of services.
- More open access to training and skills is required.
- Highest priority should be given to areas of highest need.
- Causes rather than effects need to be addressed.
- There needs to be greater development of services such as advocacy to provide a voice for the vulnerable.
- Support which builds towards independence rather than dependency needs to be developed.
- There needs to be more emphasis on improving self-esteem and self-worth.
- There needs to be more encouragement of non-judgmental working.
- High quality pre-school care and education provision must be a high priority supported by the employment of part-time teachers and inspection. (2010: 36–7)

Understanding the roles of other professionals

To work in an interagency manner with colleagues from other disciplines will demand knowledge and understanding of their roles and responsibilities. Practitioners need to be clear on how another professional can complement and support their own provision for a child and in what precise ways, how and when this support will take place. Clarity is needed on who will be responsible for coordinating the support so that each professional and the parents are fully aware of what has already taken place, what has been agreed upon, what progress has been made, what short- and long-term plans are in place and how provision is monitored.

Working with other professionals will be an essential aspect of the practitioner's role and therefore the need to establish effective working practices must be included within our planning and policies. The need to work together to understand the child holistically is summarised by Drifte:

> Working with other agencies is an integral part of supporting children with special educational needs (SEN) and their parents. This cooperative approach also provides valuable support to the practitioner, who can benefit from access to information and records that focus on a different aspect of the child's development. The practitioner can also benefit from advice and suggestions about the management of special educational needs. (Drifte, 2001: 41)

In the previous case study, we saw that Jodie's parents were working with the social worker, health visitor and drug and alcohol abuse worker. To ensure clarity of provision, the head of the special needs unit, as key worker, needed to be aware of:

- the specific difficulties experienced by Jodie, her parents and siblings
- the input offered by each involved professional
- appointments attended by the family
- further referrals made
- organising and managing review meetings
- assessments and reports written.

Having such knowledge enabled her to ensure all parties were updated with information. Sometimes confusions arise or misconceptions exist because of a lack of coordination and collaboration which can compound a child's difficulties, and this needs to be addressed.

Skills and qualities needed

Working within an interagency framework requires certain skills and abilities and, clearly, a commitment to the principles and benefits of working in this manner. If professionals believe that interagency working benefits all, but most importantly the children, then hopefully they will be able to respond positively to demands on time and working practices despite constraining influences. Interagency working is still developing and there will necessarily be trials and tribulations for a considerable time to come.

Committed professionals will be able to deal with these issues. A desire to work more effectively with colleagues from other disciplines is required, as opposed to having a duty to work with colleagues from other disciplines. Those professionals who are interested in the workings of other disciplines and are less protective of their own discipline, expertise and skills will benefit positively from the experiences of increasing their knowledge and skills, both professionally and personally.

The professionals involved

Early years practitioners may work with any of the following professionals.

The education department

The *educational psychologist* (EP) will:

- be a qualified teacher who has undertaken additional training in educational psychology
- support the identification, assessment and monitoring of specific difficulties
- suggest appropriate intervention strategies
- advise on local provision
- complete reports for statutory assessment
- offer training
- work with parents.

Sanderson (2003) discusses the move towards increased identification and assessment by teachers and SENCOs with the EPs taking a more whole-school approach, advising and supporting the development of more inclusive policies and practices. However, Sanderson (2003: 203) points out that: 'education services continue to demand that the identification and subsequent assessment of these pupils is verified by educational psychologists, especially where there are financial implications (Beaver, 1998)'.

The *early years SEN support/advisory teacher/early years advisory teacher (EYAT)* will:

- usually be a qualified teacher with SEN experience and expertise
- support local early years providers regarding specific children
- support staff in planning and providing appropriate opportunities to support specific needs
- offer staff training
- advise on local specialist provision
- support referrals to other specialists
- contribute to the statutory assessment process
- work with parents.

Most counties have the benefit of *specialist support teams* covering the areas of language impairment, visual impairment and hearing impairment. In addition, many counties offer behaviour support teams to work with individual children, groups of children and practitioners. Support team staff will generally be experienced teachers who may hold additional qualifications in their specific field.

In addition, support staff may include learning support assistants (LSAs).

Visual/hearing/language impairment and behaviour support teachers will:

- advise practitioners on specific needs of individual children
- suggest exercises, strategies and appropriate learning opportunities for individual children
- advise on specialist equipment/resources needed
- liaise with parents
- assess and monitor provision for individual children
- refer children to other specialists as appropriate
- offer advice, support and training to practitioners and parents
- sometimes contribute to the statutory assessment process.

The health department

The *general practitioner* (GP) will:

- take responsibility for family health needs
- identify and provide for medical needs/problems
- refer individual children to other specialists for specific medical assessments or treatment
- liaise with health visitors, practitioners and parents.

The *health visitor* (HV) will:

- provide primary health care for children under school age
- monitor children developmentally at regular intervals prior to school entry and identify and assess special needs when appropriate
- be informed when a child with special needs or medical problems is born
- offer support, guidance and advice to parents and professionals
- refer individual children to other specialists when appropriate
- advise on local provision and supporting agencies
- contribute to the statutory assessment process.

The *paediatrician and consultant paediatrician* will:

- monitor medical conditions in individual children
- refer individual children to other specialists when appropriate
- liaise with practitioners, other professionals and parents
- undertake a detailed developmental assessment if a child is failing HV developmental checks
- offer early diagnosis and suggest appropriate intervention and placement for children causing concern
- contribute medical information to the statutory assessment process.

The *speech and language therapist* (SLT) will:

- suggest exercises, strategies and appropriate learning opportunities for individual children with speech, language and communication difficulties

- work with individual children regarding their specific needs
- liaise with practitioners and parents
- refer children to other specialists if appropriate
- offer diagnoses of specific language impairments/disorders
- contribute information to the statutory assessment process
- monitor the speech and language development of specific children
- offer support and training to practitioners and parents.

Some *physiotherapists* specialise in paediatric working and will:

- assess and diagnose physical difficulties experienced by young children
- suggest exercises, strategies and appropriate activities for individual children with physical difficulties
- contribute information to the statutory assessment process
- offer advice and support to practitioners and parents
- advise on specialist equipment/resources needed
- refer children to other specialists as appropriate.

The *occupational therapist* (OT) will:

- support children with physical difficulties to achieve independence
- assess fine and gross motor skills
- suggest exercises, strategies and appropriate activities for individual children
- advise practitioners on the specific needs of individual children
- contribute information to the statutory assessment process
- advise on specialist equipment/resources needed
- refer children to other specialists as appropriate
- offer advice and support to practitioners and parents.

The *audiologist and ophthalmologist* will:

- assess children's hearing/vision to identify possible problems

- suggest exercises, strategies and appropriate activities for individual children with hearing/visual problems
- contribute information to the statutory assessment process
- advise practitioners/parents on individual children's needs
- advise on specialist equipment/resources needed
- refer children to other specialists as appropriate.

There is some overlap between the roles and responsibilities of the educational psychologist and the *clinical psychologist,* but clearly their underpinning philosophies will differ owing to their different training and work contexts, that is, education or health. For these reasons, referrals will depend on issues such as the structure of local services and division of key responsibilities. As an example, it may be that a clinical psychologist would be responsible for the diagnosis of attention deficit hyperactivity disorder (ADHD) in one county but in the neighbouring county the educational psychologist would diagnose. In general, clinical psychologists will:

- advise and support families experiencing difficulties
- undertake developmental assessments
- suggest strategies and appropriate experiences for individual children, siblings and/or parents
- contribute information to the statutory assessment process
- advise and support practitioners on individual cases
- monitor provision for individual children/families
- offer family/child therapy
- refer children to other specialists as appropriate.

The *child mental health* team comprises a range of professionals that may include consultant psychiatrists, child psychiatric nurses, child psychiatrists, psychotherapists, counsellors and outreach workers. They can provide:

- assessments and diagnoses
- individual or small-group therapy sessions
- within-home support and advice
- reports to support the statutory assessment process

- support and advice to practitioners
- referrals to other agencies.

The social services department

Practitioners within the SSD will have generic skills but usually work in specialist teams such as child protection, children with disabilities or children and family services. Social workers aim to enable families to help themselves, using professional expertise and resources. If a family is identified as experiencing difficulties providing appropriately for their children, social workers can assess the situation and offer guidance and support, but with the aim that their services will be reduced over a suitable period of time and withdrawn at some point in the future. In such instances, families can self-refer and thus ask specifically for help. In other cases, it may be that the family is reported as being of concern and the social worker(s) will visit the home to offer support and discuss issues and ways forwards if the parents cooperate.

The *social worker* will:

- offer assessments of family situations and subsequent support
- refer to other agencies/provision
- support local child protection procedures
- monitor children and/or families
- advise parents on the range of local supporting agencies
- contribute to the statutory assessment process
- offer direct therapeutic intervention with children.

Voluntary supporting agencies

Voluntary agencies are not directly funded by the local authority and are often registered as charitable organisations, having applied for and gained charitable status. They can be locally and/or nationally based and focus on generic or specialised areas, for example, the National Association of Special Educational Needs (www.nasen.org.uk) and National Autistic Society (www.nas.org.uk).

Voluntary agencies can offer all or some of the following to practitioners and parents alike:

- information, helplines and advice

- publications, from leaflets to books, videos and DVDs

- local support groups, networked nationwide in some instances

- respite care in the local area

- training and resources

- advocacy services

- campaigning for awareness and improved services

- special schools (boarding and day pupils)

- holiday clubs

- research databases

- links to other agencies and services (local and/or national)

- representation on local and/or national committees.

The role of the SENCO

Working together to provide for children's individual needs is required throughout the processes of Early Years Action and Action Plus, as detailed in the Code of Practice: the SENCO in every maintained setting will be responsible for:

- Ensuring liaison with parents and other professionals in respect of children with special educational needs.
- Advising other practitioners in the setting.
- Ensuring that Individual Education Plans are in place.
- Ensuring that relevant background information about individual children with special educational needs is collected, recorded and updated. (DfES, 2001c: s. 4.15)

However, I would add to this list NASEN's key areas of effective SENCO working:

- Qualities:
  - Personal impact and presence
  - A positive response to change
  - Energy, vigour and perseverance
  - Self-confidence
  - Enthusiasm

- Intellectual ability

- Reliability and integrity

- Strategic direction and development

- Supporting teaching and learning

- Managing other adults

- Interpreting data to support pupil progress

- Knowledge of legislation and management of overall provision.
  (Adapted from NASEN, 2008b)

Arguably, the most important aspect of the SENCO role is the over-all management of SEN provision within the setting, including monitoring and evaluation, but the list of additional roles and responsibilities of the SENCO is considerable, raising concerns over time constraints and workload as many SENCOs only take on this role as one part of their full-time working. In some settings, it may be a full-time role but in most it will be a part-time feature of a class-room teacher's role. In 2008, NASEN produced an overview of the 'Working lives of SENCOs' resulting from a survey of 500 SENCOs. The report revealed some illuminating facts:

1 SENCOs working in Early Years tended to have the most limited level of experience.

2 91% of respondents were teachers and 8.6% were not.

3 23% were allocated no time for the role and 2% were allocated 27.5 hours per week.

4 Lack of whole school engagement in writing/revision of SEN pol-icy.

5 Some SENCOs have sole responsibility for IEPs and intriguingly some SENCOs have no involvement in IEPs.

6 74.7% of SENCOs perceived a mismatch between what they think needs to be done and what they actually do.

7 Approximately 68% felt more money was needed to support the children effectively.

The most startling of the above facts appears to be that some SEN-COs are not involved in writing IEPs and that nearly one quarter of respondents were not allocated any additional time for this key role. These facts oppose current policy and suggest there are major prob-lems to overcome for increased success and more effective SENCOs across the UK, ensuring greater success for our young children. Clearly, there are issues to be addressed as a matter of urgency.

In 2008, the government updated the SENCO regulations (DCSF, 2008n) to take effect from September 2009. The regulations require SENCOs in 'relevant' schools (meaning 'a community, foundation or voluntary school or a maintained nursery school' (DCSF, 2008n: 1)) to be qualified teachers or they have two years to gain qualified teacher status. The government then introduced SENCO accreditation (DCSF, 2009o) for newly qualified SENCOs and those that have held the post for less than one year leading up to September 2009. Allowing three years to take the training, practitioners are directed to local training providers for access to relevant courses (www.tda.gov.uk). The guidance offered to training providers (TDA, 2009) clarifies the learning outcomes to be met by the end of this training, focusing on five key areas:

- professional context
- strategic development
- coordinating provision
- leading, developing and supporting colleagues
- working in partnership with pupils, families and other professionals. (TDA, 2009: 17–20)

It is commendable that SENCOs are now to be viewed as members of the strategic management team of their settings, but holding a nationally accredited qualification does not automatically result in increased time to undertake the role, sufficient funding to ensure appropriate provision for all children and clarification on the responsibilities a SENCO takes on board. These issues still need to be addressed.

Portage and Early Support

Portage (www.portage.org) is a home-visiting service for families of pre-school children with special needs, funded in some areas by the local health authority and in others by education. Usually following a referral from the health visitor or consultant paediatrician, a portage worker will visit the family to assess the child's needs using a detailed developmental checklist. From this initial assessment, both short- and long-term targets can be set with the worker visiting the home to work with the child and parent, supporting and monitoring progress based on strategies guided by the developmental checklist. It is anticipated that through initially working with the parent, the worker will, in time, be able to reduce input levels as the parent takes the lead in their child's provision. The parent will complete record sheets and discuss progress with the portage worker, before subsequent targets are jointly devised and planned.

Early Support (DCSF, 2009p) is the government mechanism for:

> delivering integrated services for young disabled children and their families. The programme has successfully developed into a mainstream programme, with 90 per cent of LAs either involved in it or in the early stages of using it to implement service change. As a result of its success, from April 2009, Early Support will migrate to the Department as part of its wider support for disabled children and their families, and will be managed within our wider Aiming High for Disabled Children agenda.

Planning and coordination in early years settings

Perhaps the most important consideration will be the recording systems maintained within settings. In this age of accountability, perhaps more so than ever before, we must ensure that while records should always be thorough, they should not be too cumbersome to maintain. Ease of access to records must be considered, so professionals and parents alike can interpret them easily.

The SENCO should ensure that each professional is fully aware of the roles and responsibilities of his/her colleagues within the setting, which can be supported through regular staff meetings. In addition, settings should have available a central list of agencies within the locality that can be accessed to support the setting's provision. Since the evolution of Children's Trusts, authorities should have a comprehensive list available to parents and professionals alike, but such lists need regular updating to include new and changing details.

The key-worker system will remove some of the responsibility for planning and record keeping from the SENCO as each practitioner will be responsible for the maintenance of the records for their own key-worker children, with the SENCO taking a more advisory and supervisory role. Regular progress reviews will then update practitioners, outside professionals/agencies and parents as to progress achieved and referrals made, over the past few months. The key worker will be selected as the most appropriate member of staff to work with the child, their family and other professionals, and success will depend partly on the trust and equality established within the relationship. The key worker will make sure records are updated and liaise regularly with parents, the SENCO and professionals.

Previously, the relationship between professionals and parents would have been one in which the professionals 'imparted' knowledge and skills to parents but, now, we are working within a more family-centred approach which acknowledges the parents as partners, crucial members of the interagency team and a key influence on the child and therefore future planning. Carpenter (2000a: 140) expands on this: 'The family-centred approach is not a panacea; it will not instantly bring about quality services, but it will reposition the family at the heart of service-delivery as the most informed source of knowledge about the child and its family'.

Factors affecting collaboration

A study examining interagency working was conducted by the National Foundation for Educational Research on behalf of the Local Government Association. The report (Atkinson et al., 2002), examined 30 initiatives and offers:

> analysis and discussion of the different types, or models, of multi-agency activity; the rationale for their development; agencies' and individuals' involvement in multi-agency activities, their roles and professional backgrounds; the impact of multi-agency activities; and the challenges and key factors in their success. (2002: ii)

Relating specifically to the factors affecting collaborative working, the report highlighted five key areas as consistent challenges to effective interagency working systems:

- funding and resources
- roles and responsibilities
- competing priorities
- communication
- professional and agency cultures and management.

These findings concur with those of Roffey (2001), Roaf (2002), Reed and Canning (2010) and Pugh and Duffy (2010) and also link closely to McConkey's (2002) summary of Gulliford's work on the 'less-travelled road'. Roaf (2002: 1) suggested that:

> Although schools and education services (for example, psychologists and education social workers), social services, health professionals, the police and charities all work for children, this work remains notoriously difficult to coordinate and there are often tensions which arise from the different professional and intellectual traditions that characterize these agencies. Boundary disputes

do nothing to help the inclusion of children at school or in the wider society.

More recently, Aubrey (2010: 211) links challenges for interagency working firmly within the discourse of workforce reforms, concluding that:

> reform of the workforce can cause tensions, suspicion and a reluctance to cross boundaries. A climate of organizational change, with policies and procedures focused on improved quality and delivering outcomes to specific targets increases bureaucracy and managerialism. While collaboration is called for, rivalry fed by differences in professional power, status and esteem may exacerbate territorialism and raise concerns about protecting vested interests. Acknowledging existing tensions and imbalances as well as exploring new roles, responsibilities and functions may be prerequisite to workforce reorganization.

This area will be further explored later in this chapter.

Issues for the future

Resources and training

In the current climate of supporting inclusion and dealing with considerable changes, additional funding issues arise for practitioners and local authorities. Settings may need additional resources, material and human, to provide for the needs of individual children or simply to extend current resources to account for greater diversity. There is also a need for ongoing training to ensure practitioners have the necessary skills and knowledge to provide for all children's needs within today's settings, if we are expecting mainstream practitioners to accommodate an expanding range of individual needs. As an example, it could be argued that very specialist knowledge is required to understand and provide appropriately for a young child with autism. If that knowledge does not exist, then practitioners could inadvertently be compromising the child's development. In addition, practitioners should have knowledge of local supporting agencies and professionals trained in such a specialised field to advise, support and perhaps offer staff training. In such a case, there would be an ideal opportunity for the training to be of an interagency nature.

It should be remembered that professionals are rarely trained for interagency working, so, without training planned to cater for professionals from a range of disciplines, the professional and personal skills needed may not exist or develop. Arguably, training sessions which are jointly planned, delivered by a range of professionals, attended by a range of professionals and which allow time for discussions would be the most effective. Such training would ensure that opportunities arose to discuss differing perspectives and profession-specific issues, which should lead to enhanced understanding of differing roles and the issues constraining or enhancing the work.

The SENCO national training (accreditation) is clearly a step in the right direction to ensuring all our SENCOs have relevant and up-to-date knowledge on government strategies and policies as well as effective practice. However, this will add to the existing pressures on time and funding (for studies) as indicated by the NASEN (2008b) report discussed earlier.

Joint planning for individual needs

Practitioners should be involved in joint planning for individual children in order to avoid situations, which still exist today, wherein the 'specialist' undertakes their assessments or intervention devoid of reference to the everyday provision within the setting and/or the family. Any input must be seen as a part of a complete package of provision, with components supporting and complementing each other, not working independently. Through regular meetings to discuss future targets and strategies to be used, joint discussions should occur to provide coherent provision linked to each aspect of the child's life. It is hoped that the introduction of the CAF may simplify and consolidate this process as it should ensure that all relevant information regarding a child's needs will be input centrally onto the CAF so any professional involved with the child will be aware of others that are involved and what support is in place. However, time will be needed before a meaningful review of the success of the CAF is likely to emerge. Additionally, in my role as a lecturer I work with many early years practitioners and in my sessions it is clear that very few practitioners are engaging with the CAF and, even more alarming, some have not heard of it. So clearly there are issues to be addressed.

Differing professional cultures

Each discipline will have their own philosophies, policies and working practices but these do not need to be totally diverse and practitioners do not need to 'protect' their own professional culture. Through sharing our perspectives and aims, greater awareness and understanding combined with mutual respect should emerge, but this presents its own challenges as summarised by Messenger:

Multi-agency working is often complex due to a coming together of different organizational and professional cultures and working practices. This may lead to difficulties related to a person's role, understanding the professional language of others, and ensuring responsibility and accountability of team members. (2010: 129)

Recent government initiatives to support increasing interagency working do appear to acknowledge the need to break down any professional boundaries to ensure a 'seamless' service for young children and their families, but this is not as straightforward as may first appear.

Workforce issues

Workforce reforms in the early years have long been called for and at last we are beginning to see some progress in this area under the guidance of the Children's Workforce Development Council (CWDC). Within the early years, perhaps one of the most significant areas of change relates to the Early Years Professional Status (EYPS) training which is available nationwide. Before this development, we had a range of qualifications across CACHE diplomas, National Vocational Qualifications (NVQs), Foundation Degrees (aimed at non-traditional university entrants with working experience in the early years) and BA honours degrees in Early Years or Early Childhood Studies (for more academic study). Over the last ten years, significant changes have been made but these have also brought confusion and challenges, fuelled by the speed of changes. Particularly within my own sector of Higher Education Institutions (HEIs), it takes time to rewrite programmes and proceed through quality procedures prior to commencing the courses. So with national direction changing regularly, we are constantly playing 'catch-up'. A useful example is that of the BA degrees which were originally designed to provide academic study only. Direction then suggested that practice elements needed to be included to give graduates credibility in the early years workplace so Practitioner Options were introduced. Now we are in a situation where we are encouraged to consider attaching EYPS on to the final year of our BA honours degree so graduates have evidence of thorough and detailed academic study combined with meeting the EYPS standards, placing them in a much better position regarding job prospects. All of this has happened in a relatively short space of time and created issues for staff, students and the early years workforce.

Regarding EYPS, the initial suggestion was that EYPS would be equivalent to Qualified Teacher Status (QTS) but this has since been eroded and the achievement of EYPS grants status but nothing more. So issues of pay, status and respect for early years practitioners still remain as contentious and unresolved issues which must be addressed. This should be achieved through a prolonged and carefully debated process.

Referral systems

Currently, referral systems are predominantly profession-based, depending on the professional identifying or diagnosing. For example, if the health visitor identifies a child's difficulty then a referral to the consultant paediatrician may follow, both clearly health-authority-based. Recommendations may include attendance at an early years setting which could be education-based, so perhaps there is an opportunity for greater centralisation of the referral system.

In many areas, there will be local interagency teams which meet to jointly plan future provision for individual children, following the initial diagnostic process. With input from the full range of professionals, conflicting issues can be dealt with at an early stage thus reducing time and ensuring more appropriate provision. However, professional boundaries and budgets may still impede this process, although it is hoped that the CAF will ease this process and lead to increased awareness of all professionals involved with specific children.

Summary

Interagency working has developed considerably, but issues and barriers to effective working practice still exist. The benefits to children, parents, families, early years practitioners and professionals from all disciplines are clear, so addressing these issues is of paramount importance. Changes should continue at ground level, local authority and national level to ensure the 'seamless' service we are striving for and to unify approaches. Such changes will need to be in line with the requirements of the government's range of legislation and guidance.

With greater collaboration and cooperation between practitioners, we will enhance the service we offer to parents and children alike. Parents of children with special needs already have a range of difficulties and challenges to face, but with a more unified approach to provision and effective use of the key-worker system we can, hopefully, support their needs more effectively.

Working more collaboratively with colleagues will extend our own skills and expertise, enable us to understand differing professional perspectives, roles and responsibilities, and improve our interventions with children, so our personal and professional gains will also be considerable. However, commitment and belief in the positive outcomes of interagency working from national policy level must be continued to ensure success. As Gasper (2010) concluded:

> We can and must 'get it right'. For the sake of future generations we cannot afford to lose the potential of a single child. We need the separate skills of the different parts of the Health sector, Social Care and support, Education and Community Development to enable children, parents, families and communities to reduce dependency and to achieve their potential. Experience shows it is better achieved through partnership than in isolation. Sharing, listening, valuing and respecting each other's points of view has been shown to produce innovation and more effective ways to meet individual and local needs, as well as enabling nationally identified areas to be addressed. (2010: 128)

Key issues

- Practitioners should acknowledge the benefits of interagency working.
- Positive commitment to interagency working is needed from policy level to practitioner level.
- Areas still requiring development include funding, resources, training and organisational structures.
- Respect between colleagues from differing disciplines is essential to help remove professional boundaries.
- Time management must allow for regular liaison roles.
- Workforce issues need resolution.

Points for reflection

- Make a list of all the outside professionals you are currently working with and ensure you have an understating of their roles and responsibilities. If possible, consider holding regular forum meetings to discuss common issues.
- How does your setting work with other professionals? Do you feel this could be improved in any way and, if so, formulate an action plan to ensure positive changes.
- Identify the current barriers and challenges to working more effectively with other professionals and discuss ways to implement positive changes.

Suggested further reading

Aubrey, C. (2010) 'Leading and working in multi-agency teams', in G. Pugh and B. Duffy (eds) *Contemporary Issues in the Early Years*, 5th edn. London: Sage.

Gasper, M. (2010) *Multi-agency Working in the Early Years.* London: Sage.

Roaf, C. (2002) *Coordinated Services for Included Children: Joined Up Action.* Buckingham: Open University Press.

Inclusive education for young children

Chapter objectives

To develop awareness of:

• the history of inclusive provision
• arguments for and against inclusive provision
• issues and barriers.

Introduction

Historically, early years settings have been accommodating of all children and have sought to provide effectively for each child, but in the present climate of increasing inclusion, demands on early years settings are even greater. It could be suggested that early years settings, with reduced adult:child ratios compared to schools, are better placed to provide for individual or personalised needs. However, many issues still need addressing and it is these issues that are identified and explored in this chapter using theory and research to support and inform debate. Using poverty as an example, implications for practitioners are raised and practical strategies suggested.

Perhaps the inclusive society we strive for, with its inclusive education system, is now nearer to becoming a reality. However, others might argue that the reality is still a distance away and that in the fields of early years and special education, we have to face considerable challenges to achieve total inclusion. In addition, effective provision for all children within all early years settings could be deemed unrealistic or feasible. Arguments and debate on such views will be raised.

Issues surrounding government legislation and guidance are examined and confusions highlighted. For example, within one of the guidance documents for schools, *Inclusive Schooling*, the introduction claims that:

> The Act seeks to enable more pupils who have special educational needs to be included successfully within mainstream education. This clearly signals that where parents want a mainstream education for their child everything possible should be done to provide it. Equally where parents want a special school place their wishes should be listened to and taken into account. (DfES, 2001a: 1)

This clearly indicates a need for special schools, so are we aiming for an inclusive education system or a system with some segregation but mostly inclusion? If the government continues to produce documents on 'Special Educational Needs' such as the *Special Educational Needs Code of Practice* (DfES, 2001c), *Special Educational Needs Toolkit* (DfES, 2001d) and *Inclusive Schooling: Children with Special Educational Needs* (DfES, 2001a), then immediately there is a conflict of philosophies. If there is a need to produce such guidance, then the government is highlighting the separate nature of provision for children with special needs and/or disabilities. In a truly inclusive system, should we not expect guidance purely on early years practice, primary practice and secondary practice, as this would automatically inform appropriate provision for all children regardless of ethnic background, culture and/or special need? Runswick-Cole and Hodge raise the same issues considering that:

> The language of current policy which focuses on children who are 'special' and in 'need' emphasizes individual deficits and, therefore, plays a part in constructing and sustaining exclusionary practice. (2009: 200)

Historical development and legislation

While Chapter 1 explored the history of special needs provision, this section will focus on the history and development of inclusion within early years education and care. Over the years, but most specifically in the last decade, the availability of research and literature regarding inclusion has increased tremendously. After the Warnock Report (DES, 1978), integration became a key debating issue which has since progressed to movements towards an inclusive education system for all children.

Back as far as 1913, the Mental Deficiency Act placed a requirement on local authorities to identify children aged between 7 and 16 who were deemed 'ineducable' owing to the severity of their difficulties. Many of these children were then placed in institutions and lived out their lives there. At this stage, segregation was clearly evident and reflected the philosophies of the time.

Following the 1944 Education Act (Ministry of Education, 1944), more teachers were trained to teach children with learning difficulties, but some children were still deemed ineducable and were classified as mentally handicapped, having their needs addressed by the health authorities. The segregated approach therefore continued.

Perhaps the greatest changes came after the 1970 Education Act when LEAs took responsibility for all children of statutory school age and an increased range of segregated provision arose in the UK to address the needs of all children classified as incapable of coping with mainstream schooling. At this time, medical input was still a key influence. Following the Act, an increased range of special schools emerged and debate began regarding the most appropriate ways of educating children who were not able to be catered for in mainstream schools. This debate continued until the establishment of a Committee of Enquiry to examine the education of children and young people with learning difficulties. This committee, chaired by Mary Warnock, produced its report known as the 'Warnock Report', in 1978, which was seen by many as an influential turning point for special education and special educational provision. The report offered a continuum of special educational needs as opposed to specific categories such as educationally subnormal (ESN) and moderate learning difficulties (MLD).

The ensuing Education Act (1981) adopted many of Warnock's recommendations for special education, however, there were many critics. The Act introduced the statementing process through which children with special educational needs were assessed by the LEA and a statement of their needs produced, indicating the provision required to meet their needs. Following this, and the fact that parents had no means of appealing against LEA decisions, parents' groups such as Network 81 (named after the Act) were established to lobby government, support other parents and to address the many issues that emerged in subsequent years regarding the legislation.

Another issue raised at the time was that of training. Many writers, such as Gulliford (1981), felt it was important that all teachers should receive input regarding provision for children with special needs in their initial training and that specialist courses should be available to existing teachers extending their knowledge and expertise to provide for children with special educational needs. At the same time, however, it was generally felt that the Warnock Report raised awareness of key issues and the beginnings of inclusion, and was therefore a positive.

The Code of Practice (DfEE, 1994) followed the 1993 Education Act and introduced the five-staged approach to the identification and assessment of special educational needs, culminating, if appropriate, in a statement of special educational needs produced by the LEA. In the revised Code of Practice (DfES, 2001c), this has been updated to a graduated approach which in the early years equates to Early Years Action and Early Years Action Plus.

In the same year, the international *Salamanca Statement on Principles, Policy and Practice in Special Needs Education* (UNESCO, 1994) was produced, supported by over 90 governments, including the UK, and indicating total commitment to inclusive education. Regarding children's rights, the statement clarifies that children with special educational needs should all have access to mainstream schools which can respond appropriately to their needs. Within the UK, this was closely followed by a government Green Paper *Excellence for All: Meeting Special Educational Needs*, clearly indicating an intention to move towards greater inclusion, with fewer children in segregated, special school provision:

> The ultimate purpose of SEN provision is to enable young people to flourish in adult life. There are therefore strong educational, as well as social and moral, grounds for educating children with SEN with their peers. We aim to increase the level and quality of inclusion within mainstream schools, while protecting and enhancing specialist provision for those who need it. (DfEE, 1997: 43)

The Special Education Needs and Disability Act (SENDA) 2001 (DfES, 2001b) has an underlying philosophy of inclusion. The supporting guidance document, *Inclusive Schooling: Children with Special Educational Needs* (DfES) details the current situation:

> The Special Educational Needs and Disability Act 2001 delivers a strengthened right to a mainstream education for children with special educational needs. The Act seeks to enable more pupils who have special educational needs to be included successfully within mainstream education. (2001a: 1)

The *Index for Inclusion* (Booth and Ainscow, 2002) was circulated to all schools by the DfEE as 'a way of improving schools according to inclusive values. It is a practical document, setting out what inclusion means for all aspects of schools' (Booth and Ainscow, 2002: 1).

The Index offered their model as a process that schools could work through to improve inclusive practices. This was followed by the *Index for Inclusion: Early Years and Childcare* (Booth and Ainscow, 2004) which was a revised version of the original Index written specifically for early years settings.

Since the advent of the SENDA in 2001, government initiatives have continued but have had a clearer focus on achieving success for all children, which automatically includes those with special needs. Every Child Matters, the Children Acts, Removing Barriers to Achievement, EYFS, IDP and Early Support are examples which all focus on changing the face of provision across the board, yet inclusive provision is implicit within each. A more recent government view was highlighted in the Government Response to the Education and Skills Committee Report on Special Educational Needs (HM Parliament):

> The government shares the Committee's view that inclusion is about the quality of a child's experience and providing access to a high quality education which enables them to make progress in their learning and participate fully in the activities of their school and community. (2006d: s. 28, p. 25)

Definitions and models

Models of disability have changed over the years to accommodate increased knowledge and beliefs informed by research. To appreciate and understand inclusion, practitioners need to be aware of two key models: the medical model and the social model.

The medical model

This model establishes a diagnosis of a condition and recommends the 'cure' or treatment. It does not reflect on the individual under diagnosis but focuses on the condition and assumes that treatment or special provision will ameliorate the difficulties. The child is seen as having a problem and being the problem, and the outcome is often removal from the family and community for treatment or to special provision. This model clearly labels and segregates.

The social model

In contrast, the social model perceives every individual as a part of the social community and, therefore, is more inclusive. Society has created considerable barriers which prohibit those with special needs and/or disabilities from full participation in that society. The social model acknowledges that barriers should be removed to enable access for all members of the community in all aspects of their chosen life. Crow, a disabled feminist, claims that:

> I was being dis-abled – my capabilities and opportunities were being restricted – by prejudice, discrimination, inaccessible environments and inadequate support. For years now, this social model of disability has enabled me to confront, survive and even surmount countless situations of exclusion and discrimination. It has been my mainstay. (2003: 135)

Over the past 100 years, we have slowly progressed from the medical model of identifying and supporting special needs to a more inclusive system, which is aiming for the social model of total inclusion for individuals within our society.

Definitions of inclusion

Perhaps the most helpful source of information is the Centre for Studies on Inclusive Education (CSIE, 2010a) which concluded that inclusion involves: 'the processes of increasing the participation of students in, and reducing their exclusion from, the cultures, curricula and communities of local schools'.

Within this definition, inclusion is seen as a gradual and developing process working towards inclusion for all pupils so individual settings, schools and LEAs will be at different stages of the process but striving toward the same end. The CSIE highlights the difference between integration and inclusion, which supports our understanding. Integration is viewed as moving a child into a different environment and then adapting to accommodate his/her needs, while inclusion exists where all children have a right to be able to access all facilities offered and are therefore a part of that community. The CSIE position for the future (2010a) is: 'full inclusion means the deconstruction and eventual closure of separate special schools, the transfer of resources to the mainstream and the restructuring of ordinary schools'.

An alternative view is offered by Farrell (2001: 7): 'For inclusion to be effective pupils must actively belong to, be welcomed by and participate in a school and community – that is they should be fully included'.

In summary, inclusion within early years settings is a process by which *all* children can access, at all times, all aspects of the provision. It is not a process in which practitioners welcome a child and adapt the curriculum and/or resources to provide for that child, rather that the inclusive setting will automatically be catering for individual needs and will therefore offer effective provision to every child. Provision will not offer deficit services that adapt to meet perceived or identified deficits within children but will offer equality and entitlement to all children.

Common principles of early years practice, as identified by Blenkin (1994) and Bruce (1987) among others, have now been likened to the principles suggested for inclusion in educational settings. Lloyd concludes that:

> High-quality, effective early years education can clearly be seen, then, to provide a vitally important foundation stone for the whole of education, for all children. An education system which built upon this firm foundation and used its principles as a model to underpin the policy, provision and organisation of further levels to develop a genuinely inclusive education for all, clearly would offer real access to educational opportunity to all as an entitlement. (Lloyd, 1997: 178)

Therefore for early years settings, the gap between existing and inclusive practices should not be too great. With increased knowledge and funding, effective inclusion for all children can be understood and should be feasible. These and other relevant issues will be discussed further later.

Principles

If practitioners are required to work towards an inclusive system, then we need to be clear on the underlying principles that inform our work, such as:

- access for all children in their local settings
- full participation for all children in all aspects of the provision
- appropriate opportunities for individual children to work towards their full potential
- the breaking down of barriers to access and participation
- the right to belong to the local community
- respect for all individuals.

On the other hand, the Inclusive Schooling guidance document (DfES) suggests that practitioners should use the following as 'key principles':

- Inclusion is a process by which settings and authorities develop their cultures, policies and practices to include pupils.
- With the right training, strategies and support nearly all children with special educational needs can be successfully included in mainstream education.
- An inclusive education service offers excellence and choice and incorporates the views of parents and children.
- The interests of all pupils must be safeguarded.
- All involved should actively seek to remove barriers to learning and participation.
- All children should have access to an appropriate education.
- Mainstream education will not always be right for every child all of the time. (2001a: 2)

Reasons for inclusion

If we include young children within our early years settings and they are able to progress with their neighbourhood peers to primary and secondary schools, then we will be offering them a more inclusive future. Their perceptions of each other will be influenced by individual characteristics and personalities rather than abilities, disabilities, culture or race and they will all be members of a society which has shared equal opportunities throughout childhood and will therefore expect the same in adulthood. This should ultimately lead to considerable and positive societal changes of attitudes and values. If we segregate young children with special needs from their local friends, we are encouraging a segregated existence from a very early age. All children have the right to be treated equally, valued and respected and it is difficult to satisfy these requirements in a segregated society. The benefits to individuals and wider society will be wide-ranging but should help to break down barriers and encourage greater tolerance and understanding, thus valuing diversity. As Chizea et al. suggest:

> Pre-schools are part of their local community, the focus very often of community involvement and support. The pre-school model of society, in which all members have something to offer and in which all members can find the level of support they need, can provide an inclusive approach to the needs of all children. (1999: 5)

In an inclusive early years setting, all children, including those with special needs, should therefore be able to develop positive attitudes to all children and to their learning environment, confidence, motivation to learn and positive self-concepts. Each child will be valued and acknowledged as a unique individual and his/her needs (special or otherwise) will be addressed appropriately through careful planning and the introduction of relevant, meaningful and personalised tasks and experiences. For those children experiencing difficulties, every causal factor and variable must be reflected upon before targets can be set and opportunities presented; this includes consideration of the affective as well as curricular needs of individual children. McTavish agrees with this philosophy, concluding that:

> What children need, whether they have a developmental problem or not, is to be treated as individuals in the light of their own unique, individual needs. Our focus on finding diagnostic labels obscures this and carries costs. It is time to step back and ask just how useful this approach really is. (2006: 22)

The CSIE (2010b) again offer their own suggestions as to why practitioners should support inclusive practices:

Ten reasons for inclusion:

- All children have the right to learn together.

- Children should not be devalued or discriminated against.

- Disabled adults, describing themselves as special school survivors, are demanding an end to segregation.

- There are no legitimate reasons to separate children for their education. Children belong together, with advantages and benefits for everyone. They do not need to be protected from each other.

- Research shows children do better, academically and socially, in integrated settings.

- There is no teaching or care that cannot take place in an ordinary school.

- Given commitment and support, inclusive education is a more efficient use of educational resources.

- Segregation teaches children to be fearful, ignorant and breeds injustice.

- All children need an education that will help them develop relationships and prepare them for life in the mainstream.

- Only inclusion has the potential to reduce fear and to build friendship, respect and understanding.

Enabling inclusion in early years settings

Perhaps the most obvious requirement enabling inclusive education in our early years settings is that of the commitment and support of staff and parents. All involved must be aware of further changes that could be made which will be informed by the acknowledgement of the benefits of real inclusion for all. Although the process may seem daunting, many early years settings already incorporate many features of inclusion, so when further explored the changes required may not be as great as originally thought.

If we consider some key features of inclusive practice, the existing similarities with good early years practice should emerge:

1 Awareness and understanding of inclusive practices, including legislation and guidance.

2 Commitment and support of parents and staff.

3 Effective inclusive education policy.

4 Respect of each individual involved with the setting (children and adults).

5 Physical access for all children and adults.

6 Access to all learning opportunities and resources.

7 An appropriate curriculum to support individual learning.

8 The use of teaching strategies to give all children access to learning opportunities.

9 The effective use of support staff and the SENCO to enhance inclusion and reduce withdrawal and thus segregation.

10 Effective planning and monitoring of progress.

11 Effective policies for responding to special educational needs and affective developmental needs.

12 Removal of the use of labels.

13 Positive parental partnerships.

14 Positive interagency working practices.

15 Positive adult role models.

To ensure each of these aims is met, practitioners will need to reflect on planning, monitoring and recording systems, the curriculum, the use of teaching support and physical access issues. This may result in the emergence of issues regarding training and/or funding which the setting will clearly need to address.

The Organisation for Economic Co-operation and Development (OECD) continues to instigate research into making inclusion work in mainstream settings in eight countries: Australia, Canada, Germany, the UK, the USA, Italy, Denmark and Iceland. The findings of these studies have resulted in ten key points deemed central to the inclusion process, which can be summarised as follows:

- All involved with education are to accept the responsibility of educating all children.

- Schools should be set up to be flexible learning environments, that are able to adapt, be inclusive, and have secure funding and effective training regimes.

- Teachers need to have the ability to adapt learning situations to accommodate the needs of all children.

- There is a recognised need for initial and ongoing training.

- There should be teacher recognition of the limitations of their own knowledge and skills and readiness to call in specialist support.

- There is a need for specialists to be prepared to support teachers.

- There needs to be an involvement of the whole community.

- There is a need for public accountability.

- Funding issues should be addressed.

- There should be leadership at government level for the development of effective policies. (Adapted from Evans, 2000: 37–8)

What we should remember is that in the early years we observe children, we know their abilities and strengths, we know what skill they need to develop next and can plan for this learning. We then put this intervention into place and assess the success or otherwise. This process applies to all children, including those with special needs, so sound, basic early years practice is also good special needs practice. It is not rocket science but is personalised planning which is likely to lead to success for the child. However, we must also remember that to include all children, our planning should always begin from the child and all the factors that impact on his/her learning. If we start from the demands and requirements of the EYFS and plan from the EYFS, we are less likely to reap rewards and are more likely to demotivate the child. As an example, a young boy loves playing with cars, lorries, buses and trains and we want to help him learn his colours, so it makes sense to play a game around parking all the cars of the same colour in different areas of the car park. If we tried to teach the colours using counters, matching games or threading buttons, we are less likely to see success as these are not the child's preferred activities.

The inclusion process will be ongoing and depend at times on outside agencies, for example, for the resolution of policy, training and funding issues. However, settings should ensure children their right to belong and be equal.

Issues and barriers

Early years practitioners need to be aware of these issues and potential barriers in order to succeed, but also need to reflect on the barriers to education and full participation from the children's perspectives.

The speed of change and practitioner concerns

If one of the key principles for effective inclusion is that of support of all staff involved, then clearly teacher commitment is essential. It could be suggested, however, that some teachers and early years practitioners may be concerned about the speed of recent educational changes that have been implemented, as well as having concerns about realistically being able to provide for the needs of all the children all the time while still delivering the curriculum, completing planning and recording documentation and satisfying external quality monitoring agencies. The demands are considerable and arguably unrealistic, especially when you consider that some of the learning and policy changes can only be accessed online and practitioners are not generally given time to explore them. How then can we expect them to transfer the key information into effective practice in an informed manner? At the end of the day, those that suffer will be the young children themselves and their families.

We also need to be aware that although guidance documents are stating certain practices are occurring, the circumstances have to be such that practitioners are enabled to respond to these. They will not just exist because the documentation says so!

Workforce and qualification reforms have also created confusion among early years practitioners as the vast array of qualifications linked to early years working are considerable and equivalency is not easy to match across, up or down the qualifications maze. The desire for clearer and improved qualifications is interlinked with the desire for respect and status of the workforce. 'Childcare', as the work is often referred to, is a highly skilled responsibility requiring a range of knowledge, expertise and skills and is not an 'easy option'. Those students following Early Childhood Studies degrees (ECS) or EYPS will be all too aware of the depth and breadth of knowledge required to achieve the award. Gasper concludes that:

> The need for all countries to invest in early education and care and to improve the workforce qualification levels and status are among the key findings from Starting Strong II (2006), an OECD report on 20 countries from the developed world. (2010: 112)

However, it could be suggested that over the past few years, ideas have emerged, been sent out to tender (with a very short timescale) and set in place in an equally short timescale. This raises questions about the depth of planning and informed research that has fed into these crucial developmental processes and therefore the quality of the emerging qualifications. Before these qualifications have become well established, we seem to have a new development heading out to tender, working within slightly altered goalposts. The result is simply further confusion and what is needed is a halt to any further developments and a thorough review of existing qualifications, including feedback from secondary school pupils, the early years workforce, local authorities, FEIs, HEIs and parents. If this was supported by a detailed examination of existing qualifications against quality standards, then we may be able to see a clearer direction ahead. Rapid changes however must be stopped.

Surely, what would be preferable would be a clear path of a limited number of qualifications with a range of stages where candidates can step in and at a later stage, step out, knowing they can return at a later date to continue their professional development. If this process (which would take some time) coincided with a review of pay structures for the early years, we would hopefully be more likely to have a clear career progression pathway leading to a qualification that would demand respect and status. Clearly, this would also be of tremendous benefit to all the children and families we work with and may well begin to address the lack of male early years practitioners.

Parental perspectives

Current legislation rightly offers parents a voice in the choice of school for their child, however there are many instances where this choice is diminished. Perhaps sensationalised by media, there are suggestions that children are being refused places at their chosen schools for a range of reasons. Some would suggest that the effects of the league tables and schools' accountability force some schools to be selective about their intake. For children with specific difficulties, it may be that their parents would prefer the child to be educated away from home at a specialist school in another county and are asking their own county to fund this. Practitioners need to be aware of such issues, but without significant research and clear governmental guidance (or legislation) the issues cannot be addressed and resolved.

The Advisory Centre for Education offers leaflets to parents to advise on a range of issues but regarding school choice clarify that:

> The LEA must agree to the particular maintained, mainstream or special school you want unless it can show one of the following:
> - The school is unsuitable for your child's age, ability and aptitude and the special educational needs set out in part of the statement
> - Your child's attendance would not be a good use of resources (e.g. money, staff, facilities, transport)
> - Your child's attendance would seriously affect the education of other children at the school. (ACE, 2005b: 7)

While this indicates support of parental choice, it can be seen that their choices can be, and are on occasions, overruled as the terms in which the criteria are presented make it difficult to present a reasoned argument. For example, how does one define 'good use of resources'? Further, Flewitt and Nind's research into parental perspectives highlighted that:

> some parents reported they had no real choices, or very limited choices, for a variety of reasons, including geographical location and the approach of the local educational authority (LEA) towards the funding and allocation of places for children with special educational needs. Parents had also received conflicting advice from local authority, education, health and care professionals. (2007: 429)

There are systems in place to support parents of children with special educational needs who are unhappy about the selected school for their child, including the local Parental Partnership schemes and tribunals. In addition, organisations such as the Advisory Centre for Education would be a useful source of support and information. The SENDA (DfES, 2001b) supports parental choice but the reality does not always match this governmental intention.

Children's views

Legislation and government strategies all support the view that we, as professionals and parents, need to listen to and truly 'hear' the voices of the children themselves and take this into account in our planning and provision. This is arguably most important for children with special needs and/or disabilities as we, as adults and experts (parents or professionals), seem to feel that we know what is best for the child. However, a growing body of research suggests otherwise and much can be learnt from the voices of children, young people and adults with special needs when they discuss the provision they are receiving or have received in their childhood. Jones (2005) reports that:

> One boy with cerebral palsy describes how others assume he is helpless and unable to understand anything. They talk to people beside him about him rather than addressing him directly. It is their pity he appears most irritated about: '*Many people feel sorry for me, which I don't think is right. I'm stuck with it and people feeling sorry for me isn't going to do anything for me or for them*' (Somo-gyvary, cited in Murray & Penman, 1996: 30).

Clearly then, we need to find effective ways to incorporate the child's views into our assessments, planning and provision as their views are crucial to their own holistic provision.

Funding and training

Funding appears to be a recurring issue within early years, and funding to support inclusion is no exception. Areas for consideration and issues of concern have been raised throughout the chapters of this book and funding is often present as an influential factor. One of the problems within early years is the diversity of provision and if we take the two examples of a nursery class attached to, and partly funded by, a mainstream school and a self-funding pre-school, then differences will become clear. Staff working under the school management will be able to access a range of training that will invariably be funded by the school if the relevance and appropriateness of the course is apparent. However, for pre-schools, funds for training may be limited or even non-existent. This issue needs addressing.

As we have already identified, early years practitioners need the knowledge, skills and expertise to provide for the individual needs of a range of children with special needs, so appropriate and quality assured training should be accessible to all early years practitioners if inclusion is to succeed. The theme of access to appropriate training is further supported in current legislation and guidance, and it is hoped that the move towards more integrated settings will help reduce and eliminate issues of funding for training purposes. Similarly, if the Children's Workforce Strategy attains its goals then more highly qualified early years practitioners should emerge, each having had access to training courses of high quality that ensure provision and working practice will be of equally high standards. Additionally, early years practitioners are now faced with increasing numbers of children with special needs in mainstream settings and yet the level of training they have regarding special needs and/or disability issues is often limited. As Carpenter summarises:

> There is a plethora of one-day courses designed to brief professionals on these new initiatives in policy, but in practice, are there enough professionals on the ground? What we lack in the UK is any rigorous, accredited training in early childhood intervention – courses that offer focused study and that draw together the best in early childhood education, together with our knowledge of the development of very young children with disability. (2005: 181)

This issue is also linked to the problems surrounding the early years workforce reforms and the reworking of the qualifications framework discussed earlier and until these are resolved I do not anticipate great strides being made in the key areas, rather that further confusion is likely.

The use of learning support assistants

The way in which learning support assistants (LSAs) are used and funded will greatly influence the success of inclusive practices. Many learning support workers are not qualified teachers, but in many instances the expectations that are placed on them are considerable and their success rates are to be commended. Although they receive the lowest pay and work under the guidance of the class or setting teacher/manager, they often demonstrate the greatest knowledge and effective practice for the individual children they work with. It could be suggested that, if a support worker is working with a child with Down's syndrome, he/she should have, as a minimum, knowledge of child development, special educational needs and Down's syndrome. In my experience, this is not always the case. Again training, and thus funding, are the issues to be addressed.

As inclusive education becomes more widespread, the skills and expertise within existing special facilities could be accessed and used effectively via a range of training and outreach work to ensure that support workers have the necessary skills to provide for the needs of all children and support the practitioners, but this needs to be in a coordinated and structured manner across the country. This would ensure that minimum national standards are met.

To support full inclusion, settings also need to reflect on the use of support workers, as it is important that support workers and practitioners work together to plan in a coordinated manner to ensure consistency for the child. It could be suggested that there is no longer a place for withdrawing a child into a separate area for individual work with a support worker, but there are occasions when withdrawal may be appropriate. However, there would need to be joint planning to ensure transference of skills and cohesion.

A positive outlook for early years

It can be seen that a range of issues may emerge when practitioners address the new guidance and work towards greater inclusion within their settings. These issues will all need addressing, whether at local or national level. I do not want to infer that inclusion is not feasible because there are too many barriers to be overcome. I consider inclusion is achievable, and that early years practitioners are more than capable of offering inclusion, acknowledging that successful inclusion already occurs in many settings. However, this will not be the case for all settings and will therefore depend on, firstly, the acknowledgement of potential barriers and, secondly, the motivation and support (practical and financial) to address those issues for those settings.

Lewis (2000) highlighted some important concerns with regard to inclusion, which may offer some food for thought for many practitioners. He suggests that terminology has moved from 'inclusive education' to 'inclusion', of which I am guilty within this chapter, and his concern is that we are forgetting the 'education' element of inclusion. He contends that if we are aiming to include all children within our current education system, then there is an assumption that the current education system is successful and positive, provides for all children and therefore should be available to more children. Lewis questions this assumption: if the existing system is successful then why are so many children being excluded from primary and secondary schools? If it is suggested that the existing system is not necessarily appropriate for all, then should we not be focusing on improving that system before opening it up to possibly more vulnerable children? While this may not seem appropriate within an early years book, it could be suggested that as early years build the foundations for that later learning then the issues are relevant.

Including disadvantaged children

As with any other individual need, practitioners need to be aware of the specific implications of disadvantage within an early years setting but at the same time focus on the needs of the individual child and family as opposed to the label of disadvantage. As discussed throughout this book, the most important practitioner attributes will be to reflect on a child's individual needs within the context of the setting and the family, and then to identify the most appropriate approaches. These would be developed through a process of spending time getting to know the child and family, undertaking observations, reviewing previous assessments and reports, and talking to his/her parents. From this point, the staff and parents can discuss possible strategies, outline SMART targets for future intervention and agree a review date. Then the work can begin.

However, it would be preferable for the practitioners involved to be aware of the effects of disadvantage on young children to inform their understanding of the child and the family, as well as informing planning. This should enable reflection on the child's affective development as well as general and academic development.

The limitations of the context of this chapter mean that only a snapshot of disadvantage can be presented, so I recommend that readers further their knowledge through the suggested reading and bibliography.

Background information on disadvantage

As a starting point, it is worth highlighting that in 1994 the UK had the highest child poverty rates of all the European Union countries. In addition, the Department of Social Security statistics (2000) revealed that between 1994 and 1998–99, the number of children being brought up in homes where the income was below half the national average increased over threefold, rising from 10 per cent to 35 per cent. More recently, Jose informed us that:

> In 2001 there were 14.8 million children living in the UK (National Statistics, 2004). The number living in households below 60% of median income was 3.8 million, 26% of all children (New Policy Institute, 2004). Tackling poverty may be high on the political agenda but eradicating it is not going to be straightforward. (2005: 22–3)

If the implications of this are related to early years provision, then clearly they are far reaching. Bradshaw suggests reasons for this increase:

> Our family demography does not help; a comparatively high fertility rate, low age of first marriage, high divorce rate, low mean age of child-bearing, high birth-rate outside marriage, high proportion of lone parents, high proportion of

cohabiting couples, high proportion of families with three or more children (Ditch et al., 1998). All these factors are likely to be associated with high rates of child poverty. (Bradshaw, 2001: 15)

Generally speaking, children classified as living in poverty are likely to live in temporary or council-owned properties which tend to be concentrated in large estates. Thus, the effects of poverty will affect early years settings in such areas far more than other areas of the UK. It is for this reason that the original Sure Start centres were established in areas of poverty and deprivation. However, in my experience there are many local authorities that also own rural properties which can be isolating.

The government implemented funding to a range of initiatives such as Sure Start, changes to the welfare benefits system and encouraging mothers to return to work in an attempt to remove 1 million children from deprived environments, although this is still yet to be achieved. Meanwhile, practitioners will need to support these vulnerable children.

The impact and outcomes of poverty

The outcomes of poverty can be devastating, long term and part of an ongoing cyclical process. Hooper et al.'s study, *Living with Hardship 24/7* (2007), focused specifically on the real issues facing families and identified six areas where significant changes were needed:

- Benefits: extended eligibility for access to benefits.
- Schools: extended eligibility for subsidised school activities.
- Housing: more access to low-cost housing to reduce overcrowding, poor housing conditions and inappropriate use of temporary accommodation.
- Transport: increased access to cheap or free public transport.
- Support services: services in the homes; childcare for parents under stress; support for children with behavioural difficulties; increase of counselling and support services; more rapid response for children experiencing abuse.
- Training: to enable all professionals to engage with young children and listen to their views and to recognise the many ways in which poverty impacts on families' lives. (Adapted from Hooper et al., 2007: 9–10)

Research has highlighted key links between poverty and child mortality rates, child abuse, child homelessness, teenage pregnancies, teenage drug and alcohol abuse, crime and violence, child mental health, suicide, antisocial behaviour and poor educational achievement (see Bradshaw, 2001). While schools cannot and should not be held responsible for resolving these issues, practitioners can certainly work to improve the outcomes for disadvantaged children.

The cost of poverty to the country is vast, as summarised by the Joseph Rowntree Foundation (Hirsch, 2008: 1) who concluded that: 'child poverty costs the country at least £25 billion a year, including £17 billion that could accrue to the Exchequer if child poverty were eradicated'. The facts speak for themselves – the economic impact on the country is quite staggering and the impact on the children and families themselves is immeasurable, so clearly this issue must be addressed as a matter of great urgency.

Education and poverty

Having identified the magnitude of the issue, we need to highlight the importance of effective educational opportunities to support children living in poverty and increase their chances of climbing out of poverty in the future.

The current cycle of many deprived children involves the links between academic performance and future career prospects. Clearly, if a young person leaves school with few or no qualifications (academic or vocational), then the opportunities for gaining employment will be limited. Thus, the cycle continues. This complex issue is compounded by the fact that many children from disadvantaged backgrounds become disillusioned with schools, often because of repeated failures, and are excluded for a variety of reasons. Conversely, they may remove themselves from the school situation. Either of these actions will reduce their chances for success in adulthood.

Research has historically focused on the links between poverty and academic achievement within the statutory school age range. As the early years continue to become more established, future research will, hopefully, include more data relating to this crucial period to directly inform our future planning. However, Quilgars offers a helpful summary of research evidence relating to primary-aged children:

> Other studies, including Bondi (1991) and Hutchinson (1993), also report that pupils from disadvantaged backgrounds remain behind their peers or fall further behind their peers over the primary school years. Overall, the available research consistently reveals a clear link between a range of poverty indicators and educational achievement and progress in primary school. (Quilgars, 2001: 126)

In summary, this background knowledge informs early years practitioners as to the potentially damaging effects that poverty can have on children and young people. If we can provide effectively for children from disadvantaged backgrounds in the early years, followed by continued progress throughout statutory schooling and family support, then, hopefully, we will enable more children to escape the poverty trap as adults.

Case study

A 3-year-old girl, Debbie, is referred to a pre-school group by the family's health visitor. The accompanying report suggests that Debbie's difficulties lie in the areas of social and emotional development and general developmental delay, and that the family comprises a lone-parent mother and three siblings, aged 6 years, 4 years and 18 months, living in a council flat. The family is described as living in squalid and impoverished conditions. Debbie's father is also the father of her younger sibling but the older siblings have a different father. Debbie's father is currently serving a two-year prison sentence.

A member of staff undertakes a home visit to discuss the placement with Debbie's mother who is keen for her to attend. It is agreed that Debbie will initially be observed and then staff will again meet with her mother to discuss any interventions considered appropriate.

A key worker for Debbie is allocated who then undertakes a range of initial observations to inform future planning. These highlight the following:

- Debbie loves books, stories and rhymes.
- Debbie initially found adult attention difficult to deal with but has adapted quickly and now seeks adult attention.
- Debbie is very keen to please adults.
- Debbie has a good attention span.
- Debbie's cognitive development appears to have improved considerably in the short time she has been attending.
- Debbie now shows age-appropriate skills with regard to fine motor, gross motor, hearing and speech and cognitive skills.
- Debbie finds it difficult to interact appropriately with peers as she withdraws when other children approach her or speak to her.
- Some children react negatively to Debbie.

The outcomes were discussed by the staff and the following strategies were agreed with parents:

Specific

Debbie will work initially in a one-to-one situation with her key worker for 5–10-minute periods at least three times in each session she attends. This will later be extended to include another child. In

(Continued)

(Continued)

time, this will be extended to three and four children working together, with the key worker taking less of an active role. Debbie's mother will attend local parenting classes.

General

- Debbie's love of books, stories and rhymes will be encouraged through the usual planned activities within the group.
- Staff will ensure consistent positive praise and positive reinforcement to support Debbie's social and emotional development and enhance her self-concept.
- As a whole group, the topic of friends will be developed for the next half-term to help improve the skills of all children within the group.

Before the review meeting, Debbie's key worker had liaised constantly with the health visitor and the need for support regarding basic hygiene was highlighted. Within the setting, a few children had made negative comments regarding Debbie's attire and an unpleasant aroma. This was to be addressed within the setting through a group topic, but it was felt that some support and advice from the health visitor to the mother could also help to alleviate the difficulty. At the review meeting six weeks later, it was reported that Debbie had settled very well and was improving in all developmental areas. In the areas of fine motor and cognitive skills, she was demonstrating skills above expectations for children of her age. She was beginning to interact more with her peers but this was still at an early stage of development and would be continuing. The 'Friends' topic had commenced and it was hoped that all children in the group would benefit. Staff were delighted to see that Debbie was now less withdrawn and was delighted with her 'new' clothes. She had also been very proud to share her 'new' clothes with the group at news time, supported by her key worker.

Issues arising

From the case study, the following issues can be highlighted:

- The practitioner's home visit and initial observation informed planning positively.
- Liaison with the health visitor regarding Debbie's clothing supported the work that was undertaken within the group regarding developing Debbie's social skills.

- The mother was praised at the review meeting for the improvements in Debbie's appearance to help improve the mother's low self-concept. This would indirectly enhance her pride, parenting skills and interactions with her children.

- Debbie's individual needs were identified and provided for appropriately with positive outcomes. Although the 'friends' topic was for the benefit of all the children, the intentions were clearly to support the reactions of some of the other children, which would in turn support Debbie.

- The strategies identified to support Debbie acknowledged and supported her affective development as well as her academic development.

- The setting acknowledged that they could not remove the poverty issues but responded to those issues that were within their control.

This setting addressed Debbie's individual needs effectively and with few real changes to existing planning and provision systems. The processes of home visiting, observation, identifying strengths and weaknesses/likes and dislikes, planning interventions and evaluating progress combined with parental involvement and liaison with outside professionals have all been seen to support a child's needs. Viewing Debbie as an individual and taking into account her family and their needs, her background and the effects of that background combined with an understanding of the effects of poverty and deprivation, have all helped to present an holistic understanding of Debbie. Once that stage has been reached, then informed and effective decisions can be made.

This case study highlights the effects of a deprived background on a little girl and ways to personalise planning to accommodate her needs. Debbie's individual needs were addressed, not the poverty, but through working closely with the mother improvements occurred for all family members.

Current issues for resolution

The following indicate some of the issues that still need resolving, although it should be acknowledged that current reforms and changes should hopefully address some of them:

1 Policies at local and national levels that support interagency working.

2 Equity of training opportunities for all early years practitioners.

3 Equity in pay, terms and conditions.

4 A continuation of research and developments acknowledging the importance and value of the early years.

5 A continuation of research and developments in early years special needs provision.

6 Further developments to raise the profile of early years workers.

7 Access to resources for all practitioners.

8 Equity of access to 'needs-led' provision as opposed to 'budget-led' provision.

9 A resolution of funding issues.

10 Clarification of the qualifications framework. (Wall, 2004: 145–6)

Summary

Throughout this chapter, we have explored inclusion within current legislation and guidance, as well as ways in which early years settings could begin moving towards increased inclusion. As with any changes, concerns and issues will arise, but with commitment and appropriate support these can be resolved.

Positive and purposeful training should be accessible to all those working within the early years. Although there is a range of highly appropriate courses available to pre-school practitioners, the issue of equity for all early years practitioners must be addressed. The speed at which new initiatives are implemented has been greater than the speed at which appropriate training can be organised, accessed and undertaken, so it cannot be assumed that all early years settings will be working in line with all current government strategies.

Inclusion, as an ideal, can be interpreted simplistically, but the process of inclusion is complex and requires guidance and leadership from local and national agencies as well as the total commitment of all staff and parents. If the short- and long-term benefits are appreciated, then barriers to inclusion can be identified and addressed. Inclusion is, hopefully, not too far away but in the meantime we all need to address the key issues to ensure that in the early years, all practitioners and settings are equipped to offer effective inclusion to all children and adults.

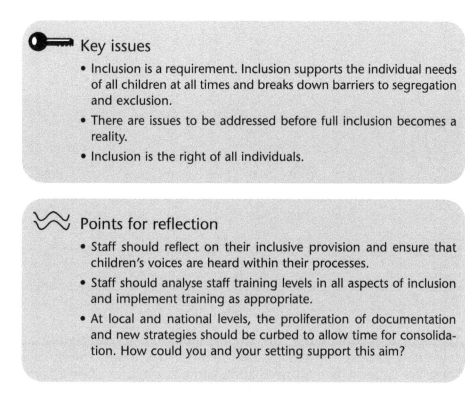

Key issues

- Inclusion is a requirement. Inclusion supports the individual needs of all children at all times and breaks down barriers to segregation and exclusion.
- There are issues to be addressed before full inclusion becomes a reality.
- Inclusion is the right of all individuals.

Points for reflection

- Staff should reflect on their inclusive provision and ensure that children's voices are heard within their processes.
- Staff should analyse staff training levels in all aspects of inclusion and implement training as appropriate.
- At local and national levels, the proliferation of documentation and new strategies should be curbed to allow time for consolidation. How could you and your setting support this aim?

Suggested further reading

Cox, T. (2000) *Combating Educational Disadvantage: Meeting the Needs of Vulnerable Children.* London: Falmer Press.

Jones, P. (2005) 'Inclusion: lessons from the children', *British Journal of Special Education*, 32(2): 60–7.

Wall, K. (2009) 'Diversity and inclusion', in T. Bruce (ed.) *Early Childhood Studies*. London: Sage.

9

Key issues for consideration

As I have worked through this, the third edition, several significant issues have emerged which are, for the most part, totally interlinked. These are issues which all need addressing as a matter of urgency at national level to have any hope of significant change being made in the foreseeable future. It is a sad reflection that many of them first emerged in 1978 in the Warnock Report and are now, over 30 years later, still demanding our time and attention. The issues are:

- SEN documentation – speed of production/change and exclusivity
- the need to listen to and respond to the voices of the families and the young children themselves
- SEN training and the funding that it demands
- early years workforce issues – lack of men in early years, status, respect and pay
- early years qualifications – clarification and streamlining needed.

Interestingly, the Select Committee Report on Education and Skills Third Report (HM Parliament, 2006a) highlighted many of the same issues and in light of these I intend to pull together some of the key threads that have emerged throughout this book and debate them further in an all-encompassing and interconnecting manner. First, however, we will explore some facts and figures taken from the Select Committee Report:

- 18% of all pupils were categorized as having some sort of SEN in 2005.
- 60% of pupils with statements attended mainstream schools in 2005.
- The number of pupils in special schools fell by nearly 30% in the 12 years from 1979 to 1991. From 1997 to 2005 there has been a decline of 4%.
- The majority of schools have between 10% and 25% of pupils with SEN.
- There is almost a fivefold difference in the proportion of pupils with statements in different authorities (from 1.08% of all pupils in Nottinghamshire to 4.83% in Halton, Cheshire).
- There are 150 systems around the English ... authorities for assessing children.
- Disabled young people are already twice as likely not to be in education, employment or training (NEET).
- 21% of disabled people aged 16–24 have no qualifications whatsoever, compared to 9% of non-disabled people of the same age. (HM Parliament, 2006a)

From these facts, it is clear to see that significant changes are needed and that change must take place sooner rather than later. For those young people referred to in the report, concluding their education with no qualifications is unacceptable and although the factors leading to this are diverse and complex, I suggest that society and the education system have let them down. Children are not born as failures but circumstances through their young lives impact on their abilities to engage with an education system that is built around targets and outcomes. As opposed to developing revised strategies and policies to address these issues in a reactive manner, it would seem more appropriate to take a breath and evaluate what has happened, why some children fail and how best we can move forwards to change the future. This, however, then takes us far beyond early years provision for young children with SEN as it includes areas such as poverty, early intervention, family breakdown, interagency working, qualifications and expertise, workforce issues and much more – certainly a challenge and a half.

For now, however, we need to return our thinking to improved ways forward for young children with SEN and their families and if we consider the cost of failing our children (see above bulleted list), we can see that to do this successfully would have a positive impact on their futures, the future of society and make economic sense. The AHDC agenda supports improvements in some areas and the *Best Practice to Common Practice* report from AHDC (DCSF) states that delivery is to be focused upon:

- the Commissioning Support Programme
- a range of skills sector and workforce agencies to support the original commitments to work with the CWDC
- regions to ensure best practice and networking happens at every point of the delivery chain

- parents and disabled children and young people to ensure their voices permeate all we do. (2009g: 2)

While these are commendable and should certainly lead to some improvements, I am unsure as to how this can happen if professionals are struggling to keep up with changes in policy and the additional initiatives that are constantly emerging. As a part of all the key government initiatives we see time and again, for example, that Early Support is the government's mechanism for supporting young children with disabilities and their families, yet some of the early years professionals I am working with regularly have not heard of this 'mechanism' nor have received any guidance or training. So the gap between front-line practice and government is evident.

Further, while the government have implemented a raft of changes for children with SEN, they have stated that three key areas still need urgent attention and these have also been evident throughout this book:

- too many children waiting too long to have their needs met
- parents lacking confidence in the system, leading to pressure for statements, and
- some children who could be taught in mainstream school being turned away.

The Committee finds it both surprising and highly concerning that these issues have still not been addressed. Evidence presented to this Inquiry has further highlighted that there are significant failings in the system that need to be dealt with urgently. (HM Parliament, 2006b)

The report then continues to suggest how these may be addressed.

So we can see that significant issues need to be tackled and, through a range of strategies and initiatives, the government is responding to each of these areas. What could be suggested is that one umbrella-type, coherent strategy could be established to incorporate each of these areas in a coordinated, interagency manner so that the drive for improvement would be clearer to follow and make more logical sense to our front-line professionals.

The CWDC has a laudable aim for 2020, but if this were to be part of a single agenda for the future then more professionals would be aware of not only their aims but the manner in which they will achieve them:

Our ambitions for 2020 mean that world class, personalized and integrated services need to be available to every child. To get there we will require sustained attention to the workforce and to culture change over the next 10 years.

> However it is important to ensure that the culture change which is needed to support further development of integrated and personalized delivery of services does not dilute the specialist skills and knowledge, or focus, of any of the people who are coming together to deliver the services. Our strategy towards the workforce must ensure that people are in the right places, and have strong understanding of their roles and responsibilities, so that by working together as a team, people from different parts of the workforce can achieve more with individual children and families than they would be able to do working on their own. (DCSF, 2008o: 14)

However, while the report states clearly that the aim is for the status of early years work to be raised, there is little indication of how this may be achieved.

The Select Committee Report summarises their proposals for their future strategy to improve SEN provision:

- a national framework linked to minimum standards
- local flexibility within a national framework
- a pupil-centred approach with SEN at the heart of personalization
- equipping the workforce: a major priority is to properly train and resource all staff
- early intervention
- partnership working
- a radical review of statementing. (HM Parliament, 2006c)

We are beginning to see great overlap with many of the other reports discussed throughout this book and even within this chapter, so does this suggest that a range of organisations is working towards similar aims and objectives? The result for me is one of increasing confusion and lack of clarity, which one consolidated focus, led by one umbrella organisation, could potentially alleviate.

Concluding comments

It would appear that key messages have emerged throughout this book to inform our future direction for all young children with SEN and their families and these have emerged through the review of current policy agendas and government initiatives, combined with my own skills and experience in this field:

- The voices of parents and family members must be heard.
- The voices of children must be heard.
- The voices of front-line professionals must be heard.
- Interagency working must improve and overcome barriers.

- Increased front-line intervention professionals (e.g. HVs and SWs) need to be available to support families from the birth of their children onwards in support of proactive, early intervention.

- The amount of legislation, guidance and reports from central government must be curtailed and a period of consolidation and reflection is needed.

- One government strategy needs to emerge which can address the diverse range of issues identified in the current raft of documentation. This would offer clarity for all those working with young children with SEN and their families.

- Coordinated, national, interagency training is essential for all professionals.

- Early years workforce issues and the early years qualifications framework should be reviewed to reduce confusion and offer a clearer professional pathway for all early years workers. This would also involve a review of pay structures.

My overriding point would be a plea for all the key players to stop and draw breath, to review all the expectations and aims of every report, strategy document and initiative and consolidate these into one consistent and structured way forward to address the key issues. The amount of reports and documentation only confuses and divides the workforce as some practitioners are engaging with some initiatives while, in my experience, other practitioners can be unaware of them. The outcome is that provision is patchy and inconsistent. We need to ensure that it is not simply by chance that young children with SEN and their families happen to meet the one professional that really engages with them and makes change happen. We need a system that ensures every parent engages with each professional they meet in an effective and empowering partnership for all parties. Whether the current national agendas will address all of these issues is, in my view, optimistic, but we have to hope that I am wrong and that in the future fewer children will 'slip through the net' and that more children, and their families, will reach their fullest potential.

We must remember that all children have the right to be respected, valued and included, so locally and nationally we must ensure that all practitioners have the knowledge and skills to offer that respect within an inclusive system and, hopefully, within a more inclusive society. Young children would no longer be classified as having 'special needs' and their families would no longer be 'different', but they would be mainstream children and families, as long as potential barriers to inclusion are confronted, debated and resolved.

Bibliography

Abbott, L. and Langston, A. (eds) (2005) *Birth to Three Matters: Supporting the Framework of Effective Practice.* Milton Keynes: Open University Press.

Advisory Centre for Education (ACE) (2005a) *Special Education Handbook: The Law on Children with Special Educational Needs,* 9th edn. London: ACE.

Advisory Centre for Education (ACE) (2005b) *Getting the Statement Right: A Practical Guide to Parents' Legal Rights.* London: ACE.

Anderson-Ford, D. (1994) 'Legal aid: how special education is defined in law', in S. Sandow (ed.), *Whose Special Need?* London: Paul Chapman Publishing.

Armstrong, F. (2007) 'Disability, education and social change in England since 1960', *History of Education,* 36(4–5): 551–68.

Atkinson, M., Wilkin, A., Stott, A., Doherty, P. and Kinder, K. (2002) *Multi-Agency Working: A Detailed Study.* Available at: www.nfer.ac.uk/nfer/publications/CSS02/CSS02_home.cfm?publicationID=370&title=Multi-agency%20working:%20a%20detailed%20study

Aubrey, C. (2010) 'Leading and working in multi-agency teams', in G. Pugh and B. Duffy (eds) *Contemporary Issues in the Early Years,* 5th edn. London: Sage.

Audit Commission (2002) *Special Educational Needs: A Mainstream Issue.* London: Audit Commission.

Baldock, P., Fitzgerald, D. and Kay, J. (2005) *Understanding Early Years Policy.* London: Paul Chapman Publishing.

Baldock, P., Fitzgerald, D. and Kay, J. (2009) *Understanding Early Years Policy,* 2nd edn. London: Sage.

Barnes, P. (ed.) (1995) *Personal, Social and Emotional Development of Children.* Milton Keynes: Open University Press.

Beaver, M., Brewster, J., Jones, P., Keene, A., Neaum, S. and Tallack, J. (1999) *Babies and Young Children. Book 1: Early Years Development.* Cheltenham: Stanley Thornes.

Beaver, M., Brewster, J., Jones, P., Keene, A., Neaum, S. and Tallack, J. (2000) *Babies and Young Children. Book 2: Early Years Care and Education.* Cheltenham: Stanley Thornes.

Behaviour4Learning (2005) *Warnock Backtracks Again.* Available at: www.behaviour4learning.ac.uk/viewarticle2.aspx?contentId=10977

Bertram, T. and Pascal, C. (2010) 'Introducing child development', in T. Bruce (ed.) *Early Childhood: A Guide for Students*, 2nd edn. London: Sage.

Beveridge, S. (1997) 'Implementing partnership with parents in schools', in S. Wolfendale (ed.), *Working with Parents of SEN Children after the Code of Practice*. London: David Fulton.

Birrell, I. (1995) 'The invisible children: a story of heartbreak and hope', *Sunday Times News Review*, 3 December: 1–2.

Blamires, M., Robertson, C. and Blamires, J. (1997) *Parent–Teacher Partnership: Practical Approaches to Meet Special Educational Needs*. London: David Fulton.

Blenkin, G. (1994) 'Early learning and a developmentally appropriate curriculum: some lessons from research', in G.M. Blenkin and A.V. Kelly (eds), *The National Curriculum and Early Learning: An Evaluation*. London: Paul Chapman Publishing.

Bluma, S., Shearer, A., Frohman, A. and Hillard, J. (1976) *Portage Guide to Education Checklist*. Windsor: NFER-Nelson.

Booth, T. and Ainscow, M. (2002) *Index for Inclusion*. Bristol: CSIE.

Booth, T. and Ainscow, M. (2004) *Index for Inclusion: Early Years and Childcare*. Bristol: CSIE.

Bradburn, E. (1976) *Margaret McMillan: Framework and Expansion of Nursery Education*. Redhill: Denholm Press.

Bradshaw, J. (ed.) (2001) *Poverty: The Outcomes for Children*. London: Family Policy Studies Centre.

Bronfenbrenner, U. (1979) *The Ecology of Human Development: Experiments by Nature and Design*. London: Harvard University Press.

Bruce, T. (1987) *Early Childhood Education*. London: Hodder & Stoughton.

Bruce, T. (ed.) (2010) *Early Childhood: A Guide for Students*, 2nd edn. London: Sage.

Cabinet Office (2005) *Improving the Lives of Disabled People*. Available at: www.cabinetoffice.gov.uk/newsroom/news_releases/2005/050119_disabled.aspx

Canfield, J. and Wells, H.C. (1976) *100 Ways to Enhance the Self-Concept in the Classroom: A Handbook for Teachers and Parents*. Englewood Cliffs, NJ: Prentice-Hall.

Carpenter, B. (ed.) (1997) *Families in Context: Emerging Trends in Family Support and Early Intervention*. London: David Fulton.

Carpenter, B. (2000a) 'Sustaining the family: meeting the needs of families of children with disabilities', *British Journal of Special Education*, 27(3): 135–43.

Carpenter, B. (2000b) in Dodd, L.W. (2004) 'Supporting the siblings of young children with disabilities', *British Journal of Special Education*, 31(1): 41–9.

Carpenter, B. (2005) 'Early childhood intervention: possibilities and prospects for professionals, families and children', *British Journal of Special Education*, 32(4): 176–83.

Carpenter, B. (with Egerton, J.) (2007) *Family Structures* (as part of the Early Support distance learning materials). Available at: www.dcsf.gov.uk/everychildmatters/healthandwellbeing/ahdc/earlysupport/training/partnershiptraining/partnershiptraining/

Central Advisory Council for Education (CACE) (1967) *Children and their Primary Schools* (Plowden Report). London: HMSO.

Centre for Studies in Inclusive Education (CSIE) (2010a) *Index for Inclusion: Developing Learning and Participation in Schools*. Available at: www.csie.org.uk/publications/inclusion-index-explained.shtml

Centre for Studies in Inclusive Education (CSIE) (2010b) *Ten Reasons for Inclusion*. Available at: www.csie.org.uk/publications/free.shtml

Charlton, T. and David, K. (eds) (1990) *Supportive Schools*. Basingstoke: Macmillan.

Charlton, T. and Jones, K. (1990) *Working on the Self*. Cheltenham: College of St Paul and St Mary Press.

Children's Workforce Development Council (CWDC) (2009a) *Early Identification, Assessment of Needs and Intervention: The Common Assessment Framework for Children and Young People: A Guide for Practitioners*. London: CWDC.

Children's Workforce Development Council (CWDC) (2009b) *Implementing Integrated Working*. Available at: www.cwdcouncil.org.uk/implementing-integrated-working

Children's Workforce Development Council (CWDC) (2010a) *Information Sharing*. Available at: www.dcsf.gov.uk/everychildmatters/strategy/deliveringservices1/informationsharing/informationsharing/

Children's Workforce Development Council (CWDC) (2010b) *Common Assessment Framework (CAF)*. Available at: www.dcsf.gov.uk/everychildmatters/strategy/deliveringservices1/caf/cafframework/

Children's Workforce Development Council (CWDC) (2010c) *Lead Professional*. Available at: www.dcsf.gov.uk/everychildmatters/strategy/managersandleaders/leadprofessional/leadprof/

Children's Workforce Development Council (CWDC) (2010d) *Setting up Multiagency Services*. Available at: www.dcsf.gov.uk/everychildmatters/strategy/deliveringservices1/multiagencyworking/multiagencyworking/

Chizea, C., Henderson, A. and Jones, G. (1999) *Inclusion in Pre-School Settings – Support for Children with Special Needs and their Families*. London: Pre-School Learning Alliance.

Clark, A. and Moss, P. (2001) *Listening to Young Children: The Mosaic Approach*. London: National Children's Bureau.

Clark, A. and Moss, P. (2005) *Spaces to Play: More Listening to Young Children Using the Mosaic Approach*. London: National Children's Bureau.

Contact-a-Family (2009) *Our Family, Our Future*. Available at: www.cafamily.org.uk/index.php?module=newsmodule&action=view&id=359&src=@random4864ff40710ee

Council for Disabled Children (CDC), Sure Start and National Children's Bureau (2003) *Early Years and the Disability Discrimination Act 1995: What Service Providers Need to Know*. Available at: www.dcsf.gov.uk/everychildmatters/publications/leaflets/757/

Court, S.D.M. (1976) *Fit for the Future: The Report of the Committee on Child Health Services, Volume 1* (Court Report). London: HMSO.

Cousins, J. (2006) 'Self-esteem in young children', *Early Years Update*. July. Available at: www.teachingexpertise.com/articles/self-esteem-in-young-children-1119

Cox, T. (2000) *Combating Educational Disadvantage: Meeting the Needs of Vulnerable Children*. London: Falmer Press.

Crow, L. (2003) 'Including all our lives: renewing the social model of disability', in M. Nind, J. Rix, K. Sheehy and K. Simmons (eds), *Inclusive Education: Diverse Perspectives*. London: David Fulton.

Dale, N. (1996) *Working with Families of Children with Special Needs*. London: Routledge.

David, T. (1990) *Under Five – Under-Educated?* Buckingham: Open University Press.

David, T. (ed.) (1994) *Working Together for Young Children: Multi-professionalism in Action*. London: Routledge.

David, T. (2009) 'Social and emotional development', in T. Maynard and N. Thomas (eds) *An Introduction to Early Childhood Studies*. London: Sage.

Davis, H. and Meltzer, L. (2007) *Working with Parents in Partnership*. Available at: www.dcsf.gov.uk/everychildmatters/healthandwellbeing/ahdc/earlysupport/training/partnershiptraining/distance/distance/

Department for Children, Schools and Families (2004) *History of Early Support*. Available at: www.dcsf.gov.uk/everychildmatters/healthandwellbeing/ahdc/earlysupport/home/

Department for Children, Schools and Families (2007a) *The Children's Plan*. Available at: www.dcsf.gov.uk/childrensplan/downloads/Childrens_Plan_Executive_Summary.pdf

Department for Children, Schools and Families (2007b) *Every Parent Matters*. Available at: www.dcsf.gov.uk/everychildmatters/resources-and-practice/IG00219/

Department for Children, Schools and Families (2007c) *Duties and Definitions: The Disability Discrimination Act 2005*. Available at: www.teachernet.gov.uk/wholeschool/disability/disabilityandthedda/dda2005/

Department for Children, Schools and Families (2007d) *The Inclusion Development Programme*. Available at: www.nationalstrategies.standards.dcsf.gov.uk/node/116691

Department for Children, Schools and Families (2007e) *Next Steps for Early Learning and Childcare: Building on the 10-Year Strategy*. London: DCSF.

Department for Children, Schools and Families (2007f) *Effective Practice: Observation, Assessment and Planning*. Available at: www.nationalstrategies.standards.dcsf.gov.uk/node/84344?uc=force_uj

Department for Children, Schools and Families (2008a) *2020 Children and Young People's Workforce Strategy*. Available at: www.everychildmatters.gov.uk/deliveringservices/childrenandyoungpeoplesworkforce/

Department for Children, Schools and Families (2008b) *Raising Standards – Improving Outcomes*. Available at: /www.surestart.gov.uk/_doc/P0002514.pdf

Department for Children, Schools and Families (2008c) *Early Years Quality Improvement Support Programme (EYQISP)*. London: DCSF.

Department for Children, Schools and Families (2008d) *The Early Years Foundation Stage*. Available at: www.teachernet.gov.uk/teachingandlearning/EYFS/

Department for Children, Schools and Families (2008e) *Inclusion Development Programme – Supporting Children with Speech, Language and Communication Needs: Guidance for Practitioners in the Early Years Foundation Stage*. London: DCSF.

Department for Children, Schools and Families (2008f) *The Bercow Report*. Available at: www.dcsf.gov.uk/bercowreview

Department for Children, Schools and Families (2008g) *Better Communication*. Available at: www.dcsf.gov.uk/slcnaction/downloads/Better_Communication_Final.pdf

Department for Children, Schools and Families (2008h) *Quality Standards for SEN and Outreach Services*. London: DCSF.

Department for Children, Schools and Families (2008i) *Special Educational Needs (SEN): A Guide for Parents and Carers*. Available at: www.teachernet.gov.uk/wholeschool/sen/parentcarers/

Department for Children, Schools and Families (2008j) *Early Years Foundation Stage: Setting the Standards for Learning, Development and Care for Children from Birth to Five*. London: DCSF.

Department for Children, Schools and Families (2008k) *Practice Guidance for the Early Years Foundation Stage*. London: DCSF.

Department for Children, Schools and Families (2008l) *Social and Emotional Aspects of Development: Guidance for Practitioners Working in the Early Years Foundation Stage*. Available at: www.publications.everychildmatters.gov.uk/default.aspx?PageFunction=productdetails&PageMode=publications&ProductId=DCSF-00707–2008&

Department for Children, Schools and Families (2008m) *Early Years Foundation Stage Profile Handbook*. Available at: www.nationalstrategies.standards.dcsf.gov.uk/print/113038

Department for Children, Schools and Families (2008n) *The Education (Special Educational Needs Coordinators) (England) Regulations 2008*. Available at: www.england-legislation.hmso.gov.uk/si/si2008/uksi_20082945_en_1

Department for Children, Schools and Families (2008o) *Building Brighter Futures: Next Steps for the Children's Workforce*. London: DCSF.

Department for Children, Schools and Families (2009a) *Healthy Lives, Brighter Futures: The Strategy for Children and Young People's Health*. Available at: www.dcsf.gov.uk/everychildmatters/publications/documents/healthylivesstrategy/

Department for Children, Schools and Families (2009b) *Next Steps for Learning and Childcare*. Available at: www.dcsf.gov.uk/everychildmatters/resources-and-practice/IG00356/

Department for Children, Schools and Families (2009c) *Your Child, Your Schools, Our Future: Building a 21st Century Schools System*. Available at: www.dcsf.gov.uk/21stcenturyschoolssystem/

Department for Children, Schools and Families (2009d) *First Frontline Children's Workers to Start using ContactPoint.* Available at: www.dcsf.gov.uk/everychild-matters/strategy/deliveringservices1/contactpoint/contactpoint/

Department for Children, Schools and Families (2009e) *Information Sharing: Guidance for Practitioners and Managers.* Available at: www.dcsf.gov.uk/everychildmatters/resources-and-practice/IG00340/

Department for Children, Schools and Families (2009f) *Disability Discrimination Act (DDA).* Available at: www.teachernet.gov.uk/wholeschool/disability/disability-andthedda/

Department for Children, Schools and Families (2009g) *Aiming High for Disabled Children: Best Practice to Common Practice.* London: DCSF.

Department for Children, Schools and Families (2009h) *Lamb Inquiry: Special Educational Needs and Parental Confidence.* Available at: www.dcsf.gov.uk/lambinquiry/

Department for Children, Schools and Families (2009i) *Sure Start Children's Centres.* Available at: www.dcsf.gov.uk/everychildmatters/earlyyears/surestart/whatsurestartdoes/

Department for Children, Schools and Families (2009j) *Talking with Families about Disability.* Available at: www.dcsf.gov.uk/everychildmatters/healthandwell-being/ahdc/earlysupport/inpractice/delivery/talkingaboutdisability/talkingabout disability/

Department for Children, Schools and Families (2009k) *United Nations Convention on the Rights of the Child: The Articles.* Available at: www.dcsf.gov.uk/everychildmatters/_download/?id=3265

Department for Children, Schools and Families (2009l) *Progress Matters: Reviewing and Enhancing Young Children's Development.* London: DCSF.

Department for Children, Schools and Families (2009m) *The Inclusion Development Programme – Supporting Children on the Autism Spectrum: Guidance for Practitioners in the Early Years Foundation Stage.* Available at: www.nationalstrate-gies.standards.dcsf.gov.uk/node/173893

Department for Children, Schools and Families, (2009n) *The Protection of Children in England: Action Plan – The Government's Response to Lord Laming.* Available at: www.publications.everychildmatters.gov.uk/default.aspx?Page-Function=productdetails&PageMode=publications&ProductId=CM+7589&

Department for Children, Schools and Families (2009o) *The Education (Special Educational Needs Coordinators) (England) (Amendment) Regulations 2009.* Available at: www.opsi.gov.uk/si/si2009/uksi_20091387_en_1

Department for Children, Schools and Families (2009p) *Early Support Programme.* Available at: www.dcsf.gov.uk/everychildmatters/publications/documents/esprog/

Department for Education and Employment (DfEE) (1988) *Education Reform Act.* London: HMSO.

Department for Education and Employment (DfEE) (1993) *Education Act.* London: HMSO.

Department for Education and Employment (DfEE) (1994) *Code of Practice on the Identification and Assessment of Special Educational Needs.* London: HMSO.

Department for Education and Employment (DfEE) (1997) *Excellence for All: Meeting Special Educational Needs.* London: Stationery Office.

Department for Education and Skills (DfES) (2001a) *Inclusive Schooling: Children with Special Educational Needs.* Nottingham: DfES.

Department for Education and Skills (DfES) (2001b) *Special Educational Needs and Disability Act 2001.* London: HMSO.

Department for Education and Skills (DfES) (2001c) *Special Educational Needs Code of Practice.* Nottingham: DfES.

Department for Education and Skills (DfES) (2001d) *Special Educational Needs Toolkit.* Nottingham: DfES.

Department for Education and Skills (DfES) (2002) *Autistic Spectrum Disorders: Good Practice Guidance.* London: DfES.

Department for Education and Skills (DfES) (2003a) *Every Child Matters.* London: DfES.

Department for Education and Skills (DfES) (2003b) *Every Child Matters: Change for Children: Facts and Figures.* Available at www.dfes.gov.uk/everychildmatters

Department for Education and Skills (DfES) (2004a) *Every Child Matters: Next Steps.* London: DfES.

Department for Education and Skills (DfES) (2004b) *Children Act.* London: HMSO.

Department for Education and Skills (DfES) (2004c) *Removing Barriers to Achievement: The Government's Strategy for SEN.* London: DfES.

Department for Education and Skills (DfES) (2005a) *Children's Workforce Strategy (Consultation).* London: DfES.

Department for Education and Skills (DfES) (2005b) *Common Core of Skills and Knowledge for the Children's Workforce.* Available at: www.dcsf.gov.uk/everychildmatters/strategy/deliveringservices1/commoncore/commoncoreofskillsand knowledge/

Department for Education and Skills (DfES) (2007) *Early Years Foundation Stage.* London: DfES.

Department for Education and Skills and Department of Health (DfES and DoH) (2002) *Together from the Start: Practical Guidance for Professionals Working with Disabled Children (Birth to 2) and their Families.* London: DfES.

Department for Education and Skills and Department of Health (DfES and DoH) (2003) *Together from the Start: Practical Guidance for Professionals Working with Disabled Children (Birth to Third Birthday) and their Families.* London: DfES.

Department for Education and Skills (DfES)/Sure Start Unit (2002) *Birth to Three Matters: A Framework to Support Children in their Earliest Years.* London: DfES.

Department of Education and Science (DES) (1970) *Education (Handicapped Children) Act.* London: HMSO.

Department of Education and Science (DES) (1978) *The Report of the Committee of Enquiry into the Education of Handicapped Children and Young People* (Warnock Report). London: HMSO.

Department of Education and Science (DES) (1981) *Education Act.* London: HMSO.

Department of Health (DoH) (1991) *The Children Act Guidance and Regulations. Volume 2: Family Support, Daycare and Educational Provision for Young Children.* London: HMSO.

Department of Health (DoH) (2004) *National Service Framework: Standard 8.* Available at: www.dh.gov.uk/en/Publicationsandstatistics/Publications/PublicationsPolicyAndGuidance/Browsable/DH_4094479

Department of Health (DoH) (2009a) *National Service Framework for Children, Young People and Maternity Services: Executive Summary.* Available at: www.dh. gov. uk/en/Publicationsandstatistics/Publications/PublicationsPolicyAndGuidance/DH _4089100

Department of Health (DoH) (2009b) *Getting it Right for Children and Families: Maximising the Contribution of the Health Visiting Team – 'Ambition, Action, Achievement'.* London: DoH.

Department of Social Security (2000) *Households Below Average Income: 1994–1998/9.* London: Stationery Office.

Directgov (2009) *Sure Start Children's Centres.* Available at: www.direct. gov.uk/en/Parents/Preschooldevelopmentandlearning/NurseriesPlaygroupsReceptionClasses/DG_173054

Disability Rights Commission (DRC) (2005) *Special Schools Debate July 2005.* Available at: www.83.137.212.42/sitearchive/drc/library/policy/education/special_schools_debate_july_20.html

Dodd, L.W. (2004) 'Supporting the siblings of young children with disabilities', *British Journal of Special Education,* 31(1): 41–9.

Draper, L. and Duffy, B. (2001) 'Working with parents', in G. Pugh (ed.), *Contemporary Issues in the Early Years*, 3rd edn. London: Paul Chapman Publishing.

Drifte, C. (2001) *Special Needs in Early Years Settings: A Guide for Practitioners.* London: David Fulton.

Drifte, C. (2010) *The Manual for the Early Years SENCO*, 2nd edn. London: Sage.

Edwards, A. and Knight, P. (1994) *Effective Early Years Education: Teaching Young Children.* Buckingham: Open University Press.

Emad, H. (2000) 'The vital link between home and school', *Early Years Educator,* 2(7): 48–9.

Evans, P. (2000) 'Including students with disabilities in mainstream schools', in H. Savolainen, H. Kokkala and H. Alasuutari (eds), *Meeting Special and Diverse Educational Needs: Making Inclusive Education a Reality.* Helsinki: Ministry for Foreign Affairs of Finland.

Farrell, M. (2004) *Special Educational Needs: A Resource for Practitioners.* London: Paul Chapman Publishing.

Farrell, P. (2001) 'Special education in the last twenty years: have things really got better?', *British Journal of Special Education,* 28(1): 3–9.

Flewitt, R. and Nind, M. (2007) 'Parents choosing to combine special and inclusive early years settings: the best of both worlds?', *European Journal of Special Needs Education,* 22(4): 425–41.

Gasper, M. (2010) *Multi-agency Working in the Early Years: Challenges and Opportunities.* London: Sage.

Goldenberg, I. and Goldenberg, H. (1985) 'Family therapy: an overview', in B. Carpenter (2000) 'Sustaining the family: meeting the needs of families of children with disabilities', *British Journal of Special Education,* 27(3): 135–43.

Goodall, J. (1997) 'All young children have needs', in S. Wolfendale (ed.), *Meeting Special Needs in the Early Years: Directions in Policy and Practice.* London: David Fulton.

Gorrod, L. (1997) *My Brother is Different.* London: NAS.

Gulliford, R. (1981) 'Teacher training and Warnock', *Special Education Forward Trends,* 8(2): 13–15.

Harnett, A. (2002) 'Developing children as independent and confident learners: personal, social and emotional development', in I. Keating (ed.), *Achieving QTS: Teaching the Foundation Stage.* Exeter: Learning Matters.

Hayward, A. (2006) *Making Inclusion Happen.* London: Sage.

Herbert, E. and Carpenter, B. (1994) 'Fathers – the secondary partners: professional perceptions and a father's reflections', *Children and Society,* 8(1): 31–41.

Hickman, C. and Jones, K. (2005) 'Inclusive practice for children with special educational needs,' in T. Waller (ed.), *An Introduction to Early Childhood: A Multidisciplinary Approach.* London: Paul Chapman Publishing.

Hirsch, D. (2008) *Estimating the Costs of Child Poverty.* Available at: www.jrf.org.uk/publications/estimating-costs-child-poverty

HM Parliament (2006a) *Select Committee on Education and Skills* Third Report: *SEN Facts and Figures.* Available at: www.publications.parliament.uk/pa/cm200506/cmselect/cmeduski/478/47805.htm

HM Parliament (2006b) *Select Committee on Education and Skills* Third Report: *Failings within the SEN system.* Available at: www.publications.parliament.uk/pa/cm200506/cmselect/cmeduski/478/47809.htm

HM Parliament (2006c) *Select Committee on Education and Skills* Third Report: *Future Strategy.* Available at: www.publications.parliament.uk/pacm200506/cmselect/cmeduski/478/47810.htm

HM Parliament (2006d) *Government Response to the Education and Skills Committee Report on Special Educational Needs.* Available at: www.teachernet.gov.uk/docbank/index.cfm?id=10429

HM Treasury, with Department for Education and Science, Department for Work and Pensions, Department of Trade and Industry (2004) *Choice for Parents: The Best Start for Children: A Ten Year Strategy for Childcare.* London: HMSO.

HM Treasury with Department for Education and Skills (2007) *Aiming High for*

Disabled Children: Better Support for Families. London: HMSO.

Hohmann, M. and Weikart, D.P. (1995) *Educating Young Children*. Ypsolanti, MI: High Scope.

Hooper, C.-A., Gorin, S., Cabal, C. and Dyson, C. (2007) *Living with Hardship 24/7: The Diverse Experiences of Families in Poverty in England*. Available at: www.nspcc.org.uk/Inform/research/Findings/livingwithhardship_wda52842.html

House of Commons (2001) *Education and Employment First Report: Early Years – Quality Assurance, the Early Years Workforce*. Available at: www.publications.parliament.uk/pa/cm200001/cmselect/cmeduemp/33/3308.htm

Hurst, V. (1997) *Planning for Early Learning: Educating Young Children*. London: Paul Chapman Publishing.

Hutchin, V. (2010) 'Meeting individual needs', in T. Bruce (ed.) *Early Childhood: A Guide for Students*, 2nd edn. London: Sage.

Independent Panel for Special Educational Advice (IPSEA) (2005) *Inquiry into Special Education Needs*. Woodbridge: IPSEA.

Johnston, J. and Nahmad-Williams, L. (2009) *Early Childhood Studies*. Harlow: Pearson Education.

Jones, C. (2004) *Supporting Inclusion in the Early Years*. Maidenhead: Open University Press.

Jones, P. (2005) 'Inclusion: lessons from the children', *British Journal of Special Education*, 32(2): 60–7.

Jose, N. (2005) 'Child poverty: is it child abuse?', *Paediatric Nursing*, 17(8): 20–3.

Keenan, T. (2002) *An Introduction to Child Development*. London: Sage.

Lambley, H. (1993) 'Learning and behaviour problems', in T. Charlton and K. David (eds), *Managing Misbehaviour in Schools*, 2nd edn. London: Routledge.

Langston, A. (2003) 'Togetherness and partnership = empowerment', *Early Years Educator*, 5(6): 53–5.

Lee, K. (2005) 'We must support the parents of children with SEN', *Early Years Educator*, 7(6): 65–7.

Lewis, J. (2000) 'Let's remember the "education" in inclusive education', *British Journal of Special Education*, 27(4): 202.

Lindsay, G. (1997) 'Values and legislation', in G. Lindsay and D. Thompson (eds), *Values into Practice in Special Education*. London: David Fulton.

Lloyd, C. (1997) 'Inclusive education for children with SEN in the early years', in S. Wolfendale (ed.), *Meeting Special Needs in the Early Years: Directions in Policy and Practice*. London: David Fulton.

Long, R. and Fogell, J. (1999) *Supporting Pupils with Emotional Difficulties: Creating a Caring Environment for All*. London: David Fulton.

Macintyre, C. (2006) 'Early identification of additional learning needs', *Early Years Educator*, 7(9): 59–61.

Mallet, R. (1997) 'A parental perspective on partnership', in S. Wolfendale (ed.), *Working with Parents of SEN Children after the Code of Practice*. London: David Fulton.

Maynard, T. and Thomas, N. (eds) (2004) *An Introduction to Early Childhood Studies.* London: Sage.

Maynard, T. and Thomas, N. (eds) (2009) *An Introduction to Early Childhood Studies,* 2nd edn. London: Sage.

McConkey, R. (2002) 'Reciprocal working by education, health and social services: lessons for a less-travelled road', *British Journal of Special Education,* 29(1): 3–8.

McTavish, F. (2006) 'With children there is no such thing as normal', *Early Years Educator,* 7(9): 20–2.

Messenger, W. (2010) 'Managing multi-agency working', in M. Reed and N. Canning (eds), *Reflective Practice in the Early Years.* London: Sage.

Milbourne, L. (2005) 'Children, families and interagency work: experiences of partnership work in primary education settings', *British Educational Research Journal,* 31(6): 675–95.

Miller, L., Cable, C. and Devereux, J. (2005) *Developing Early Years Practice.* London: David Fulton.

Ministry of Education (1944) *Education Act.* London: HMSO.

Mortimer, H. (2000) *Playladders.* Lichfield: QED.

Mortimer, H. (2001) *Special Needs and Early Years Provision.* London: Continuum.

Mortimore, P., Sammons, P., Stoll, L., Lewis, D. and Ecob, R. (1988) *School Matters.* Wells: Open Books.

Moyles, J. (1989) *Just Playing? The Role and Status of Play in Early Childhood Education.* Milton Keynes: Open University Press.

National Association for Special Educational Needs (NASEN) (2000a) *Policy on Partnership with Parents and Carers.* Available at: www.nasen.org.uk/policy-documents/

National Association for Special Educational Needs (NASEN) (2008b) *The Effective Role of the SENCO.* Available at: www.nasen.org.uk/information-sheets/

National Strategies (2007) *Effective Practice: Observation, Assessment and Planning.* Available at: www.nationalstrategies.standards.dcsf.gov.uk/node/84344

National Strategies (2008) *Areas of Learning.* Available at: www.nationalstrategies.standards.dcsf.gov.uk/node/84045?uc%20=%20force_uj

Nutbrown, C. and Carter, C. (2010) 'The tools of assessment: watching and learning', in G. Pugh and B. Duffy (eds), *Contemporary Issues in the Early Years,* 5th edn. London: Sage.

O'Connor, U., McConkey, R. and Hartop, B. (2005) 'Parental views on the statutory assessment and educational planning for children with special educational needs', *European Journal of Special Needs Education,* 20(3): 251–69.

Office for Standards in Education (Ofsted) (2008). *Early Years: Leading to Excellence.* London: Ofsted.

Owen, G. (1928) cited in S. Northen (1999) 'Recognition of early years takes its time', *Times Educational Supplement,* December: 15.

Paige-Smith, A. (1997) 'The rise and impact of the parental lobby: including voluntary groups and the education of children with learning difficulties or disabilities', in S. Wolfendale (ed.), *Meeting Special Needs in the Early Years: Directions in Policy and Practice.* London: David Fulton.

Policy Analysis Unit (1986) *Voluntary Organisations and Childcare: Issues and Challenges.* London: NCVO.

Primary National Strategy. (2005) *Excellence and Enjoyment: Social and Emotional Aspects of Learning – Guidance.* London: DfES.

Pugh, G. (ed.) (2001) *Contemporary Issues in the Early Years*, 3rd edn. London: Paul Chapman Publishing.

Pugh, G. and Duffy, B. (eds) (2010) *Contemporary Issues in the Early Years*, 5th edn. London: Sage.

Qualifications and Curriculum Authority (QCA) (1999) *The Early Learning Goals.* London: QCA/DfEE.

Qualifications and Curriculum Authority (QCA) (2000) *Curriculum Guidance for the Foundation Stage.* London: QCA/DfEE.

Qualifications and Curriculum Authority (QCA) (2008a) *Early Years Foundation Stage.* London: QCA/DCFS.

Qualifications and Curriculum Authority (QCA) (2008b) *Early Years Foundation Stage Profile Handbook.* London: QCA/DCFS. Available at: www.testsandexams. qcda.gov.uk/17852.aspx

Qualifications and Curriculum Development Authority (QCDA) (2009) *P Scales.* Available at: www.qcda.gov.uk/8541.aspx

Quilgars, D. (2001) 'Educational attainment', in J. Bradshaw (ed.), *Poverty: The Outcomes for Children.* London: Family Policy Studies Centre.

Reed, M. and Canning, N. (eds) (2010) *Reflective Practice in the Early Years.* London: Sage.

Rennie, J. (1996) 'Working with parents', in G. Pugh (ed.), *Contemporary Issues in the Early Years: Working Collaboratively for Children.* London: Paul Chapman Publishing.

Roaf, C. (2002) *Coordinated Services for Included Children: Joined Up Action.* Buckingham: Open University Press.

Roberts, R. (2010) *Wellbeing from Birth.* London: Sage.

Robson, B. (1989) *Special Needs in Ordinary Schools: Pre-School Provision for Children with Special Needs.* London: Cassell.

Roffey, S. (2001) *Special Needs in the Early Years: Collaboration, Communication and Coordination*, 2nd edn. London: David Fulton.

Rogers, C. (2007) 'Disabling a family? Emotional dilemmas experienced in becoming a parent of a child with learning disabilities', *British Journal of Special Education*, 34(3): 136–43.

Rogers, C.R. (1983) *The Freedom to Learn in the 80's.* Columbus, OH: Merrill.

Rotter, J. (1966) 'Generalised expectancies for internal versus external control of reinforcement', *Psychological Monograph,* 80: 609.

Row, S. (2005) *Surviving the Special Educational Needs System. How to be a Velvet Bulldozer.* London: Jessica Kingsley Publishers.

Rudge, C. (2010) 'Children's Centres', in G. Pugh and B. Duffy (eds), *Contemporary Issues in the Early Years,* 5th edn. London: Sage.

Runswick-Cole, K. and Hodge, N. (2009) 'Needs or rights? A challenge to the discource of special education', *British Journal of Special Education,* 36(4): 198–203.

Russell, F. (2003) 'The expectations of parents of disabled children', *British Journal of Special Education,* 30(3): 144–9.

Sanderson, S. (2003) 'The role of the educational psychologist in the inclusive process', in C. Tilstone and R. Rose (eds), *Strategies to Promote Inclusive Practices.* London: Routledge Falmer.

School Curriculum and Assessment Authority (SCAA) (1996) *Desirable Outcomes of Children's Learning on Entering Compulsory Education.* London: SCAA.

Smith, H. (1996) *Procedures, Practice and Guidance for SENCOs.* Tamworth: NASEN.

Spenceley, L. (2000) 'Communicate if you want to educate', *Early Years Educator,* 2(4): 50–1.

Suffolk Local Authority/DCSF (2009) *Early Years Foundation Stage Profile: eProfile v3.1 September 2009.* Available at: www.teachernet.gov.uk/teachingandlearning/eyfs/profile/eyfsppv31/

Sure Start (2002) *Supporting Families Who Have Children with Special Needs and Disabilities.* London: DfES.

Sure Start (2003) *Area Special Educational Needs Coordinators (SENCOs) – Supporting Early Identification and Intervention for Children with Special Educational Needs.* London: DfES.

Sure Start (2008) *The Childcare Act.* Available at www.surestart.gov.uk/resources/general/childcareact/

Swick, K.J. and Hooks, L. (2005) 'Parental experiences and beliefs regarding inclusive placements of their special needs children', *Early Childhood Education Journal,* 32(6): 397–402.

Tassoni, P. (2003) *Supporting Special Needs: Understanding Inclusion in the Early Years.* Oxford: Heinemann.

Training and Development Agency for Schools (TDA) (2009) *Specification for Nationally Approved Training for Special Educational Needs Coordinators (SENCOs) New to the Role, Leading to the Award of the National Award for SEN Coordination.* Available at: www.tda.gov.uk/upload/resources/pdf/s/national_senco_training_specification.pdf

Together for Children (TfC) (2006) *Children's Centres FAQs.* Available at: www.childrens-centres.org/Topics/FAQ/CCFAQ.aspx

Together for Disabled Children (TfDC) (2008) *What's New.* Available at: www.togetherfdc.org/default.aspx

Towers, C. (2009) *Recognising Fathers: A National Survey of Fathers who Have a Child with a Disability.* Available at: www.learningdisabilities.org.uk/our-work/family-support/fathers/

United Nations Educational, Scientific and Cultural Organisation (UNESCO) (1994) *Salamanca Statement on Principles, Policy and Practice in Special Needs Education.* Paris: UNESCO.

Van der Eyken, W. (1967) *The Pre-School Years.* London: Penguin.

Wall, K. (1996) 'Welfare and liaison', in K. David and T. Charlton (eds), *Pastoral Care Matters in Primary and Secondary Schools.* London: Routledge.

Wall, K. (2004) 'Inclusion and special educational needs', in T. Maynard and N. Thomas (eds), *An Introduction to Early Childhood Studies.* London: Sage.

Wall, K. (2005) 'Singing from the same hymn sheet benefits children', *Early Years Educator,* 7(8): 42–4.

Wall, K. (2009) 'Diversity and inclusion', in T. Bruce (ed.) *Early Childhood Studies.* London: Sage.

Wall, K. (2010) *Autism and Early Years Practice,* 2nd edn. London: Sage.

Ward, U. (2009) *Working with Parents in Early Years Settings.* Exeter: Learning Matters.

Webster, A. and McConnell, C. (1987) *Special Needs in Ordinary Schools: Children with Speech and Language Difficulties.* London: Cassell.

Weinberger, J., Pickstone, C. and Hannon, P. (eds) (2005) *Learning from Sure Start: Working with Young Children and their Families.* Maidenhead: Open University Press and McGraw-Hill.

Whalley, M. (2007) *Involving Parents in their Children's Learning,* 2nd edn. London: Paul Chapman Publishing.

Wheeler, H. and Connor, J. (2009) *Parents, Early Years and Learning, Parents as Partners in the Early Years Foundation Stage: Principles into Practice.* London: NCB.

Whitaker, P. (2007) 'Provision for youngsters with autistic spectrum disorders in mainstream schools: what parents say – and what parents want', *British Journal of Special Education,* 34(3): 170–8.

Wolfendale, S. (1989) *Parental Involvement: Developing Networks between Home, School and Community.* London: Cassell.

Wolfendale, S. (ed.) (1997) *Working with Parents of SEN Children after the Code of Practice.* London: David Fulton.

Wolfendale, S. (2006) *Meeting Special Needs in the Early Years: Directions in Policy and Practice.* London: David Fulton.

Index

978-1-84920-554-2

978-1-84920-578-8

978-1-4129-2309-5

978-1-84920-464-4

978-1-84920-196-4

978-1-84860-197-0

978-1-84920-116-2

978-1-84920-520-7

978-1-84860-997-6

Find out more about these titles and our wide range of books for education students and practitioners at **www.sagepub.co.uk/education**

EXCITING EARLY YEARS AND PRIMARY TEXTS FROM SAGE